ASTRIDE TWO CENTURIES

ASTRIDE TWO CENTURIES

The Life of Bob McKergow

"Up in the saddle, down on the farm;
Master of Foxhounds, Yeomanry Colonel;
on stage, on safari, always on the go"

PETER MCKERGOW

Quiller Press

First published 1999 by
Quiller Press Ltd, 46 Lillie Road, London, SW6 1TN

Copyright 1999 © Peter McKergow

ISBN 1 899163 52 2

Designed by Jo Lee
Printed by Colorcraft

Contents

BIBLIOGRAPHY

Chapter 1
Wood. W., *A Sussex Farmer*
Jonathan Cape 1938 4

Parry D, *English Horse Drawn Vehicles*
Warne 1979

Chapter 5
Jennings A, Robson J. & Weller L. *300 Years of Hunting in Surrey and Sussex*
Sotheby's 1991

Surtees RS, *Handley Cross or Mr Jorrocks's Hunt*
Illustrated John Leach
Bradbury, Agnew & Co Ltd 1854

Bradley, Cuthbert, *The Reminiscences of Frank Gillard*
Edward Arnold 1898

Sassoon S., *Memoirs of a Fox Hunting Man*
Faber & Gwyer Ltd 1928

Sassoon S, *Memoirs of an Infantry Officer*
Faber & Faber Ltd 1930

Sassoon S, *The Old Huntsman and Other Poems*
William Heinemann 1917

Chapter 6
Sitwell, Osbert, *Great Morning*
Macmillan & Co & The Book Society 1948,

Powell Edwards H.I., *The Sussex Yeomanry and 16th (Sussex Yeomanry) Battalion Royal Sussex Regiment 1914-1919*
Andrew Melrose Ltd 1921

Chapter 8
Sparrow G, *The Crawley and Horsham Hunt*
The Sporting Gallery (Limited Edition) 1930

Chapter 10
Churchill W.S, *The Second World War, vol 2, 148*
Cassell 1949

~ *Acknowledgements* ~

I would like to express my thanks to my family who started the idea of a 'Life' when they sorted the box of letters into date order and promptly suggested that there might be a wider interest in them than just ourselves.

In due course it became clear that other records derived from newspaper cuttings, hunting diaries and the like, did in fact, supply sufficient background for a reasonably comprehensive biography of my father.

My thanks are also due to the Publishers and Hugh Barty-King for their skill and consideration in preparing the manuscript for publication.

I am also grateful to Mr Leslie Weller, Chairman of the Crawley and Horsham Hunt, for permission to quote extensively from the Sotheby's book on the History of Hunting in Surrey and Sussex.

Finally, nothing could have appeared without the word processing of Sue Cooke who succeeded against all odds in deciphering the hundreds of sheets of scrawl.

~ *McKergow Family Tree* ~

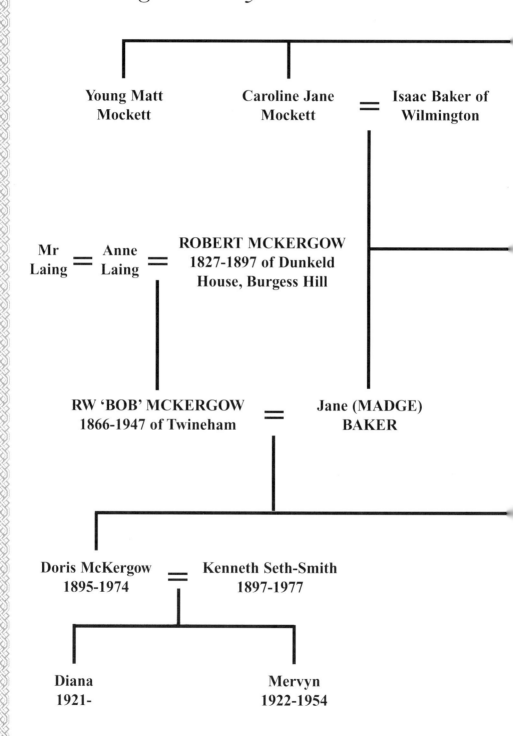

Young Matt
Mockett

Caroline Jane
Mockett = Isaac Baker of
Wilmington

Mr
Laing = Anne
Laing = ROBERT MCKERGOW
1827-1897 of Dunkeld
House, Burgess Hill

RW 'BOB' MCKERGOW
1866-1947 of Twineham = Jane (MADGE)
BAKER

Doris McKergow
1895-1974 = Kenneth Seth-Smith
1897-1977

Diana
1921-

Mervyn
1922-1954

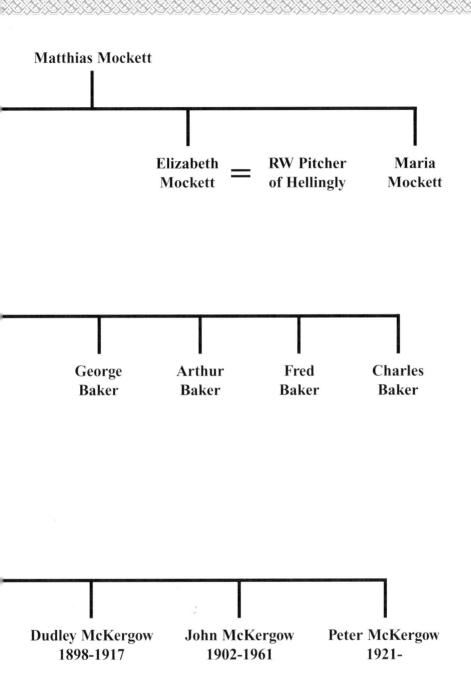

Matthias Mockett

Elizabeth Mockett = RW Pitcher of Hellingly   Maria Mockett

George Baker   Arthur Baker   Fred Baker   Charles Baker

Dudley McKergow 1898-1917   John McKergow 1902-1961   Peter McKergow 1921-

Riding out
of the
Nineteenth
Century

1866-1900

~ 1 ~
Growing Up

In 1859 Robert McKergow left Glasgow to start a wine and spirit business in the South East. He had learnt the trade with Findlater Mackie & Co and progressed to managing the firm's Manchester branch. The company wanted to extend their trading opportunities by having a new business launched under their name but effectively run by McKergow. The directors of the company made funds available to purchase premises and, in addition to the interest on mortgages, would receive a share of the profits.

The company had a similar scheme running in a fashionable part of London under the direction of Bruce Todd, who added his name to the backers. Robert McKergow was told to find a base on the South Coast. He travelled down to Brighton by train and went out from there to east and west. It did not take long to conclude that Brighton had the best future and by October 1859 he was in business, occupying properties on the corner of Prince Albert St and Nile St. The idea of installing a business which involved handling casks and crates on such a cramped site is difficult to comprehend. To make matters worse storage was in rented cellars under Middle Street, but nothing changed until after Robert's death. It is intriguing to find that he never sold the local beers. This was probably a well calculated decision based on the consumers he was aiming at - the day tripper.

Town Council elders had hoped that Brighton, the Queen of Watering Places, would attract a wealthy and refined clientele once the railway link with London was established in the 1840s. They were not totally disappointed, but the crowds that packed the excursion trains were cheerful cockneys ready for a good day out. They would have been delighted to find beer and stout from Truman & Co (London), Bass and Allsopp from Burton-on-Trent, and Guinness from Dublin. Robert must have been an excellent negotiator because he succeeded in getting his beer into the popular outlets. He could hardly have been welcomed by the existing suppliers but sales improved strongly. The item 'Goodwill' appears from the beginning which suggests he took over an existing business. Goodwill cost him £300 a month initially and occasionally increased to £400 or even £600 a month. The largest fixed items of expenditure were the interest payments to those who had advanced money on the security of his business property. By January 1862 he was paying out the following substantial sums to his backers each month.

1

John F. Corscaden	£1308-0-5d
I. Mackie	£1349-18-9d
Alex Findlater	£1286-7-11d
B. B. Todd	£701-11-3d

By 1869 these sums had increased to £3188-18s, £2140-10-5d, £2746-1-2d and £3156 respectively. It is surprising that, apart from some early payments, Findlater Mackie & Co of Glasgow do not feature in the accounts. Someone must have been supplying his whisky and brandy, and it would follow that the firm whence he came was the most likely source. Robert's special whisky supports this idea. It was sold with a yellow label on the bottle depicting a sort of Monarch of the Glen with the superscription 'Findlaters V O Whisky Guaranteed 10 years old'. Nothing throws any light on a wine supplier.

Robert's own drawings from the business were around £500 a month in the first year, rising to £800 in 1861 and over £2,000 a month by 1864. In due course he invested in both property and stocks. A list drawn up in 1890 shows rents coming in from 19 properties and dividends from 26 companies. The properties were a very mixed lot and are probably an indication that what we would regard as good commercial freeholds hardly existed. Robert did manage to secure some shops in the main thoroughfares but most of the time he was content with houses, which included lodging houses. To be fair on them, they paid their rents regularly.

The shareholdings are again quite typical of the period and positively alarming. We can hardly imagine consigning our savings to Egyptian Bonds, Argentine Railways, Spanish silver, Portuguese Bonds and the Llanberis Railway. The Australian Banks and the various London banks were rather more secure but the investor only had small companies to choose from and none of them were seriously in the 'Blue Chip' class.

Meanwhile back in Glasgow there was little prosperity around for the McKergow family. His brother Adam died in 1881 and left £577 and his married sister lived in 'reduced circumstances'. Robert devised a scheme of financial help which cannot be unravelled at this distance but basically consisted of the purchase of 33 Capital and Counties shares at £33 each which he held in his own name with an IOU in favour of his sister. There may have been another investment, as the cheque he sent every half year was for more than the Capital & Counties dividend.

One letter survives:

16 Prince Albert Street
Brighton
8 May 1886

Dear Mary
Enclosed is cheque value £17-10/- as usual. I hope you and your family are all well and getting full employment. Your acknowledgement for (illegible) will oblige.
Yours affectionately
R. McKergow

Robert gives the impression that he is rather fed up with this family even though his sister is part of it. Lack of employment was Mary's husband's problem and Robert had evidently no expectation that things were getting any better. Only 6 years after setting up business he was a man of sufficient prospects to marry. The bride was Anne Laing, a widow with a young daughter, living at Oakwood Villa, Burgess Hill. No letters or memoirs remain that throw any light on how they met each other.

The wedding took place at the Presbyterian Church, Church Street, Brighton in November 1865 when they were both 38. Robert moved into Oakwood Villa from his bachelor quarters at 16 Prince Albert Street and the following year Robert Wilson was born there. Neither Robert nor Anne had much interest in the social graduations of Burgess Hill, but as a man of some wealth he had to establish himself. An important house was a step in that direction and Robert followed fashion in building a mansion in white stucco with a pillared porch christened Dunkeld House. It had all the Victorian accoutrements such as conservatory, stables, coach houses and staff accommodation, with a butler to open the door. At the same time Burgess Hill station was only a short walk away so he could travel to Brighton quite easily for business.

Taking his place in Society also, he found, meant worshipping at the parish church of St John's. After a Presbyterian upbringing the Anglo-Catholic rituals were not to his liking. There was also a distinct flavour of snobbery among the congregation. These ladies, he protested "are more interested in criticising each other's hats than in the service".

Burgess Hill had what passed for high society, but it also had a big slice of low life represented by the unfortunate brickyard workers. Bricks were a major industry for the town. An early photograph from the southern boundary has the parish church rising like a ship above the rows of drying sheds. There was very little security in the trade even in good times, so when demand fell away the brickyards were closed and the labourers dismissed.

Anne McKergow joined with other ladies in organising soup kitchens and clothes distributions. She spent many hours at her sewing machine making night-shirts so voluminous that, it was jokingly said, two men could get inside. Her relief work began to cost Robert a bit of money and he decided to investigate. He found his back door besieged by a none too well behaved crowd of men, women and children. He tackled his wife politely about it. "My dear, I think the relief is not well organised. As far as I can see the men are getting one parcel, then going into the back of the crowd and coming up for another." Anne was outraged. "Robert, how could you say such things about my men!" He had to retreat. "Very well my dear, I will say no more."

Robert Wilson (Bob) grew up at Dunkeld House as a rather fierce little boy who would pitch in to any other boys who crossed his path. He started his education at a Brighton prep school conventionally enough and then transferred to Streat Rectory, where the Reverend Paget Davies ran a school for a few boys who boarded in the house. There were public schools available, but for some reason his father never sent him to one. Bob's asthma was quite troublesome at the time and could have been the reason for his private education.

Robert must have been distinctly disappointed that Bob's interests developed solely along sporting lines. By the age of 18 or 20 he was hunting regularly, had his own pack of beagles and enjoyed shooting, evidently with the support of a youth in a curly brimmed bowler who acted as groom, kennelman and whipper-in by turns. By 1887 he had decided it was time to spread his wings and suggested to his father that he should go up to Cambridge University. Robert was still trying to interest him in the business and would have thought the university had nothing to contribute in that direction. Instead Bob was persuaded (or firmly told) to assist George Laing, Anne's eldest son, in being a Beer, Wine and Spirit merchant in Nottingham. It was not a success.

He found the Laing household very straightlaced. There was hunting with Lord Harrington's foxhounds which no doubt had its satisfying moments but he found the country dull. The length of his sojourn in Nottingham is not recorded. It was as short as he could make it.

The young man with a bit of money behind him often found social life at home a bit frustrating; his parents had friends but they were much older and even if they had sons and daughters they could well be extremely dull. 'Get away from home' was the answer and there was no better place to meet excellent fellows than the universities of Oxford and Cambridge. The fathers were often less approving. It was well known, or so they thought, that all sorts of bad behaviour went on at these establishments and their carefully brought-up son could well be at moral risk. This state of mind was so prevalent that there was even a farcical novel published, *The Adventures of Mr Verdant Green*, that milked the topic for as many laughs as the author could muster.

Robert McKergow could not have been in the least enthusiastic when Bob put forward the idea that the experience of Cambridge University would be valuable. In fact it is most surprising that he agreed to it at all. He could not understand his son. His own life was of clockwork regularity. He caught the same train to Brighton each working day, walked the same route to the office, dealt with the business of the day, walked back to the station, caught the same train back to Burgess Hill, walked to Dunkeld House, placed his top hat on the hall table, moved to the dining room for a glass of water (carafe and glass were in position) and finally entered the drawing room where Anne was ready to greet him. Bob, on the other hand, was all over the place. Hunting with his beagles, shooting with friends, organising tennis parties in summer and out in the evenings taking part in theatricals. No harm in it, of course, but Robert did have to step in pretty often to point out that there were things to do at Prince Albert Street.

Nevertheless Robert did give way over Cambridge and sent him off to Downing College in the autumn of 1888. It would have been a big operation, involving as it did the packing of a full dinner service of Limoges china, a tea service, a humidor of cigars, clothes for all occasions, some silverware and ornaments, and pictures. Robert had contributed to these in the form of a set of prints based on Hogarth's *The Rake's Progress* updated to Victorian times. This was the Verdant Green story but with an unhappy ending. The naive undergraduate is led astray, but instead of learning his lesson and triumphing over his temptors, he gets into deeper trouble and, presumably in debt, faces being sent down. The last print in the series is full of Victorian sentimentality. It shows the haggard undergraduate, after a sleepless night, drawing the curtains of his bedroom and gazing at the tower of the College Chapel, for the last time of course. Ahead clearly lies the dreaded interview with the Senior Tutor, followed by the journey home to face the pater himself. Whether or not this pictorial sermon had any effect we cannot tell, but Bob never got into the slightest trouble during his varsity days.

There was plenty of enjoyment; that was all there was to do. Bob joined the ranks of those undergraduates who used the university as a finishing school and had no intention of obtaining a degree. It is thought that at the turn of the century at least ten per cent of undergraduates were in this category. How they managed to fill their days, when their friends had lectures to attend and essays to write, is a mystery.

Bob joined the College Rowing Club and progressed to being captain of the 2nd boat and rowed at 5 in the First Boat which had some successes in the Lent and May Races during his time. The hunting he found dull but he improved his skill as a whip by getting instruction in driving tandem and four-in-hand. In March 1890 he was commissioned as a Second Lieutenant in the Volunteer Battalion of the Suffolk Regiment.

The University was a remarkably small society. Later in the 1890s a so-called Sketch Book of University characters was published, and Bob had no difficulty in identifying them. Among those included was J. B. Close coaching the Trinity Boat from his horse. "Now boys! I want you to come sl-o-wly forward and SHARP BACK." Butler, Master of Trinity, appears in various Butlerian situations. Mrs Billings, Bedmaker of Trinity, gets her full repertoire of

"That you 'ev"

"That oi 'ev-ent"

"That you did"

"That oi never"

A bedmaker or "bedder" made the young gentlemen's beds in college and generally 'did' the rooms - later, highly respectable ladies.

Professor Stanford of C.U. Music Society was lampooned with a barrel organ and monkey. The lady students, quite a rarity and not of undergraduate status, were treated in the books quite gently. Obviously gentlemen would not ridicule respectable ladies but the impression was given that they were not really in the right place.

It was a hearty male society with the old element of Town v Gown still in evidence. Town objected to being ground down by an overmighty Gown, who, in turn, felt it right and proper to teach the mannerless louts a lesson every now and then. Downing College men one year found a good target in the pantomime being performed at the New Theatre opposite the College gates. A group of them bought seats for several nights and made a set at Neptune. "What Ho!" he would cry, emerging from the wings, "I am Neptune of the vasty deep." His problem was that the hecklers got the words out just ahead of him. After a night or two of this the choleric Neptune exchanged abuse with his tormentors who exited in triumph. No doubt Town also shared his annoyance. Among the other college companions the waggish 'Bunny' Vincent and the over meticulous Turner went on taking Bob's boisterous friendship in good part for years later.

The family at Burgess Hill must have been relieved that their son did not intend to live far afield and abandon the Brighton businesses once the Cambridge interlude was completed. He aimed at more independence but was quite happy to be living within a few miles of home if a suitable house and farm came on the market - and subject to his father approving the property and putting up the money. It was most unusual for a young unmarried man to set up house on his own and not many of them wanted to farm the land attached to the residence, but these considerations would be attended to as and when they arose.

First he had to do a year, starting July 1891, as a farm pupil. Farming, in what was then classed as 'a substantial way', provided a living without too much exertion. But income was too dependent on the weather and agricultural prices for the farmer ever to feel safe financially. That was their excuse for their notorious parsimonious behaviour, of course.

William Wood in *A Sussex Farmer* put it well. "The farmer whose home I tried to describe (the man, with three hundred acres or so, his own property) did not work so hard as his wife - in terms of manual labour he did no work at all. He looked after his farm, and controlled his labour, he went to market and fairs, he knew the value of what he had to sell, he was a good judge of the sheep, cattle and horses he had to buy, but of actual work on the farm he never did a stroke; why should he when he could get all the hard work done for him at the rate of two shillings or half a crown a day, and for some part of these years for eight shillings a week? Such a farmer could not afford to work, it was only a waste of his time."

The farmer pupil acted as an interested observer while his master demonstrated his management skills and business acumen, although the pupil might conceivably volunteer to give the shepherd a hand in the lambing pens for an hour or two. At the same time he was probably encouraged to keep a hunter and turn out with the foxhounds when they met in the district. In the summer there would be tennis. A pleasant existence for a young man who enjoyed the countryside.

As soon as he came down from Cambridge in the summer of 1891 Bob arranged to join R. W. 'Squire' Pitcher of Grovebridge, Hellingly as a pupil. He was probably warned in advance that Squire was a rough diamond but grew a good variety of crops and knew how to get the best deal for his sheep and cattle. Socially, though, life at the farm was a disaster, and Bob probably wondered how he was going to survive twelve months. The reality was entirely different.

One can imagine master and pupil riding into the yard one lunchtime and spotting a small dog cart near the stables and a pony tied up inside. Directly they were in the house Bob would be hurried into the front room and introduced by Mrs Pitcher to 'Miss Baker, my niece'.

It is unlikely that they fell instantly in love at that moment but certainly Bob found Jane Baker lively and very good looking, while the lady was undoubtedly struck by the polished manner and enthusiasms of the young gentleman. He in turn was probably astonished to hear later that Jane was only 15 years old, as she had seemed so self-possessed. Marriage was a long way off, but in the meantime social life was not going to be a problem with Jeanie turning up in her trap as often as possible - or proper. Ladies did not pursue men in the eighteen eighties.

Who was she and how did it happen that she turned up five miles from home so opportunely? She was half a Mockett by birth and much more than half by upbringing.

In the 17th century the Mocketts were probably ironmasters in Kent, casting the guns for the English fleet. Coming forward to the 19th century Jane's grandfather, Matthias, had been a prosperous yeoman combining being the licensee of the White Horse, Willingdon with farming, sheep breeding and ownership of the Windmill at Polegate, four and a half miles from Eastbourne, with a nice house adjoining. He had one son and three daughters. Caroline Jane married Isaac Baker, a farmer at Wilmington Priory. They had four sons, so there must have been huge delight when a daughter was born in May 1876 - delight turning to great sadness when Caroline Jane died of puerperal fever within a few days. Maria, Matthias's unmarried daughter still living at Polegate, came over in a farm delivery cart in the night and carried off the baby to her house. Fifteen years later the baby, Jane Elizabeth Madeline, was catching everyone's eye at Polegate.

Matthias had passed away some years earlier and his son, Young Matt, was killed in a shooting accident. His daughter Elizabeth (Lizzie) married firstly a Mr Philpot and after his death R. W. 'Squire' Pitcher of Grovebridge. So it was quite natural that Jane should go back and forth between Polegate and Grovebridge.

Two of her brothers, George and Arthur, moved away from the district and set up as estate agents and auctioneers at Horley in Surrey. Arthur soon dropped out of active participation, however, and merely called in once a week for his 'expenses'. Fred stayed at Wilmington with his father, who married again. Charles, a cheerful and popular character, worked for Stricklands the agricultural merchants and lived with Maria.

He later secured his future prospects by marrying Miss Strickland, his boss's daughter.

At Burgess Hill Robert and Anne continued to live at Dunkeld House. Her two daughters by her first husband, Alice and Harriet, had their own house nearby. George ran his Nottingham Wine Merchants in partnership with Robert. Jack, his brother, went to Canada, married and had children who were orphaned at a young age when both parents died of influenza and were eventually returned to England to be in Robert's care.

Bob's closest friend at Burgess Hill was Tom Maynard whom he had known from boyhood. Tom was very much the opposite character. Poor eyesight, no interest in sport or horses, he could barely drive one horse in a cart, but kindness itself, an excellent solicitor and helpful to every organisation starting up in the town.

Getting around in those days was done either sitting astride a horse or in the seat of a carriage drawn by one. The dog cart, at its most extreme, was the sports car of the day. The early 1800s design provided for a flat body mounted above two 55-inch wheels. The driver and passenger sat up in front, and at the back there was a louvered compartment for the dog, which could be unfolded to make a seat and foot rest for two passengers facing backwards. With two horses in tandem as the motive power, the outfit was fast and required a lot of skill from the driver and horses that would respond.

By the end of the century the dog compartment had become a small luggage boot and the vehicle usually only carried the driver and the liveried groom or, best of all, the driver and a pretty girl. Dog carts were also made with a low slung body that could carry four passengers.

The standard four wheeled carriage was the brougham that could be used as an open carriage or closed by a hood and drawn by one or two horses according to one's wealth. It was also the standard London cab. Until he married, Bob did not own one, as he always drove himself. At the top of the range came the private drag or four-in-hand coach. These were purely used for the sport of driving four-in-hand, and the enthusiasts usually belonged to the Coaching Club formed in 1870.

~ 2 ~
Courting by Post

After that first meeting at Squire Pitcher's in the summer of 1891, up to May the following year, Bob and Jeanie were able to meet frequently. Then Bob ran out of excuses for continuing to stay with the Squire at Grovebridge, the house in Hellingly, and felt obliged to fall in with his father's wish to return home to help with the negotiations to buy Twineham Grange.

So the two had to part, promising to write to each other as often as they could - as often, that is to say, as they considered socially permissible. Twice a week? That all? Surely no-one could possibly accuse them of improper behaviour if they wrote three times a week? And presumably a conventionally fond letter of farewell before parting would not count?

Keeping the correspondence clandestine was obviously going to be difficult, but not impossible. It would depend on how you went about it. It was just a matter of taking care.

Bob told Jeanie he was writing his goodbye letter under difficulties, "as Birnie is whirling round me".

> Well 'old lady', how are you? I hope you have no headache… I never knew Grovebridge was such a dull place before. There seems to be a great deal missing since Friday night. I felt extremely dull coming home from Polegate but it was worse when I arrived here. Yesterday I attempted to pack but it was rather a failure.

He was leaving the next day. He hoped she would be able to come and see him off at Polegate station. His train came in at 3.43 and left at 3.58, giving them 15 minutes to say farewell. "I have never wished before that the train should fit in badly, but I do this time."

> The Squire has kept up a continual chaff, but it's like 'water off a duck's back' with me. The Squire informed me while at dessert that Miss Mockett was in a dreadful state about you. I hope this is not true or else I shall hear something to my disadvantage when I meet her… Goodbye darling, hoping we shall meet at the station tomorrow afternoon if all's well.

I remain your affect. old Mac.
Likelihood of a talk with Tom Maynard "over the little Polegate girl with the little dimples".

Once back at home, Bob received the first letter from the little Polegate girl with the dimples three days later, telling him she was probably starting singing lessons in a week or two, and beseeching him not to forget the photo. "I want it very very much, but the original more." As a token of her love she sent him a pair of embroidered braces. He told her that he wanted Tom Maynard to be the first of his friends to know of their acquaintanceship.

Bob turned up in Eastbourne a week later, as he warned her he might, on an errand for his father, who wanted him to inspect a house there. Entering gleefully into the spirit of conspiracy that now coloured their relationship, Jeanie told him she would meet him at Eastbourne station "quite by accident".

Every so often Bob's sisters had as their guest a French count. He was a musician who had all the ladies of Burgess Hill at his feet. He was asked everywhere to Musical Afternoons. "He is a very decent fellow, but distinctly French," Bob told Jeanie by way of light relief before giving her the unwelcome news that the business of buying Twineham Grange, which kept them apart, was still far from settled - "everything seems wrong with it."

The count has come back here for a few days. He and the girl have amused themselves this afternoon by painting, one canvas and the other on glass. He has spoilt her dress through fooling with the paint, so they have been having a good deal of civil conversation.... Now, if the Grange falls through and I cannot buy it, I am going to ask the Squire if I may come back till I find another farm and house to suit me. I suppose he has no other pupils in view yet.

When they next met, Jeanie thought it should be as a couple known to be betrothed. "Since our engagement is an absolute secret," she wrote to Bob on July 9, 1892, "I owe it as a duty to my father to acquaint him with it, rather than he should hear it from some other source." She also felt Bob would be pleased, incidentally, to hear that the Blue Hungarian Band was playing in Eastbourne. A week later she told him:

Father will probably give me a blowing up because I had not seen him since I returned to Grovebridge. The Aunt [Maria Mockett]... told him that perhaps some day you might want to be a thief. He said 'Oh oh Jeanie's very young (it seems to be the cry), but I thought there was some attraction at Grovebridge but I did not know which one."

The cat was swiftly emerging from the bag. In his letter of July 12 Bob told Jeanie he had mentioned "the whole facts of the case" to his sister, and that she replied that she had expected it for some time, and was sure who was the lady concerned.

After the 'accidental' meeting at Eastbourne railway station, Jeanie confessed to Bob she had "lost herself"; and Aunt Maria had been very nice and said heaps of lovely things about him. What about meeting at Brighton Show? Fine, said Bob. "The gov informs me tonight he thinks he will be at the Brighton Show on Friday next, also I believe my sister intends to come, so I suppose I shall have to dance around with them to a considerable extent." He always called his father 'Gov'.

It was something Jeanie had to face up to. "Intend to come to show train arriving London Road at 11.01 am, and shall walk to Preston Park. Shall go to look at Southdown sheep. Quite afraid at the prospect of meeting sister, "she wrote on August 18. Her fears were premature. "Dreadfully disappointed at not being able to see you today - too wet and headache," she wrote next day. Bob agreed.

> Horribly wet yesterday. Quite wise not turning up. How about the Eastbourne Flower Show? I will do my best to come over for it, but you know if the gov thinks I ought to go somewhere else I shall have to go, as I cannot very well put forth the excuse 'Please I want to go the Eastbourne Flower Show', to which he would remark 'Bosh, how long have you taken an interest in gardening?' I suppose the Aunt will be away. Who is coming with us? We must have a chaperone as I am shy.

More frustration followed a week later. For Jeanie, that is.

> I feel so mad I can scarcely explain myself. Aunt Kate called me this morning worse luck! and coolly informed us that she and her party consisting of four were coming here to dinner and tea on Wednesday. Extreme rage - do you want to meet this crowd.

Bob was not to be thwarted.

> I must say 'Bother the Browns' but don't let your passions rise my dear. I will be at Polegate Station at 2.14 pm. If I am not I shall be already at Eastbourne and will meet you at the station instead... I have not mentioned at home that I am going to Eastbourne yet. I shall mention it casually to the mater tomorrow.

He kept his father in the dark. "I heard the gov was rampaging around wondering where on earth I had gone to," he told his fiancee on September 1. "The mater remarked, 'Well you are a nice boy to be so late. Wherever where you?'"

Bob's half-sisters Alice and Harriet were desperate to meet the cause of all this ferment - and if possible help their brother cope with it. "Sisters want to see you. My sister is very pleased to come and keep house for me" (September 2). But it was going to be some time before there was a house to keep. "Very bad tempered. The workmen don't seem to get on with the house [Twineham Grange] a bit. It will be Christmas before I get settled over there." (October 5)

At least he had managed to get the animals installed. "Horses taken over to the Grange from Burgess Hill. Took six men to take them out of the field, arrived at the Grange being led by different men."

More irksome than the laziness of the builders were the overbearing demands of his father. "Bother the gov. I wish he would go away for a day or two, and then Hark! Forrard! to Polegate. I heard our under-gardener whistling 'Love's Old Sweet Song'. I suppose he has heard me singing or shouting it in my bedroom when I am dressing."

At this juncture, for some reason that is not entirely clear, Bob started calling the object of his affections by a different name: no longer 'Jeanie' but 'Madge'.

Both of them found ways of compensating for the lack of opportunities to be with each other. For Madge it was Good Works. "I find that I am to go on a Working Party for the London Poor every Thursday. Isn't it awfully funny to think of me at such a meeting taking tea and gossip!" Bob took to the stage. "I have been asked to take part in some amateur theatricals," he told Madge on October 19. And then, four days later:

> I heard this morning from a lady of my acquaintance here, that I and another fellow were to act the whole of *The Rivals* by ourselves. Now we both may be very great performers but I don't see how we can possibly do that. No doubt you have seen *The Rivals* acted, but you know it takes about a dozen people including several females.

The Rivals, as Madge will have known, was the 23-year-old Richard Sheridan's first play, produced at the Covent Garden Theatre in London in 1775.

If their trysts were to remain clandestine, Bob had carefully to stage manage every meeting. But things did not always go according to the script.

> I returned to Keymer Junction in safety where I changed trains to go on to Burgess Hill, when I found my respected parent looking out of the window to see why the train did not go. So I withdrew into the shadow of darkness and did not go on to Burgess Hill by the train, but quietly walked up to my sister's and there found my mother… I went home with the mater and eluded all conversation as to what I had been doing yesterday. (October 28)

Other members of Bob's family had to be handled with equal care, and their advice heeded, as he warned Madge a couple of days later.

> You seem to be very frightened that my sister will think me not reasonable. Of course not seeing one another for only one month is no good as it is not long enough apart. But still, we will if you like try that first; just see how it seems… I have not had a talk to my sister about it yet. She agreed with me that we should most probably have to go three months without seeing one another when my people knew. I think it is awful nonsense.

A new distraction was having a go at driving tandem. When on October 30 Bob told Madge he had sent to London for the two-horse harness, she retorted she thought it a silly idea, "but I might think differently if I saw you doing it." His reaction was instant.

> My dear girl, tandem is not a silly game; it is very nice to drive in that way, I can assure you. If the leader does not insist upon turning to look at you just when you want to show to advantage.

The harness arrived within a week, and Bob told Madge he intended trying the two horses together the next morning. "I hope they go alright as I am going to put them in my best cart, and I don't want that smashed up." When he drove the tandem over to the Grange, "The horses looked awfully well," he proudly reported to Madge on November 8, "and went splendidly together. We simply had no bother at all. They might have been together all their lives. There was only one thing wanting to make it look a very swell turn-out indeed, and that was a pretty girl beside the driver."

Madge was content to watch horses on her feet.

> We went to the meet and enjoyed it very much, only it was a little cold. I am going to a matinee at the Devonshire Park Theatre on Saturday with Miss V to see Terry in *The Rocket*. It is rather unfortunate as I saw that piece in town when I was last there.

Bob's preparations to move into his own house went full steam ahead. On November 3 he told Madge he had been in Brighton the day before with his mother buying furniture.

> My gov objected to me going to Maples; he said we ought to deal in Brighton as there are such good shops there. Hanningtons have the most beautiful things, and you can see them all laid out in suites. I don't know what my gov will say when he sees the bill. We bought yesterday five bedroom suites, the dining room, and also the hall furniture, so I thought we did fairly well.

Not only fairly well but less expensive than Maples in Tottenham Court Road. Keeping the Hannington suites in prime condition would be the pride and joy of whomever Bob managed to engage as housekeeper. The task was now to find a woman ready to accept the wage he had in mind.

> The housekeeper I thought of having wants £27 a year, and I am only going to give £25, so that would not do for her. If Miss Mockett ["The Aunt"] should hear of a housemaid, please let me know. I am going to give her £15, and I think that is enough, don't you?

Madge was not paid a penny for teaching the class which the rector had talked her and Aunt Maria into teaching at the Sunday School. "I have a nice lot of little boys, who can read, to teach." And Bob's play-acting was equally unpaid. He had also to put up with the inevitable frustrations of local amateur theatricals - "I went to have a rehearsal [of *The Rivals*] last night but found the Institution taken up with the Choral Society meeting."

The Grange was steadily taking shape. "The workmen are not yet out," Bob told Madge by way of a situation report on November 10. "There were seven painters at work there yesterday in the house. One day last week there were 24 men at work in the place." And it was full steam ahead for the game shooters and carriage drivers. "We had a very good day's sport yesterday," Bob told Madge on November 12.

> Stanford of the Court shot with us; he is a ripping shot. Dick and myself returned home last night with the tandem in the dark and it also was very foggy so I could hardly see the leaders head; and to add to the excitement one lamp went out, so we had to feel our way home, Dick blowing the post horn like blazes. Excuse the expression but I cannot find another. When we arrived the gov was out at the gates; thought we had smashed up bottom of a ditch somewhere.

Madge was suffering from clerical pressure and the Aunt's disapproval of her cooking.

> Our clergyman was more erratic than ever yesterday. He wants the Aunt and I to go and have tea with him on Thursday and meet some other Sunday School teachers to arrange a course of lessons… On Wednesday the Aunt is going to have 20 little girls to tea who belong to the Girls Friendly Society. I am sure they will eat a dreadful amount of cake and I have to make it tomorrow. I made some wonderful kind of cake today. The Aunt says it's not fit to eat. (November 14)

Bob's somewhat intermittent rehearsing for his part in Sheridan's *The Rivals* in no way detracted from it being All Right On The Night of November 22. "The performance went off splendidly," he proudly reported to Madge. "The room was bang full; something like 300 people there. We in our piece got on very well indeed. But people would laugh, so it rather put you off." Presumably in the wrong places. So only half All Right? Apart from the inappropriate mirth, he was distracted by the rage he had over losing his cigar case, and the workmen at the Grange telling him that the cistern was leaking and would have to be replaced - and the carpets were coming tomorrow. Gadzooks! There was no hitch however in the staffing arrangements.

> Harrie and I have been interviewing servants during the afternoon and evening and I think we have picked out two rather decent people. The housekeeper is rather a small woman but seems a good tempered sort. The housemaid is rather a nice looking girl and ought to understand her work… Now old lady, I am not much of a fellow to compliment you I am afraid, but I never saw you look so well in all your life as you did yesterday. I am sure you are in better health, which makes you look prettier than ever in

my eyes, which I hope and believe you care about a little. (November 29)

In spite of the compliment, next day Madge felt depressed. "I feel rather like soda water with all the fizz gone out of it… I ought to have gone to a meeting yesterday concerning the Sunday School treat, but I felt too 'flat'." It was a metaphor to which she became particularly attached, and used it many times again. Bob shared her depression.

> I have also felt a sort of flat feeling, although I have had a lot to do and think about. I wrote for one housekeeper's character and found her neither trustworthy or clean, so I had no further correspondence with her. But luckily we had another one 'hanging' on, whom I saw on Monday, a very nice sort of woman but rather inclined to be a bit doleful I should imagine…. My gov is going over to the Grange this morning. We told him a little bit how we had been spending money on furniture. He was very good about it indeed, and when I told him I thought the smoke room would look bare, he said see how it looks first and then you can have more if does not look well. I thought it awfully decent of the old chap. (December 1)

Bob could not share his fiancee's merriment over his attempts to find staff. "I can't help laughing about the housekeeper - I hope the next one will suit," she had written; to which Bob replied, "You seem much amused about the servants. I have really got this time a decent sort of housekeeper. Anyway I have engaged her for better or worse."

He anticipated less amusement from the news he gave her on December 6.

> Now I have got another piece of news which I am afraid you won't like and that is that I am going to act with the Misses Griffiths and Jago in *As Cool as a Cucumber*. There is also another fellow going to take part named Hammond, who Miss G knows well. The beauty of it is he has to make love to her. Tom Maynard is at this point furious about it. He says he would not mind me making love to his girl but cannot stand the chap.

Whatever threat the doubtless flirtatious Miss G might be, what about Miss V? This young woman, Madge told Bob on December 10, had come to see her that afternoon concerning her ball dress.

> She is going to the Hospital Ball on the 6th and to another one at the Hotel Metropole in Brighton. She asked me if you were going. She seems very anxious to see you…. J.B. of Friston ran into the Archdeacon's carriage with his cart the other day. Of course he says that the Archdeacon's carriage ran into him, but the paper said differently.

From his letter of December 16, it seems that Bob was not yet out of trouble over his servant appointments, although it is far from clear just what the trouble was this time.

I am in a nice fix now. My housemaid disappointed me last night after the housekeeper had come and we had taken the man away who has had charge there. So we had to pack off one of our servants from here about 9.00pm last night.

Earlier Bob had written that he was taking his sister Harriet over "to try and put things a bit square over at the Grange or we shall never get in by next summer if we go on like this". Yet ten days later he was telling Madge on writing paper headed 'The Grange, Twineham':

My sister and I drove over yesterday afternoon with the tandem. I have not driven for some time, but it was the easiest way to get the two horses over… It seems awfully funny living here.

He liked the housekeeper. She seemed a very decent sort of woman, she kept the place clean and tidy. He was too tired to go to church. To mark the great occasion of the first time he had stayed in his new house, he sent the girl who hopefully one day would be mistress of Twineham Grange a present, and received a gracious letter of thanks.

A short letter to thank you very much for the sweet and lovely cloak that has just arrived. If that is your sister's taste I think it is superb. It will be fifty times more useful to me than a tea gown, and it is just the colour that suits me best. In fact the loveliness of it is past explaining. (December 19)

Surely etiquette would allow them a closer acquaintanceship than the exchange, by leave of the General Post Office, of parcels and letters? It was not a step to be taken without due deliberation. Bob's sister Harriet who was keeping house for him was naturally the first to be consulted. She agreed with him, he told Madge, "that you ought to be heard of soon by my people [parents], and she sees no reason why you, with Miss Mockett [The Aunt], should not come over to see me here". Harriet would issue the invitation "so I will have nothing to do with it at all". Madge talked it over with her parents and told Bob she thought they had reached the right conclusion.

They agree that it would be best for me not to come over to the Grange till I am 17, but as soon after as you like. The reasons are Firstly: that it would be known in Burgess Hill that I visited your house, which would be considered, after what has already passed and is pretty well known, more or less equivalent to an engagement because I am unacquainted with your family and friends. Secondly: that as our affaire de coeur is so well known, people would at once put two and two together. [December 23]

So that is how they played it. And then it was Christmas. Now that he was Lord of the Grange, she told Bob, he would have to go to morning service in church. "I do hope we shall have a frosty Xmas. I don't think I shall do much in the way

16

of church decorating this year as we had such dreadful colds after it last time." Bob not only had a new place to live in but a new one to worship in, with which he was at pains to familiarise himself. "I went out for a ride to the post office for my sister and found where our pew was in church." Unable to be with his beloved, Bob could only express his feelings in writing:

> Wish you a Merry Christmas and a Happy New Year and many of them sweetheart and may your shadow never grow less. Harrie and I are going to spend our Christmas together in a quiet sort of way. I wish you were here and then we should be all right. (December 24, 1892)

Bob was on his own for a bit immediately after Christmas - Harriet went off to spend a couple of days with friends - and all alone in the Grange he was far from merry. Village cheerleaders gave him no cheer at all.

> I have just been disturbed in my letter with some musicians, I suppose they call themselves, and I never heard such a ghastly row. I cannot make out what sort of instrument would give such unearthly noises. The man who made it ought to be compelled to play it till the end of his days, The people of Twineham seem to have a very good idea of keeping up Christmas in the good old style... A nice thing has happened today, the mater's housemaid which we have here has been taken home in the carriage this afternoon ill, so I am left at home by my little self tonight as my sister will not return until tomorrow. [December 26, 1892]

Circumstances conspired to keep Bob in a state of melancholy. At least he could write to his dearest one in Polegate to tell her the cause of it, in an effort to cheer himself up - though probably in vain.

> I have not got another housemaid yet which is an awful bore. The Rector and his daughters called this afternoon. I am glad I was out. Another set of musicians have just arrived, another ghastly row. They certainly have peculiar instruments in these parts. I wish we had not got this moonlight ice business on tomorrow night. I suppose you will be skating at Hailsham tomorrow. I wish I could join you.

Any kind of music got on his nerves. Even the anthem the choir sang in Twineham church was "a bit dreadful". His depression was partially lifted by reading the letter which Madge wrote to him from Wilmington Priory the day after Christmas.

> I wore the cloak over here yesterday because it was so cold. I felt as warm as possible and I blessed you from the bottom of my heart darling for the Aunt was fearfully cold. We are all going to Exeat for a few days skating. You can skate for a mile or two there.... Auntie, Arthur, George and myself went to see an old woman in this village yesterday when I gave her some

money that I had collected at dessert. The poor thing insisted on scrambling up to make a curtsey to me. I must tell you that she lives on 2s 6d a week, 6d of which she pays for rent.

Things were still not yet going right for Bob at the Grange. On January 1, 1893 he wrote to Madge:

> I have just finished my dinner all alone and have also polished off half a bottle of champagne. Feeling rather shaken up today as the wheel of my dog cart came off last night as I was coming home through Burgess Hill and pitched me across the road on my elbow. My groom boy never let go of the cart at all as I never let go of the reins, but made the horse what had bolted drag me along the road behind the cart. He soon got tired of drawing 12st 13lbs and gave in, so the horse was not hurt at all. It was an awfully lucky get-off for me. I might have broken my arm as the road was not too soft to fall on I found. I went home and told my sister to keep it if possible from the mater. The gov got in an awful temper, told me to burn the cart, no business to have such a cart on the place. So I then proceeded to get our men, with the help of the coach builder, to carry it home on a truck, as it was too much broken up to wheel home.

Trouble was not confined to the daytime.

> Last night [December 31, 1892] I had another adventure. I had just gone to bed when I heard a tremendous thumping at the back somewhere. It was about 12 o'clock. It sounded like someone kicking a door with heavy boots. I sprang out of bed, went to the window and listened. It still went on, so I was just off downstairs when I met the housekeeper awfully frightened saying there was someone breaking in at the housekeeper's room. I went back to get a six-chambered revolver loaded, and proceeded to open a window above and shouted. No response. So I then went down and went all round the house; could find no one at all. I cannot make it out. I believe it was done for a joke by some drunken beggar as it was Christmas Eve [by which he meant New Year's Eve]. If the housekeeper had not lit a light I should have had them to a cert… Stanford is coming tonight to have a cigar with me…. I ought to go to a concert here tomorrow night, as I understand I am an honorary member of the Working Club it is in aid of. Miss Knowles of Grovelands is going to act I believe.

Bob was not a happy man, and it saddened Madge to hear it. "How dreadfully unfortunate you have been of late," she wrote to him on January 3. By way of keeping from dwelling too long on his mishaps, she hoped he would be pleased to know that Eddie Gower was engaged to Nellie Green of the baker's shop in Hailsham, planned to set up a home in South Africa, return to Sussex, wed her and take her back with him to start a life of married bliss across the seas. "Sounds all very nice, doesn't it?"

It did, but it did little to alleviate the concern that he, and everyone else, had for the failing health of his mother.

> The mater is still awfully bad. The gov came over yesterday and said she will not eat anything. All she fancies is cream that I take over. So I am going over tomorrow with some again. She has been having turtle soup and oysters, and seemed to be getting on well. Now she says she doesn't want that. I don't know what they will do.

On top of it all a burst pipe flooded the stables, and the staff did nothing. "Then a log falls out of the grate and burns a hole in the dining room rug." It was all gloom at the Grange. On the other hand, when Madge was in peril of breaking a leg on an over-polished floor, she thought it hilarious.

> It was very <u>funny</u> at the dance last night. To commence with we were very late, and I think Howard had been trying to improve the floor and had put a lot of wax on it. The consequence was that it was simply a work of art to get off without leaving your shoes behind you. The waltzing was also very funny, a good deal of dipping with very little waltz.

Bob derived none of the comfort he expected from attending the parish church services, nor from the good behaviour he believed he would find in a nephew.

> My young nephew is coming to stop with me on Thursday, an uncouth sort of schoolboy, all legs and feet. I am just going to lick him into shape a bit while he is here. I am going down to the post with this this afternoon if the snow does not get too deep. I have also to go to Bolney to see a man. There were sixteen people at church on Sunday afternoon. I never saw such a congregation in any church in my life. This place is positively disgraceful. The people grow up perfect heathens. We really want a change of parsons to do any good. The rector here is a very nice man to talk to and a clever man, but you know the rest concerning him.

What raised his spirits and lifted him out of these black moods was surrendering to the tinsel glamour, the bawdy jokes and the rousing choruses into which he could lose himself on a night out in Brighton.

> We went to the Theatre. It is a very good pantomime at Brighton Theatre Royal this year. There were eight of us in the party, four Miss Gs, T.M.[Tom Maynard], my sister and self and a fellow called Bridge who was up at the Varsity the same time I was. He lives near Keymer. I knew him up at Cambridge. I was awfully surprised at seeing him… I fancy I rather startled Harrie by a statement made on the impulse of the moment when we were driving home last night from Burgess Hill "that I really did not see anything at all in the girls and that I could back Madge against the lot".

Singing music hall songs was more invigorating than intoning hymns in church where, he told Madge, "it is an awful service, I wish there was an alteration there".

> Yesterday there came by post a large roll of songs with Dick's scrawl on the outside. I found it contained nearly every "Coster Song" that was ever written by Chevalier [Albert not Maurice], and in his letter he said he hoped I would learn them, as it would be a change from my usual melody of *Beauty's Eyes* etc. The old beggar he is, thought he would take a rise out of me.
>
> P.S. Postmen have struck in this part of the world owing to the increased number of letters to be delivered.

Madge was scouring the shops for suitable numbers.

> I bought some songs from Eastbourne on Saturday. I don't think much of them but I think I shall keep two. One is called *The Flights of Ages* and the other is *The Plains of Peace* which is a kind of half sacred one. The roads down here are half thick in mud; it is really not safe to go out unless you have very thick boots. [January 23, 1893]

Bob said he would bring down *Bedouin Love Song* and *Beauty's Eyes* but wanted more. Madge knew just the thing.

> I know some rather nice songs that would suit you, some that George had at Christmas viz. *The Yeoman's Wedding, The Drinkers* and *The Jolly Monk*. I like the two first-named but they are all good and not too dreadfully sentimental. The Aunt is shrieking for me to come and make buns, so goodbye dearest.

Like his friend Dick Reece, who wrote to tell him he had been appointed an Inspector to the Local Government Board, as Master of Twineham Grange Bob wanted to feel he had influence in the way the village was run. On January 23 he told Madge he was going to a Conservative dinner at Burgess Hill.

> I have interviewed a man of this parish this morning who informed me that the Vestry [what became the parish council] meeting for Twineham was in March. I tell you I am going for several of them on that occasion. Firstly I think the schools are most abominably managed in this parish, a perfect nonentity for a school mistress not qualified at all for such a post. I expect I shall get sat on but I don't care about that a bit. I will have my say.

At the Conservative Dinner, attended by 50 or so, the speech given by the man chosen to respond to the toast of the Town and Trades of Burgess Hill was not one that Bob would wish to emulate. He told Madge how the man had begun by saying he quite agreed with the last speaker, and that he had never made a speech in public before. The rest of the speech went something like this: "I ought to say before anybody before - ahem! - so of course I don't know what to say in a speech, but I quite agree with the last speaker that the trade of Burgess Hill is in a very good state at least ever since I have known it. But as I said before, we have a good water supply and a good gas supply (he had not in fact mentioned it before). I have been asked to make a speech before, but I never have done. But as I said before, I quite agree with the last speaker, and I think as I have no more to say I will sit down." He sat down amidst more great applause.

Bob's own aspirations for playing a part in local politics, which necessarily involved speech-making, were hampered by his suffering from asthma. To relieve the effects of it, he told Madge he would take the advice of his doctor friend Dick Reece.

> I have to knock off all beer and drink Burgundy. I don't mind that much; no doubt you think that will be a bit of a hardship. He [Dick] says its no use dosing myself with medicine. He wants me to try the other way first. [February 1]

Madge said the Aunt had suggested another way.

> The Aunt says she wonders that you do not try Bournemouth, as that is always considered a good place to cure asthma, but she supposed that yours is a heart complaint as well. She also says that the roads here are very bad, and that if you go to Eastbourne she expects they will disappear altogether from the wear and tear they get. If you go to Eastbourne and stay at the Queen's till the 10th, you will be there for the Hunt Ball which takes place that day.

Braving the crumbling roads, a party of Madge's relations drove over from Wilmington to Polegate when, Madge told Bob, "We had some very good fun. The Baker Band gave selections, the Aunt acting as audience: two violins, 2 banjos and two people hammering away on the piano. We made a good noise if we did nothing else."

In the middle of February, Bob went to Eastbourne for a holiday with Madge - "lovely times I have had while you were down here" [February 15]. For Bob too it was a memorable occasion, as he told Madge on his return home.

> I arrived home alright. I went up to see mother. She seemed much better. She asked me if I had enjoyed myself. I said yes thanks, I sang the Coster songs last night, it was a funny entertainment of course, these songs went down well. No doubt you will receive Harrie's invitation when you receive this.... Miss Knowles is getting up some theatricals for Easter and has asked me to take part. I also want to get up a concert for the Cricket Club. Will you perform on the banjo? It would simply fetch them if a lady played. You might easily do so.

Madge disagreed.

21

I am very sorry but I am sure that I could not play at your concert. I should be so frightened darling. And besides, I can't play nearly well enough to perform at a concert... I don't think I envy your sister going to the Exhibition [in America]. I should not mind if you could go by train but to go all that distance by sea would be dreadful.

She was always able to face the hazards of a drive over to Twineham - not only the surface of the roads but the reception she would get from her future in-laws. Bob never hid his views on the latter.

Harrie went to Burgess Hill today with me and informed the mater that you were coming to pay us a visit. She took it well, better than the other parent I expect. I did your letters up in bundles tonight; 105 in number now. I told Harrie, who said I'd better publish the correspondence, it is a pity it should be wasted... I have not had asthma for three nights now. I hope I am going to get rid of it. This is a funny parish actually. There is an entertainment going to be given tomorrow night at the Rectory, and a sort of comic song entertainment I presume. Rather peculiar is it not? (February 21)

Madge concurred. "I think one must be a very strange clergyman to go in for comic song entertainment in Lent." On February 22 she heard of the change of date for her visit, coupled with a further plea to bring her instrument.

Can you come on Tuesday which is the 7th of March instead of the 9th, that is if you can get your dress ready which I believe you are having built just now... I am extremely sorry we are rather hard up for looking glasses. We have one which goes the round of the house. Each person is allowed five minutes to finish that part of your toilet which necessitates a looking glass. Will you please bring your banjo. My sister wants to hear you play, in fact we all want to hear you play. Learn up something and do bring it, also some music and songs.

And then followed some tips on how London society were grooming themselves, based on the night of gaiety he spent at the Hotel Metropole in the new Northumberland Avenue off Trafalgar Square, from which he was writing.

Have just sat down to breakfast. Time 11 o'clock, and feel a bit fagged out. I am going down to Burgess Hill by 12 o'clock train if I can manage it. We had a splendid dance last night. The suite of dancing rooms are grand. We supped in the big salon. About 250 there were. Turner was staying here. We did not go to bed till 20 minutes to six this morning, talking over everything. Reece had a very jolly party last night. I have brought back all the latest fashions in my eye, and describe the best dresses to my sister who always wants to know a lot. I can give you a tip as well, and that is fringes are <u>gone</u> out, so for goodness sake don't go cutting your hair again. There was hardly a girl in the room with a fringe. I think they look much better now without them. I will tell you [how] to build your hair when you come out. If you bring your banjo, you must play it. We shall insist upon that. Also bring the pretty song you mention.

"I can see from what you say," replied Madge, "that you intend to turn my hair off my forehead; I am sure it would suit me a bit. I am now doing my hair in a rather tight twist at the back. How did the London ladies do it?"

Once back in Twineham, London and its problems seemed remote and irrelevant. For Bob, as he told Madge, there were more pressing matters to attend to, and of a different, country character.

March is coming in like a lion today; I hope it will go out like a lamb. I am just going to write old Turner about a horse, and inform him how to feed it, as he wants to know. I don't know if he thinks the horse eats sawdust or cinders. He has just been most awfully done buying horses, so he wants me to get one for him…. I hope he will come when you are here. He would make you laugh.

I had a letter from the Squire [Pitcher] the other day with advice how to treat sheep. The new pupil had two falls over jumps that day. He's making a pretty good start. The other one's horse is laid up. (March 1, 1893)

Madge had an even more eventful occasion to relate.

Mr Simonds has won a bet for £1. He said that he could swim from Long Brook Bridge to Marks Bridge in his ordinary clothes, nail boots etc. He accomplished this feat while the others ran along the banks with hop poles and waggon ropes… There was a good deal of excitement caused.

Bob was appalled at such folly.

I think Simonds is rather a fool to go playing the goat like that, as [I] know how that brook rushes down when there is a flood on, as no doubt there was when he swam it.

Madge got herself wet, but less sensationally.

We went to Eastbourne to do some shopping yesterday and came as usual laden with parcels. The Aunt has gone in for a kind of cart which she drags about. It is very nice as she takes all my parcels in it and won't let me carry it. I went to Eastbourne this morning for my singing lesson and got rather wet, but I found was dry by the time I got home.

Madge's all-important 18-day visit to Twineham was imminent, and Bob made sure nothing went wrong. There was little he could do about "the simply awful singing" in the parish church which he found really hard work to listen to, as he told her in his letter of March 5, if she insisted in going to mattins.

I hope you will come by the 11.50 Keymer Junction. I will be there to meet you (not tandem) if all goes well. If I do not appear on the platform you will know I cannot leave my horse. If I can get anyone to hold him I will go up to the train.

P.S. Please inform Miss Mockett we (Harrie and I) will do ourselves best to take care of her darling during her stay with us, and we will be very careful she is not thrown amongst young men (thieves) who will tempt her away from her Aunt's watchful care.

Madge was looking forward to it, but left him in no doubt about her willingness or ability to play for him. "I have not touched the banjo for over a week, so I can't play anything," she wrote the day before her departure on March 9. And when it was all over, she sat down after the tiring journey back to Polegate to write him a letter of thanks.

I arrived home quite safely and feel like a bottle of soda water that had had the cork out for several days. An old man got in at Hassocks, a very queer looking individual. It made me feel quite creepy when we came to that long tunnel. I met Charles alright at Lewes. The Aunt was on the station when I arrived.... I know I did not half thank you old dear sweetheart for my very pleasant visit to you, please accept my best thanks now. I am quite longing to get to bed and have a good weep.

She was glad the next day to receive a sincere letter signed 'H C Laing' from Bob's sister Harriet who was responsible for the smooth running of Twineham Grange and had done everything in her power to make the visit a success

I am glad you got home safely and that your Aunt thinks you're looking well. I bought my dress home in triumph and am very pleased with it. The skirt feels heavy in the hand, but I do not notice it when on. The sleeves are decidedly voluminous. I must get used to that first, and then I shall like the dress... We miss your ripple; the house seems quiet without you. I enjoyed your visit very much and shall look forward to another some day. (March 28, 1893)

Posting his letter to Madge, Bob met Old Blake who told him he, Bob, had been elected Churchwarden on Saturday, as he expected Bob had heard. He had not.

I said I had not the least idea of it. He said, 'Oh yes. T W Helme has resigned as, he said, you lived here in the parish so it would be better.' I have not the remotest idea what a Churchwarden has to do. If he has to take the money, I am there as it will provide pocket money for several days.

Madge thought he was quite the proper person to be Churchwarden. "If they keep appointing you for everything, you will be quite an important person. You now have something to do with the Church, School and Cricket Club." [April 1, 1893]

Few of Bob's activities as a member of the Twineham Cricket Club, outside his performances at the wicket, demanded as much of his attention as choosing the song he was to sing at its concerts. For the next one he had no hesitation in settling for *Mrs Jones's Musical Party* and *Simon the Cellarman*, although in the event he substituted *Our Little Nippers* for *Mrs Jones*. The room was 'crowded to suffocation' and the *Nippers* number went down the best of the two.

Less easy was deciding whether to join Dick Reece's party for the Downing College May Week Ball at Cambridge. He thought about it on long tandem drives and while watering his shrubs, but had difficulty in making up his mind.

Spring was in the air, and from all quarters came the cry 'Anyone for tennis?' He retrieved his tennis racquet from Burgess Hill. He was invited for tennis at Shermanbury Rectory, and looked forward to having a game "with the aid of Miss Knowles and another lady; I expect I shall drive everything into the next parish".

Bob told himself that Madge would have little to worry about his partnering Miss Knowles on the rectory tennis court, but what would she think about the character he had been asked to play in *Second Thoughts*? "It seems I have to make violent love to two ladies; I hope you don't mind."

What had she to lose? She was as good as engaged to Bob - but only 'as good as'. The delay in making official announcement of their engagement came from the McKergow side, and, as Madge told Bob, the Aunt was determined to remove it.

> The Aunt had a talk with Father yesterday. He said he thought from what he knew and had heard, that you were a <u>very</u> <u>good</u> <u>sort</u> (sounds as if you were a horse). Do you want me to call you 'Bob' now, or not? I will do so if you like. (April 7)

"Please impress it on your parents," she wrote the next week, "that I am very old. Don't forget about my fading beauty."

It was not a matter of feigning old age for the parson at Twineham. When Bob went to the rectory on April 18 he "heard a very bad account of the Rector - they think he will not live many days".

Bob's other concern was how best to fill the gap occasioned by the parson's absence.

> It is an awful bore finding a parson for Sunday next. I have written for one today, but really don't know if I shall be able to get one in time. If not I must read the service myself with the help of 'Muster Gander'. I saw him this morning. He says this is all new to me sir, you must be head man and arrange affairs, and it seems to me we have a good deal on our shoulders at present.

Bob never expected the Reverend Molyneux to return to his parish duties, but it was no less of a shock when the rector died on April 20. "I don't know what the poor family will do," he told Madge, "it is very bad for them." She could not but agree. "It is very sad to think of the Rector's death, but at the same time it is a great relief to the parish. I can't think what the family will do, as I believe the daughters, who are at home, have scarcely any accomplishments."

Perhaps Molyneux was not all that old, and his stipend the family's only income.

The Rector's death only seemed to compound the trouble Bob was having with his estate staff,

> I sacked Stoner at a minute's notice for loafing, and when told spoke in an insolent fashion. So I told him to put down his tools and go there and then. He wanted his money, so I politely told him to go to blazes. I then went into the stables and threatened to thrash the life out of Heath for neglecting the old horse which was standing in the stable dripping down with water. (April 17)

Within ten days he appointed another groom - "there is a difference in the stable already, it is most neat and clean." And in another compartment of his life, Bob was finding his part in *Second Thoughts*, with all that love-making, trickier than he had thought.

> Yesterday we had our fourth rehearsal. I don't like my part, but I suppose I must do it. Barrie has to take part in the "—— Woman" as they cannot get anybody round here.

Bob put himself out to help the grieving daughters of the late rector by inviting them to the Grange for a musical evening at which the pièce de résistance was the French count whom he brought over from Burgess Hill,

> The Misses Molyneux are coming to dinner tonight, in a quiet way of course, as it is so soon after their father's death, to be introduced to the Count, as she is a 'musicker' also, and heard him play in town some time ago at a concert.

Madge could do better than that. She told Bob she was going to London to see the leading actor of the day perform in his latest historical melodrama at the Lyceum Theatre. "We are going to a matinee of *Becket* today. I hope I shall like it. I think it is my duty to see [Henry] Irving act, as I have never done so."

Becket was a verse play by Tennyson about the archbishop and chancellor murdered on orders from Henry II in Canterbury Cathedral. It was first produced at the Lyceum in the Strand on February 3, 1893. Ellen Terry played the female lead and her son Edward Gordon Craig, better known as a scenic designer, had a small part in it. The critic Clement Scott thought his performance in *Becket* was "the crowning point of Irving's career... the more one sees of the performance the more one is rivetted and fascinated by it". The play was "one of the most perfect artistic productions of our time". Madge will have been glad she saw it, and is likely never to have forgotten it.

Actor Robert McKergow was easing into the part in *Second Thoughts* which he had once felt uneasy in. After dinner with the Sales family, which must have enabled him to shed his inhibitions, he had, he told Madge, "a very good rehearsal - I made love in quite an approved style". It was, once again, All Right On The Night.

> The theatricals went off very well indeed. The prompting in the first piece was awful, but it went very well indeed. Miss Sale acted splendidly. I made love to Miss K wonderfully. It quite fetched the rustic mind. What do you think - the mater and some Burgess Hill drove over for the show. What a giddy old thing she is.

Madge was spectator not player in the spectacle of Queen Victoria opening the Imperial Institute that day in May 1893, when she watched the procession "from Moyle Bretton's room at St George's Hospital [at Hyde Park Corner]."

> Hicks and Cis [Bretton] met us at Victoria [Station]. When we arrived at the hospital, we at first could not find Moyle's room, but when at last we did arrive, we found Moyle had just finished shaving. He had been called out during the night, and was then finishing his toilet. His room had two windows, and we saw the Queen beautifully twice. After the procession was over Hicks went to see what he could find to eat, and at last came back with frock coat tails filled with lemonade bottles and carrying a large bag of the famous hospital bath buns. Althoug her [Altogether?] we had great fun.

Churchwarden Bob was making slow progress in his task of finding someone suitable to take over as rector, someone able to perform in the pulpit in a way the congregation would find stimulating.

> I have also been awfully busy with Churchwarden business. I was disappointed in the clergyman today, so had to rush off to Brighton on Friday to get one. He was an old man, but preached a very nice sermon and made allusions to the death of the late rector which sent the congregation into tears. We had him up to dinner today. Turner and I went back to church afterwards and did not stop to the service.... I have come to the conclusion that being Churchwarden is awful hard work. [April 30]

It was a matter of providing stop-gaps.

> I have got McDermott to take the services next Sunday. I wrote to his Rector and asked him to let him come. He is a very good sort - a great musician. The last time he came he played all the latest operas through [doubtless the Savoy Operas of Gilbert & Sullivan]. I am glad we were far from the madding crowd. Who do you think arrived here the other morning? Stanford by Jove. He asked me to play cricket this season for Bolney. He said Hodgson had asked him. I declined with thanks. He said he was

not going to have anything to do with the Flower Show this year, as when he took anything in hand he liked to do it well. So I said we have some very good new men on the committee so it is alright.

Madge continued her culture trips to London, where The Season was in full swing, with a visit to Burlington House.

We enjoyed the Academy very much and got rather tired. There is a portrait of the Master of the Eridge Hunt. My cousin Annie has a painting hung this year but it doesn't look anything wonderful to me.

At last the McKergows saw the need to end the ridiculous situation arising from their reluctance to let it be known formally that Bob and Madge were engaged. Bob gave Madge news of the breakthrough on May 4, 1893.

The mater I understand told the gov on Saturday that I was to be engaged this month, which made him jump considerably. He talked for a few minutes rather vigorously, but it seemed to end fairly calmly, expounded on the youth of the lady and so on.

The actual announcement was not made for another two weeks. "We have been engaged a week, darling," wrote Madge on May 27, "and it seems a fortnight since you left." Bob turned his mind to how he should mark the occasion in the way everyone would expect him to.

Now the next thing is what we are to do for you to meet people (friends). Either a picnic must be given or a dance. I am going for the latter tomorrow with the gov and I think it really would be best as people come readily for that. I suppose you would also like that best. What do you think?

Madge loved the idea.

Either a dance or a picnic would be a lovely way of meeting your friends. Of course I think it would be delightful, only won't it give you and Miss Laing an awful lot of bother? I quite expect the friends would prefer a dance. A picnic depends so much on the weather that it is rather risky,

Making plans for his life as a married man was no reason to let up on the social engagements and sporting activities which came with this time of year.

I have just had supper tonight after having got wet through at the fishing party. We did not catch much except the ladies who no doubt have all caught colds.

And at long last he no longer had to worry about filling the vacancy at the rectory.

I have heard very good news today that the Rev. J Paget Davies of Streat is going to get the living of Twineham, my old tutor. It will be very nice as he is an awful good sort and also his wife. I am glad I am churchwarden when he comes as we get on well together. It will be rather funny for one of his rowdiest pupils to be his Churchwarden. I hope he will not remind the people of the district of some of the scenes at the rectory when I was there. Harriet told the servants here today that I was engaged and that you were coming to stay.

The supper party with which they planned to celebrate their betrothal, Bob told his fiancee on May 30, would take place next Friday week. "I suppose you will have your gown by then, ready to be the belle of the evening, and makes us all fall at your feet." And this letter, for the first time, he signed not 'Old Mac' but 'Bob'.

~ 3 ~
Truly Engaged

Everyone now knew of Bob and Madge's engagement, not just the favoured few who had to talk about it in hushed tones among themselves and never to anyone who was not 'in the know'. Madge could go about openly as Bob McKergow's fiancee, but never without a chaperone who on most occasions was Bob's half-sister Harriet Laing.

When Bob returned from playing tennis at the Aubers in the first week of June 1893, he was able to tell Madge, "They wished you had been there and hoped I would bring you to see them." And incidentally, he added, she did not need to bring her banjo for Tom Maynard's party if she did not want to.

Members of the McKergow clan clamoured for more information on the young lady who was soon to become one of them, and wrote to welcome her and offer their congratulations. Bob's niece Katie Laing wrote from Bart's Hospital on June 4:

> It gave me great pleasure to hear of your engagement to that lucky uncle of mine. You must forgive me for not writing before, but when I am off duty I do not as a rule feel in the humour for letter writing. Today is a quiet day in surgery where I am, and we were allowed to read and write. This is being written on a ward with only two beds in it, but the patients are not suffering from anything infectious - but accidents. Sometimes I see awful sights brought in.... I think I am going to Cheshunt next Sunday. It is my long day, which we all have once a month. I like this life immensely. We have a jolly time, but I can't say I am very fond of attending operations but I am getting more accustomed to it already.

Bob's many varsity friends sent separate invitations to Miss Baker to join their parties for all end-of-term events at Cambridge. Dr Barclay Smith and Dr Dick Reece requested the pleasure of her company to watch the May Races on board their houseboat on June 13, and take food afterwards in Dr Perkins's Rooms in Downing College. She and Bob were two of 60 or so who lined up to be photographed before things became too boisterous.

It was an exhausting, noisy experience for the newly engaged couple, with all the conventional undergraduate shenaniganing, and the next day seemed a bit empty.

"My very dearest Bob," wrote Madge when she got home, "quite safely after a very hot journey." She saw S.M. at Brighton, she told him, and he hoped they had enjoyed their visit to Cambridge together. "Now don't be dull my sweetheart. I daresay it will not be long before we can meet again."

After reaching home at 6.40 the Morning After, Bob had to confess he felt very dull indeed. He had become hooked on Madge's favourite metaphor. "This place feels like a bottle of soda water with the cork left out for an hour." He was in no state to rid his mind of the fears he had about the outcome of his mother's surgical operation due to take place on June 17. "I do hope Mother will get over tomorrow all right. I am simply dreading the business. I hate seeing her before they commence. I don't think I can do it."

Madge was equally anxious.

> I hope the operation has passed off well. I have not received the telegram yet but no doubt shall do so before long then... I have been vaccinated today. Mr Farnell congratulated me twice on my engagement. He said don't have a silly engagement of 4 months. He said, 'You must wait till a year next September or I shall make a fuss.' I said I should only wait until August, so he passed it for then.

Sixty-six-year-old Mrs Robert McKergow, Bob's mother, was operated on in a room at Dunkeld House with Dick Reece in attendance, and Bob moved over there until she was fully recovered. From there, on June 18, he told Madge:

> I came over yesterday and they said I had better stop the night as Dick could not come back to Twineham with me as they wanted him to stop in the house all night to be ready in case of anything happening... Mother really is a brick. She went through the whole affair splendidly, walked into the room smiling so Dick said. There were four doctors and the nurse present. They took threequarters of an hour over it. She was very delirious when she came to; she struck out and hit Dr Richardson wildly. Then Dick was sent for and he got her quiet. And again Dick gave her some sleeping stuff last night as she was very restless, but she is progressing favourably now... I don't want many days like yesterday. I had to help set out the room for the operation which was rather ghastly. They seem to think mother will be about a week or ten days in bed; then you will be able to come back to Twineham.

"Your mother is indeed plucky," wrote back Madge.

> I am so glad to hear all is going on well. Don't forget to give her some of my love when she is strong enough to be talked to. What a comfort Dr Reece must have been.... The Aunt is going to take twenty little girls

(GFS) on the hills to tea and games on Thursday. I hope it will not be as hot as it is today... I had a letter from 'Dr Dick' this morning in which he says that Mrs McKergow has for some time promised him she would give a fancy dress ball; and I think that when she is well, he will begin to talk to her about it. He is always on the look-out for some fun isn't he?... I heard Louisa [her maid] say au revoir to Florence yesterday as she was going down the road - they are getting quite educated now, see.

Bob went back home to Twineham to cope with the entertaining that went with the induction of the new rector. He told Madge it was all getting him down.

I feel horribly cross about this affair altogether. I never knew such a rotten affair with alterations of days etc.... The mater is up and trotting about and received ten visitors because Harrie was away, and knocked herself up rather. Mother thinks of coming over to Twineham in a cab on Saturday. (June 29, 1893)

It was Bob's dog that made Madge cross. For him it was a bit of a joke - "I shall bring this beautiful beast down with me to devour your cats when I come." But not for Madge. "Please don't bring that awful dog with you; wait and let me see him at Dunkeld first. I don't want him here to kill my cats."

However both were looking forward to spending days together at Twineham Grange that hot summer of 1893. "The house seems quiet as a grave tonight - no little girl to spoon, so I shall have to turn in," wrote Bob on July 7. When Madge returned to Polegate she at once sent a note which began, "I have arrived home quite safely," and ended, "Now goodbye dearest, thanking you very much for the delightful time I have spent with you."

Animals became a major preoccupation. "The Aunt," Madge told Bob on July 23, "says that Jack is the most wilful dog she has ever seen. She had to beat him because he tried to bite the butcher; but she thinks he will soon make a very good dog."

Madge was happy to leave canine-control to Aunt Maria; she now set her sights on acquiring the art of equitation.

I am very much looking forward to seeing you my darling on Saturday. I have mentioned that I wish to ride, and they are thinking about it.... The Aunt told Fred the other evening that I wished to learn riding, and that after I had had a few lessons I should want him to take me out. He said he should be pleased to help me when they had a suitable horse. So that is alright.

To ride comfortably and safely she had to be properly dressed - and à la mode. She disliked black Melton cloth, and thought little of 'safety' riding habits which left your skirt on the horse if you fell off. Bob pleaded with her to avoid a serge riding habit which would stretch and look horrid at once - "You cannot beat the Melton cloth for style," he insisted. Her taste might differ from his, but she believed she was unlikely to go far wrong if she took the advice of the tailors at Nicholls in London's Regent Street. Bob's mother and Madge's aunt had hit it off with one another, so the matter of the design and material of Madge's first riding habit was soon settled to their mutual satisfaction. If it was not to Bob's taste he would have to lump it. He was fully occupied in any case with a very different kind of animal. "I am going to dip 60 sheep tomorrow if fine, so I anticipate getting into a good mess." He was already in a bit of a mess over his domestics. He told Madge she would be glad to hear that at least one of them, Wickham, had agreed to stop on.

> I had a card from that girl I saw on Saturday saying she had taken the Brighton place. I first of all interviewed Mrs P[artington] on the subject who told me Wickham had not got the place in the lunatic asylum, so I then asked Wickham whether she would stop till I was suited. I said I thought it was a great pity she was leaving and talked to her like a father. She then said I will promise to stop on. I was put out because Mrs P. would not let me out on Sunday evening, so I said I would put that right. I am awfully pleased really; she is a splendid waitress. She waited well the other night, and I always have a feeling that she will not upset the soup down the guest's neck or anything like that.

With the aid of the steady-handed Wickham, Bob felt able to relax at home, but was overdoing it, in the view of one of his friends, he told Madge when it came to the church.

> Davidson was up fussing around yesterday afternoon in great form, saying he thought we were doing too much at the church without having a faculty for doing the same. I agreed with him, but still at the same time reminded him I had done nothing but that the Rector was doing it himself without consulting anyone which I thought was a mistake. (August 3)

Aunt Lizzie, Madge told Bob, was having poultry trouble.

> When we arrived at Grovebridge, Aunt said she had had 8 of her best chickens stolen. Mr Pearless went off to Hailsham and 3 policemen came up and hunted for a few hours, then gave it up as hopeless. About 6 in the evening, when we were playing tennis, these lost chicks walked through the hedge very calmly, greatly to our amusement. Won't the policeman laugh? (August 4)

To Madge's dismay her favourite cat turned thief, for which there was only one penalty.

> 'Nigger' is dead. He stole the breakfast and was then sent away to be shot. I have another lovely rough kitten that the Viccaji's have sent, I shall bring it with me when I come for good, so it's no use what you say darling!

Work hard and play hard was the lifestyle at Twineham in the eighteen nineties, with plenty of choice for how to spend your playtime. Bob told Madge of the cricket match about to take place in the park on August 7 with a team from Brighton, but that he would not be present.

> We've got the Flower Show on Wednesday next. I intend buying you a white shawl which is being worked for the show. Miss K says I must make you a present of it as it would suit you so well... George, Fred and I amused ourselves at the Fair today having shots at bottles after I had stood about three hours trying to sell my lambs. I did not succeed, so sent them home again to Burgess Hill... Well I must close and go to bed as I have to be up early about the Show tomorrow. Mrs P thinks she is going to have the first prize for butter. I don't know. What did you think wrong with it when you were over?

Perhaps it melted too quickly in the August sun? He was nearly killed with the heat of the Show, he told Madge.

> It went off very well indeed. Mrs P got second prize for butter. She gave a very close run for the 1st. I went into Knowles after supper and we then went back to the Show, after people had cleared, to get the needlework out of the tent. Your shawl is beautifully worked I must say.

Mrs McKergow came over for the Show, obviously fully recovered from her debilitating operation, firing on both barrels - not however at the targets in the shooting booth but her son.

> Mother gave me an awful lecture yesterday about seeing you so often. She said it was absurd to be always going over to see you; that we saw far too much of one another; that you would think far more of me if I saw you less, and that we had annoyed the gov very much by walking about arm in arm at Dunkeld. She did not think it at all nice of us. (August 10)

"Your father is an old silly," retorted Madge. "He will have to put up with it after we are married." The parents' shocked attitude to their son's open display of his affection for his bride-to-be was merely absurd so far as Bob was concerned, and had no effect on the pace of the social round into which he plunged during his last days as a bachelor at the Grange. Madge was kept fully informed.

> Dick and Bunny are coming and next Saturday night I anticipated having a very fine dinner party. I have made out the menu and am going to give it to Mrs P to carry out. We have discussed the situation at some length already. I am going to ask the following, Miss K, the Misses K and friend a Scotch lady, Mr and Mrs Sale, Dick, Bunny and myself. The friend, as you notice, rather upsets the show as she is stopping with the Ks. Of course there is no alternative.

It was a roaring success.

> The dinner went off very well indeed. You should have heard those fellows going ahead. They would make any dinner party go well. I told them they were both to be charming and, by Jove, they laid themselves out for it. I am sure everyone thought I had two very nice friends. Bunny and I went to Church yesterday in the morning; Dick would not go the old beggar. Mrs P cooked the dinner very well indeed, and we had both the Matthews girls to help in the background. (August 21, 1893)

The dinner party was a welcome distraction from the words of would-be advice which his mother had shot at him so explosively that afternoon at the Show. But he could not entirely dismiss them from his mind. Was she perhaps right? What - or who - had prompted her to do it?

> I told Harriet the remark mother made, and asked her if she had anything to do with it. She said, 'Of course not; I think she talks nonsense.'

To demonstrate their disregard of Mr and Mrs McKergow's views of how they should conduct themselves, Bob went ahead with the overnight visit to Polegate which he had planned for August 25. He was in light-hearted mood when he told Madge, "Please mind the dog does not bite me or I shall shoot him. Ta-ta till we meet then. I shall have more news."

He picked up Harriet at Burgess Hill on his way back to Twineham after the visit, and swiftly passed on to Madge the inside information which had come to the ears of his sister from an obviously authoritative source in the world of *haute couture*.

> Harriet says don't have a new dress if you can help it yet, as there is going to be a great change in dress. (August 29, 1893)

Just in time. His letter clashed with hers telling him, "I have bought the material for a new dress today." It was mercifully followed by a second letter that read, "I need not have my dress made yet if you think it will be better not." (August 31)

With the beginning of September came the moment to take shot guns out of their case in the Gun Room, stock up with cartridges and clean out the game bags. By the first of the month Bob had five invitations to partridge shooting. One of them was from Charles to shoot at Wilmington on the 4th. This was a good opportunity to stay with Madge and the Aunt. When he got home he put the final arrangements in hand for his own shoot.

He had, by this time, thoroughly fallen out with Stanford of the Court whom he suspected of being sufficiently unsporting to shoot any of the Grange partridges that flew on to the Court land. Matthews was instructed to station men in Bob Lane ready to shout and wave their arms about to deflect the partridges from the Stanford territory. How successful this was is not mentioned, but the day was 'ghastly' and everyone shot badly.

At Polegate Madge was starting to learn to ride with Mr Weeks and his 'riding masters'. She found trotting quite easy, but she could not get the hang of cantering. Mr Weeks suggested a two-hour downland ride from Eastbourne to Jevington for the next lesson, and gave it as his opinion that she would be able to ride in six weeks.

At Twineham making preparations for the dance, first mooted in May and now fixed for October 3, became top priority. Waiters had to be engaged, musicians had to be booked and beds found for them. There was debate about the dance floor - should it be stained as well as polished? Harriet was in charge of decorations, considered hanging fans on the walls trimmed with ribbons, but abandoned the idea.

Typically Dick Reece stirred things up by sending a list of his friends whom he would like Bob to invite. No way, said Bob, they had more than enough friends of their own. Bob reminded Madge that he would necessarily have to dance with many of the ladies as a duty, but that he would yield to no-one to take her into dinner. She took that for granted; it was all part of what the Upper Crust called Good Form, the Done Thing. She did not feel required to make any comment however on the report she received from Bob of the conversation which his mother had with a Dr Murtagh and his wife. Mrs Murtagh had said she had married at a young age when her character was not formed, but her husband had 'done it for her'.

In all this time Bob had lost touch with his one-time mentor Squire Pitcher of Grovebridge who had married Maria Mockett's sister Elizabeth. He was surprised therefore to receive a letter from him, dated September 23, suggesting he came to the sale he was holding at Beestons on October 7, and offering to send him a catalogue.

> I hope you will come down and spend some of yr _profits_ of this yrs farming. There are a nice lot of sheep, about 460 and a lot of horses and colts and some good tackling. When you get a catalogue you will see what there is. What a summer it has been. I have not quite finished hay making and a little more harvesting to do.
>
> October 7th comes on a Saturday and if you can manage it perhaps you could stay over Sunday or perhaps you wd prefer staying at the house of a certain 'maiden lady' of your acquaintance. This I will leave [you] to have your own opinion about, but come to my sale you must _and shall_. We have no end of partridge this season - they are frightfully wild and I do not get much time to shoot them. Pearless has been out several times but not with much success. I am finishing hop-picking today - ta-ta.

Bob did not go. He had become increasingly aware that 'Squire' Pitcher was a very good salesman. If he had ventured down there he would have been welcomed boisterously - and sold some sheep he did not really want.

Madge's acquisition of the art of riding a horse was taking time - slow and painful, as she told Bob on October 11.

I enjoyed my ride very much but it gave me a dreadfully bad headache. I was really too tired to ride… Coming home my horse was nearly thrown. A little boy sent a hoop across the road just as we were passing(trotting). It got muddled up in my horses's hind legs, but I stopped quickly and another boy came and got it out… The Working Party begins tomorrow - ta-ta my dearest sweetheart.
With love.

A month later she had an even more unpleasant experience. During her first riding lesson her horse almost fell in the street, but she managed to remain seated. For the Master of Twineham Grange, life took its less hazardous but enjoyable autumnal course.

I have just been out shooting with the gov this morning. I have just seen a covey of 12 going across the Park… We had a meeting in the schoolroom last night very well attended by the villagers about the heating of the church. We collected about £50 on the spot which was good. I must close as I have to ride down to the post to pay the men. I was elected President of the Working Men's Club last night in place of Mr Knowles. I have to be home to take the chair at the Annual Supper held on Nov 2nd. I have also a public dinner on 1st and another meeting of the church business as soon as I have come back, so I am fairly full up.

But not so full up that he could not fit in a healthy ration of sight-seeing and theatre-going in the capital.
From his room in the prestigious Hotel Victoria in Northumberland Avenue off Trafalgar Square, he penned a note to Madge: "I am just going to have my [silk] hat ironed, then dress for dinner [white tie and tails of course] and on to a theatre." A fuller account followed in two days:

I went down to Woolwich yesterday and I went over the whole of the Arsenal. It is a wonderful place. The best of it, I got in without a ticket from the War Office, my personal appearance etc. We went to see *Gaity Girl* [sic]; dined at Blanchards [169 Regent Street] first. The night before I saw *Charley's Aunt* at the Globe [in Newcastle Street off the Strand].

Then up to Newbridge near Wolverhampton for a few days shooting with his friend John Rose.

We had a splendid day's shooting. We killed sixteen and a half brace of pheasants, eight and a half of partridges, two brace of pigeon, one hare and four rabbits, total head of 61. It was the best day's shooting I have had. I am shooting with another party tomorrow, where we expect to have a good day. I am going to ride a friendly horse out cubbing on Tuesday. The people here are always very hospitable to me.

He posted what Madge in her letter of thanks called 'a pair' of pheasants, which she said arrived in perfect condition. Three days later Bob joined a shooting party in Poynton in Cheshire.

> I had some fine shooting yesterday: 87 pheasants and sundry other things. You never saw such shooting, and we only shot the small coverts. Turner's uncle and friends have between 5 and 6 thousand acres. I got in an awful funk I should make a fool of myself, especially when the ladies turned up, but I shot better than ever.
>
> You must excuse me not writing to you but I have been rushed about so we had to stay the night at Turner's uncle's. We dine in a big public dinner in Manchester the night before. I am going over to Turner's cotton mill this morning and they want me to go down a coal pit but I fancy it is a bit rough on the clothes.

Bob came back from his shooting parties with a bad cold and an even worse temper. The garden was in 'a disgraceful state' and Willie the groom was going to be 'given beans' for using the best hunting saddle for exercising the mare.

He was relieved to find that the Working Men's Club dinner was going to be put off until December 7 as the Committee wanted to make it a bigger affair. Matthews, the farm foreman, improved the atmosphere by saying that there were a great many pheasants in the wood so a shooting party was arranged 'to have a bang at them'. The gov was invited and unexpectedly recommended that Bob should get himself a new gun. On the day of the shoot the gov had a bad knee and was unable to walk much. It was a fair day's sport with a bag of 31 head.

There were more servant problems. They were upset at 'late dinner' being started again; and then Mrs Partington the housekeeper gave notice on account of the Grange being such 'a hard place'. Bob could not agree; the Matthews girls were always available to be brought in to help. He and Harriet decided to try and get a good cook, rather than a housekeeper who was 'only for ornament'.

This somewhat fraught atmosphere was relieved by the arrival of the gov and Harriet's sister Alice with an extraordinary story. The gov had got to know an elderly French gentleman who was determined to marry off his daughter to an Englishman. This character had come to the gov saying he had heard of his son. Would he give him a photograph of Bob to show to his daughter? He offered the gov the use of his chalet somewhere in France for the summer in which the two young people could become acquainted and, in the event of it all ending up with their getting married, he would make his daughter a present of thirty thousand pounds. "You've never heard such a joke!!" chortled Bob.

The sore throat that Madge kept mentioning was decidedly worrying. When Bob begged them to take a look at the Park Croft water supply, as the possible cause of it, the Aunt hesitated but was eventually persuaded to take the necessary action. It did not deter Madge from persevering with her riding lessons, and demonstrated how keen she was to become an accomplished horsewoman, no expense barred, by deciding to buy a new saddle. She had Fred go to a harness-maker's sale and he came back with one costing six guineas. It did not suit her however, and after she had tried and rejected two or three others, she settled on one at ten guineas. Bob was not to be outdone, and ordered a new hunting rig-out from a tailor in Brighton including a frock-coat - "shan't know myself". In the meantime he felt sufficiently well fitted out to attend a swagger meet at Bolney.

Bob hoped he could persuade Madge's brother Charles Baker to play his violin at 'this wonderful Club dinner' at the next village of Wineham, but Madge thought this unlikely. When Bob and his pals met in the Mission Room at Wineham to plan the evening's programme and he saw he was down to sing twice, he suggested giving them renderings of *Private Tommy* and *The Nipper's Lullabye*.

He was enjoying life at the Grange, but as he confessed to Madge it seemed to be costing an inordinately large amount of money, and it had him worried. He felt he had to tell the gov that since September 1892 he had spent £3,434 on running the place, and the farm was still not in profit. Should he give it up? Not a good prospect. He and Madge were planning to get married in 1894 and live at the Grange.

It was a dilemma that brought Madge hurrying over to Twineham to help Bob sort things out. After staying a few days, it appears that the two of them, and presumably the gov, decided how best to meet the situation and the crisis passed. By the end of November 1893 Bob was busy ferreting. After two days, he, the dogs and the ferrets were worn out. They had killed 18 rabbits which, he had to admit, was not going to reduce the population very significantly.

If Madge was to sing in the anthem in church on Christmas Day, as the Polegate vicar wanted her to along with Aunt Maria, she would have to get rid of her sore throat. "For goodness sake have the water seen to," said Bob, convinced that was the cause of it. Bob was invited over for Christmas and looked forward to hearing some good choral music.

The Aunt made Jack the dog a blue dress - "he does look so funny" Madge told Bob. Later in the month she took Jack to her Working Party, and they were highly amused at his costume. Turner and his groom came to stay at the Grange to get some hunting. It was all rather exhausting. They nearly got as far as Wilmington with the hounds. They had got up at 6.30 and never got back till seven o'clock at night. After the hunt they had to ride from near Seaford to Lewes to catch the train to Burgess Hill and then ride back from there. Bob thought Turner would have good reason for remembering hunting in that part of the world.

As Bob went down to the shop to get change to pay his men, he called in at the church and was worried to find it in an awful mess with the builders still working. Would it be ready for the opening service on the Sunday evening before Christmas Day? he asked the rector whom he found in the nave. He seemed confident that it would, and took the opportunity of raising with Bob the matter of his joining the robed choir of men and boys which was in the course of being formed. Bob foresaw a great crush in church when it was opened, but told Madge that he was leaving it to Gander to organise things.

Bob and Turner planned another exhausting day in the hunting field of the kind they had done last time, which once again meant having to take a train from Burgess Hill to Lewes and then riding out to Beddingham some three or four miles further on. Turner said he was hanged if he would go if it was wet. They would have to leave the Grange at 7.45 to catch the 9.03 at Burgess Hill as the horses must go steady. It was a pretty big business going all that distance but he wanted to show Turner some sport.

The dinner and concert of the Working Men's Club went off very well. Bob sang *The Nipper's Lullabye* and *Private Atkins* (or *Tommy*) which, he told Madge, seemed to fetch the audience a bit. Miss Hunt accompanied fearfully badly - even the people at the back noticed it. Never again would he sing without someone he knew playing for him.

On December 12 differences of opinion arose between Bob and Madge on various matters - quite a rift. The first was over Bob's fretting at the prospect of shutting up the Grange over Christmas. Since he would be at Polegate and Harriet at Burgess Hill, and Wickham wanted to go home, it seemed inevitable. Cook could not be left there alone. Madge's view, expressed somewhat brusquely, was that he must think them a dull lot at Polegate if he could not stay more than four days; an extra day or two would not affect what happened at the Grange.

Then there was the question of whether he should join the proposed church choir. Did Madge want him to turn down the rector's invitation or not? Her view was that singing in the choir would not suit him because he disliked turning out in the evenings for 'practices'. He could not but agree that that might be so, but he was much put out by Madge's further reason for his not joining, that he was not as good a musician as Simmons. It was a bit thick, he told her, to compare him to the village grocer. When he had heard Simmons sing at the recent concert, he had felt a perfect 'Teddy Lloyd' to him. Madge granted Bob had the better voice, but held to her opinion that he knew nothing of the *theory* of music.

It was time to back down. Bob wrote that his remarks about Simmons were jokingly meant, and he conceded that Simmons knew more about music than he did.

When, as already arranged, within a few days he visited Polegate, and the two of them were able to indulge in talking, instead of merely writing, to each other, all differences of opinion were smoothed over, disagreements were settled and "everything was all right".

Bob was back again at Polegate for the Christmas season, stayed until the 28th and then received a letter from Madge saying she was looking forward to coming to Twineham on January 8. She hoped he had had a good day's hunting. It was a good run from Burgess Hill to the Hill, he told her, but he came down over a fence and lamed the mare.

One of Bob's worries about shutting up the Grange while away at Polegate had been having to leave the farm men unsupervised; he would have to leave written instructions. He did not need to worry. Things were as usual on the farm after he had been away, he told Madge - one man on the drink all week. "Blow Christmas!"

On New Year's Eve 1893 Bob went to church twice. The services went very well and the singing did not sound too bad. Davidson was there in a cassock, played in the morning and read a lesson in the afternoon. His letter bringing her these last titbits of village news for 1893 ended with him wishing her a Very

Happy New Year - "ought to be the happiest - I hope it will."

On New Year's Day 1894 Madge reported that the Aunt was ill in bed with the 'influ', which was what everybody called influenza. Her brother Charles had a bad headache. The next day he looked really ill - there were cases of typhoid at Willingdon. On January 2 Bob also went down with influ and took to his bed, although he felt better next day. His doctor insisted that his bedroom fire be kept in all night, and Harriet and Wickham had taken it in turns to keep it stoked up. To relieve, if not cure, the Aunt's influ, the doctor had prescribed Tonic and Oysters, and they had worked wonders. She was well on the way to recovery.

It started snowing again at the end of the week, and they were skating on the Crumbles in Eastbourne. Madge expected Bob would not have sufficiently recovered from his bout of influ to cope with her visit to the Grange planned for January 8. She was right. He suggested it was postponed for a day. All his taps were frozen up. Since it was no weather for riding. he advised her to leave her saddle at home but to bring music and skates. Bob gradually got the better of influenza, comforted by the warm fire in his bedroom grate now kept in at night, not only by his two lady stokers, but also by George King.

The time came when he was well enough to entertain his fiancee, and she stayed with him and Harriet at the Grange for some 18 days that cold January of 1894 - until the 28th. On her return to Polegate she wrote and told him she had reached home safely, and Bob replied that it was strange to be writing to her again.

And then he followed up this loving letter with one that was tactlessly bound to annoy her. In it he said that he had 'heard' that his family were concerned that Madge had not had a wider education, had not been abroad for a year for example. Not surprisingly Madge was very upset. She told Bob he was not 'manly' to be swayed by such talk. His family, she said, were showing themselves to be 'deceitful' in outwardly giving her a welcome, but apparently being unkind behind her back.

Once raised, it was not a matter that would quickly be dismissed. In the exchange of letters that took place in the opening days of February, Madge was to learn that the McKergows not only regretted the restricted nature of her education up to now, but felt that since she was failing to improve her mind, which they partly put down to the limited society of Polegate. Bob thought it was essential to get her away from there. He had to concede however that Twineham did not have much to offer in terms of intellectual company either.

It is not entirely clear, from the correspondence of the two at this time, just how all this arose. What may have happened was that the Laing sisters. Harriet and Alice, and Bob's mother (née Anne Laing) were surprised at Bob's social success at Twineham. They may have thought he would be even more influential in the years ahead, and that he would therefore need the support of a gifted wife. He was however engaged to a 17-year-old farmer's daughter, very pretty and lively but inexperienced. That, they might have thought, could be a disadvantage.

Someone outside the family picked up on such comments, and passed them on to Bob, no doubt well embellished.

Madge saw at once it was not the sort of talk she should pretend had not come to her ears, but that she should bring it out into the open and not allow it to lie festering - and grow.

She had no hesitation in telling Bob he must ask his father if it was true that he and his wife disapproved of her. But of course Bob was so nervous of his father that he did not dare question him in that way. So it was never mentioned who thought what. So far as is known, such questioning, as there might have been at that time of the level of Madge's education and intellect, never affected the long-term relationships of the two families. As far as is known, there was never any unkindness after the wedding, and Madge became one of the most admired host-esses in the county.

It needed more than the gov's apparent fear that Madge's 'inexperience' would render her incapable of acting as his son's chatelaine to divert Bob from his social round, visiting his beloved Madge as often as he could and pressing on with all that was needed to be done to make sure the wedding place took place - and with-out a hitch - on the appointed day.

And there was certainly no interruption in the non-stop letter-writing.

> I have just come in from Church. The Rector did not preach, worse luck; we had an awful duffer instead… I suppose Dick's wedding will soon be along now. I had a wire yesterday from him wanting me to come to dinner tomorrow night. I suppose you have discussed the wedding question since you have been home at some length. I should like to know the ideas for a wedding present to Dick.
>
> The gov is coming over tomorrow to shoot rabbits. The pony has got a sore elbow but I hope she will be better in a day or two.
>
> I have had to leave off at this point in the letter as Capt Lously has come to dinner. I don't think you ever met him; he is a great hunting man and a regular caution. He whistles splendidly and plays the piano at the same time. (February 4, 1894)

Madge was not yet entirely reconciled to forgetting the slur which her future father-in-law had apparently cast on her ability to take her place at the head of Bob's household, and wrote to Bob to tell him once again, although tucked in at the end of a letter conveying the usual village news, how he must take the action she had previously urged him to take.

> I don't think you know the Mr Mayfield we met. He is brother to the one who married Miss Jackson. He is a broad faced creature with a bored expression and hunts three times a week and is just off to Palestine on a riding tour… I wish you would have the conversation with your father.

Bob was set on enlarging the estate which was to be become the family home of the new generation of McKergows, and giving the Grange the grander image which he believed was more appropriate to the marital status he was about to assume.

I had a letter from Mr Seth-Smith's estate agents today offering that field of his by the lodge. I have written and told them to send me particulars of price etc. I hope I shall get it, as it really ought to go with this place. I expect you will say Bother the land. I know you bar the idea of buying land.

I am going to ride to hounds tomorrow if all's well… We shall probably have some noisy scenes here soon concerning politics. I am trying to get [George] Goschen [later made a viscount and Chancellor of the Exchequer] to address a meeting, and as Stanford is running Goring, things will soon look up.

For Madge, the time leading up to the day when she would leave the circle in which had spent her childhood, was taken up with seeing as much as possible of the friends and relations who for so long had made up her world and she was about to exchange for the new set of which she would become a part as Mrs Bob McKergow. "I am pleased to hear," she wrote to Bob on February 10, 1894, "that you are thinking of coming on Monday."

It will be quite convenient to us. The Viccahji's are coming to dinner on Monday and it is the day on which Aunt L is coming, so we (Cis and I) have been to the meet at Willingdon this morning and have only just got back… We had a very jolly evening with the Wilmington people. Fred sang The Nipper's Lullaby and played the banjo. We (Cis and I) presented Chaws [her brother Charles] with an 'address' in red ink, and the razor case, on bended knee when we offered it. His exclamation was "What the plague is this!" which we thought was very rude.

Bob would not have to make the same adjustment. After his wedding day he would continue to live in the same world, and enjoy the country life in the community into which he had been born - the fishing and shooting and in particular the hunting. Madge knew the sort of life she would be sharing with him, and if she was ever in any doubt, his flow of letters giving her daily accounts of what he was up to, made it all plain.

I had a very fine run with the Warnham Staghounds yesterday from W Grinstead to Burgess Hill where I pulled up. I left off right opposite to Maynard's house so I called. Mrs Bourne is there, had lunch, gruelled the mare and then jogged home. The mare was awfully done. Stanford tried to show off in front of me at a brook and got in, which rather made me smile. The hounds looked like going to Lewes when I left them. One lady got in the brook, we went through here like blazes. I feel perfectly stiff all over this morning. (February 15, 1894)

No wonder. Bob was right, the hunt did finish at Lewes, which meant a run of at least 20 miles, one of the longest Warnham Staghounds ever had. Apart from the moorland hunts, stag hunting in the nineteenth century was artificial, in the sense that the stags were tame. The so-called 'carted' stag released at the meet, and the hounds laid on to the scent after a suitable pause. The stag stopped when it thought it had galloped far enough and was held at bay by the pack. A blood-thirsty scene was brought to an end somewhat lamely by the stag being restored to its cart and taken home to recover for the next outing. Stag hunting gave some storming runs, but the genuine fox hunters always preferred the uncertainties and subtleties of their sport. The Warnham Staghounds were dispersed during the Great War of 1914-18.

From this letter of February 15 Madge also learnt more of Bob's fight to keep the running of the farm on an even keel.

> As soon as I left on Monday, one of the men went off and got drunk; he was working piece work. Fred found it out, so I sacked the man on the spot. It seems jolly hard lines never to be able to leave for a moment. H Sayers is laid up with influ, so I am pretty well off for men. I bought the cob off James on Tuesday. They had had another accident, the whole dog cart turned over by a bicycle. I have an awful lot to do today. I must ride down to the schools to see how the work is getting on, also arrange for Goschen's meeting on March 2nd.

Fitted in between the charitable and political work was the no small matter of earning a living, of bringing in the money which would pay for running the house and the far-from modest lifestyle to which he was accustomed.

> I have had a good morning's farming and sold 20 sheep before breakfast which is energy… The piece of land I want near the lodge, they are asking £100 an acre. We paid £25 for this. They think they have a mug on I expect.
>
> We commenced lambing yesterday, so old Matthews has had rather a rough time… I called on Davidson on Friday to arrange about the meeting. Of course no end of people called, so I had to talk tommy rot about an hour as I could not get hold of Davidson to tell him what I wanted.

Bob knew only too well of the need to keep a tight rein on his outgoings and never to allow his taste for the best of everything to run away with him, nor the wish to cut a fine figure in the eyes of the Twineham community as Master of the Grange.

> I had a look at a brougham last week but the price rather put me off, £75. So I said I thought I could manage this winter without one as it is nearly over. It is a pretty turn out but wants doing up badly. The dog cart, since it has been done up, looks slap up, yellow wheels and blue body, my dear. They will see me coming now… I am sending the book and also the tooth powder which pleased me. I am sure you will like it.
>
> Tell the Aunt I am surprised at her ending her letter with such a perilous sentence as 'ta-ta dear boy'. Why, if I was not already engaged I should almost imagine she was mashing me. I would not allow it if I were you. No

wonder she forgot to pack my bag. I expect she was alla flutter 'giddy old thing'.

I am going to hunt tomorrow, Ditchling Common. I don't fancy I can get over for the Hellingly meet. I will see how the mare is.

Madge made sure Bob did not miss out on what were regarded as the latest scientific aids to good farming.

Charles says I am to tell you that he has read in *Farm and Home* that 'Basic Slag' is a good thing to improve mossey pasture land, and says perhaps it would be as well for you to try a portion of one of your fields with this year. Next month is the time of application.

Basic Slag was a by-product of steel making. It was a popular phosphatic fertiliser for grassland at this time. Bob took Madge's advice and had Matthews spread the dust by hand, badly blistering his arms in the process. It all made the arduous side of Bob's life as a farmer that amount more arduous.

I have a nice hard day before me as Matthews is laid up and young Will is hardly fit to be entirely by himself. I was down at the farm till eleven last night, and I suppose I have got to have another bout of it today....

I have asked Dick [Reece] when the blue blazes he is going to look a poor beggar of a farmer up. Just give him a prod up when you are down and tell him, although he is to be married, he need not cut all his old friends before. We expect it afterwards to a certain extent, according to Turner's ideas... Why always stamp your letters with 2 half penny stamps! Do you get more for your money?

Goodbye darling with love. (February 20)

For Bob theatre-going in London was proving as exhausting as farming in Twineham.

Dog tired after visiting the theatre. I think *The Second Mrs Tanqueray* a most immoral piece but at the same time the acting of George Alexander and Mrs Patrick Campbell was superb. I did not care for Maude Millett much yesterday, she was not graceful in her movements on the stage, she rolled about when walking. I think I rather stepped into something yesterday; the tickets were 7/6d each and not to be had for love or money for days.

Sir Arthur Pinero's play *The Second Mrs Tanqueray* had opened at the St James's Theatre in London in May the year before, and startled the town. As A V Cookman writes in the *Oxford Companion to the Theatre*, in the theatrical world of the time "so much and so long given over to farce, burlesque and melodrama, Pinero's play was revolutionary. It was a serious English play with an idea - and it made money... It had the effect of breaking down a host of fearful prejudices and clearing the intellectual air." No wonder Farmer Bob found it tiring.

I wonder if on his way home he dreamt of mounting *The Second Mrs Tanqueray* in the hall at Twineham with himself in the George Alexander part? It would be more of a sensation than *Second Thoughts*. But how would Madge take it? Nothing to worry about - just a dream. It was going to be the real, down-to-earth world next day, and lord knows it had plenty of problems waiting to be solved without adding imaginary ones.

> Matthews is much better, thank goodness. I wish this frost would clear. I wanted to hunt tomorrow with the Crawley and Horsham at Shermanbury but the ground is like a brick... We have now placarded the whole of the adjoining parishes with posters about the meeting. The room is now enlarged and makes a splendid big room, first rate for private theatricals.

~ 4 ~
Truly Wed

From now on, as she showed in her next letter to Bob, Madge's mind was on the proper stage-managing not of theatricals but her wedding.

> Mrs Foster [of Eridge Castle] was spending the day here yesterday. She says that all that is given at an afternoon wedding is a reception, and as soon as the bride leaves everyone does likewise. She is in charge of the castle for Lord Abergavenny, with Lord and Lady Henry Nevill under her thumb to a great extent.

Bob appreciated that such matters had to be settled, but for him it was a tedious distraction from a day with the hounds.

> I quite agree that it is necessary to have a reception after a wedding, but you cannot have it in the road or street. My idea was to make it more of a family party by going to the theatre afterwards, but I leave it entirely in your people's hands as I don't see how we can receive guests when there will be, as I take it, very few above our two families.
>
> I was hunting yesterday; we had a fair run. Goring's party are coming to hold a meeting at Twineham soon after we have had ours. He was out hunting yesterday, he rides straight.

Madge pressed on. A chance came to bring Bob to heel on what for her was top priority while staying with friends in Edgware.

> Now for my question. Miss Perkins has asked me if it would be possible for you to come here on Friday. Ada drove me to Bushy this afternoon to consult Miss Levison [the chief bridesmaid] about the dresses. She invited us to a fancy dress ball at the studio and we accepted. Will you come and see that we don't run away or get lost. Miss Perkins says she will be very pleased to put you up for the night. Do come if you possibly can, darling, and wire me in the morning.

All that the men need wear is masks and dominoes, it is only a small affair so don't get anything expensive... You need only wear evening dress under the dominoes. The bridesmaids'' dresses will be very fine. Pale blue satin trimmed with purple velvet, hat to match, tan colour shoes, stockings, gloves. This will cost me £10 at least as Ada's dressmaker will charge 8 gns for the dresses alone.... The dance is at the Art Studios at Bushey. Miss Levison is sharing a studio with a girl there. There will be heaps of men as the men's studio is very close.

Bob sounded out his mother, who was ill and he was visiting, on how best to complete the decor of the most important room at the Grange. He told Madge:

I asked her how much she thought furnishing the drawing room would cost as a preliminary canter. She said she knew you wanted some chairs like the girls in their drawing room and we had a little chat. Miss Davies said yesterday she heard I was to be married this spring. I said that was quite incorrect information.

I suppose you are up to your eyes in dressy talk... I had a church meeting which lasted three hours yesterday. We had all the accounts to settle. Mr Davidson was nursing a cold yesterday at home, hope he liked it.

As for Madge's fancy dress idea, it was not really going to be convenient. Politics called.

Please thank Miss Perkins for her kind invite. I should like to be there, but you know I cannot throw the meeting etc over; it is you know tomorrow night. I have been shooting all day with the gov and am writing this in haste before the gov goes. I am very pleased you are going to the dance and I hope you will enjoy yourself. What a great extravagance you are going in for with regard to the bridesmaids' dresses! Well goodbye darling. Think of me sometimes when you are in the midst of the mazy waltz.

He was finding his legs in the world of politics, and hob-knobbing on the same platform with the likes of George Goschen did much for increasing his self-confidence.

I have just come back from the meeting which has been a success. Goschen is a very nice man and made a very good speech. I proposed the vote of confidence in him and made quite a long speech much to my own surprise. I felt when I got on my legs that I could have spoken for half an hour. Our dinner tonight went off very well indeed. Wickham waited splendidly. I am going to support Goschen at the club on Monday night. Davidson did very well in the chair.

I hope you enjoyed the dance. I wish I had been there. I have thought of you many times... I hope I shall get all my people to see that it would be better that I should be married this summer. I really feel we shall be more happy now together.

Sidbury Lodge, Edgware, where Madge was staying, was a good base from which to drive to the shops of London where she was gathering in all that was needed for the wedding.

At the beginning of March 1894 she had a tiring day, which began at 9.30 in the morning with the dressmaker, to make final decisions on what the brides-maids were to wear.

The main design of their costumes had been fixed for some time. They fea-tured pelisses of pale cornflower blue faced cloth, with a petticoat, showing all down the front, of lace over pink They were to wear pale pink chiffon vests with a cravat of pale pink chiffon edged with lace. Mother-of-pearl buckles, buttons and trimming. The lace was costing £22s a yard - expensive. But Madge had been reminded that her costume would make a handsome visiting dress after she was married. She and her bridesmaids were to have cream picture hats with crowns of blue velvet trimmed with cornflowers shaded from blue to pink.

After conveying all these details to Bob after returning to Sidbury Lodge, Madge ended by telling him she was brimming over with new ideas for drawing rooms and dresses since she had been at Edgware. And, as one after another tum-bled through her mind, she quickly added them in the form of postscripts:

PS   5 bridesmaids who will each leave church with a groomsman
PS   Dinner at 7
PS   Dr R wears a smoking coat,

For his part Bob discussed drawing room furnishing with his mother, and gave thought to whether £27 represented the true value of Harriet's grand piano which she had offered to sell him and he would have loved to have bought. He told his mama the good news that the Seth-Smiths had dropped the price they were ask-ing for their field by about a half. So should he buy it? Now that his father had finished stocktaking, might that not be the moment to ask him for the larger allowance which he felt should go with marital status?

Once again Bob had to allay any fears that he always felt Madge might have about the romantic parts that his friend Jago asked him to play in local amateur dramatic society productions. "My part is very good; they say it suits me which is rude; there is a lot of lovemaking in it. I hope you don't mind." Madge was used to responding to this familiar rhetorical question. She was looking forward to see-ing him act, she wrote, but, as ever, added words of warning about too violent lovemaking. She will have repeated them to his face when he came down to Polegate to hunt, returning home on March 13.

There had been no question of a row over the ardour he put into his stage romances, there never was. Back at the Grange however he had an unholy row with his half-sister/housekeeper Harriet. She greeted his return by announcing that she would like to invite Miss Knowles to dinner that night, and would send George King right away with a note to her.

George King? But he is doing the cricket pitch, expostulated Bob. In that case, said Harriet, she would have Willie do the errand, and sent for him. When Willie told her he was getting the master's horse ready for him to go hunting on, she insisted that first of all he must take her invitation to Miss Knowles. So when Bob went to the stables to collect his hunter, Willie was missing. Bob exploded. He strode back to the house and gave Harriet a piece of his mind. She was more trouble than she was worth, he told her. *She must leave.*

Two days later she had done just that - left the Grange and gone to Dunkeld House at Burgess Hill. She told her mother what had happened. and that she saw no reason why she should go back to the Grange, at least for the time being.

George had done a good job on the cricket pitch in the Park, Bob told Madge; it now looked promising. He and his men were taking all the turf off and re-turfing - "in fact great alterations are going on at the Grange." At the school meeting he was about to attend he would be asking one or two most important questions.

He was feeling very stiff after another long run with the Surrey Staghounds. At the end of it, after loading the deer, the surviving followers besieged a public house to gruel their horses. The landlord and lady lost their heads, and the party had to help themselves. Bob boiled the kettle in the kitchen to get hot water and collared things wanted. Miss Corbett, he thought Madge might like to know, went right through the run with them.

The gov came and stayed a night at the Grange, but Bob did not feel able to raise the matter of increasing his allowance. He accompanied Bob to Twineham church for the morning service. "I was surprised he did not think we were going to Rome; he seemed very pleased with the service."

The cricket pitch was still progressing favourably. He hoped Twineham would be able to raise a good team, and that he would have a go at last of being one of them. "I am rather afraid of again trying to handle the 'wiley willow', but am going to try now it will be so near home."

Bob had another 'ripping run' with the Surrey Stag on March 20. They finished just at the top of Bob Lane, Twineham. The old horse was nearly done, so Bob let him find his own way home and helped load the stag. Those at the Grange thought he was injured, and his mother and Harriet drove out in the carriage to find him. But all was well, and a few days later he was hunting with the Surrey Staghounds at Ditchling Common.

He was now firmly in the church choir and, on returning from the hunt, attended choir practice in the church for what they were going to sing on Easter Sunday. Of greater interest to Madge was his account of the discussion he had had with his mother about arrangements for the wedding. Since Harriet, who must have agreed to return after the row, was now planning to leave permanently and go to Miss Brace after Easter, Mrs McKergow approved an early marriage, and saw the urgency of having everything in place in the drawing room. The sooner Madge and the Aunt came over and lent a hand the better.

This was just the news that Madge had been waiting for, and she told Bob how excited she was to know that they would soon be wed. Would it be June or July? Bob had even better news. After a fruitless session with his father at Burgess Hill, the old man had come across to Twineham the next day, after apparently thinking things over, and had another talk. The outcome, he told Madge, was excellent, the gov agreeing with everything proposed - "no mistake he is an old brick." What a relief! "Your letter yesterday," replied Madge, "made me spend a very happy Easter, dearest."

On March 30 Bob wrote that he had received an invitation from the Woods at Hickstead to an afternoon dance "for you and me". "Have you a dress, or black velvet skirt and silk or chiffon blouse will do. Would you like to go?" In any case he thought she should come over soon "to begin this room" - presumably the drawing room. "I want you and I and the mater to go and see some Chippendale that a lady at Hassocks has for sale." He was only lukewarm about the Woods's invitation. "I think afternoon dances are rot and I have no clothes fit to go in, so shall take pyjamas and a tall hat." More to his liking was the prospect of going to hunt with the Stag at Bolney on Tuesday, and his coming visit to Polegate. Madge shared his distaste for afternoon dances, but told Bob she would go to the one at Hickstead with him if a refusal would give offence. "I believe it is the correct thing for ladies to keep their hats on at afternoon dances, which will be horrid." But she put a brave face on it - or under it - and loyally supported her future husband at the Wood family's country *thé dansant,* which did nothing to improve her health.

> I arrived home quite safely yesterday and was met by Charles. The Aunt has a dreadful cold and mine is not much better yet. I suggested luncheon for the members of your family before the wedding, but they are dead against it. They say it would not be at all the right thing, and they won't do it. I can't do anything with them. They will worry me into fiddle sticks before the wedding comes off. The answer from the Grosvenor Hotel [at Victoria Station] is satisfactory, but they have no private entrance and do not supply carriages. So we have written for the Buckingham Palace Hotel terms.

Bob was getting on with putting the house straight at Twineham.

> The staining of the floor is to be finished this week. I have taken two of the mater's pictures to be remounted today. Dick thinks the same about the luncheon as I do, and says that if your people don't do it, he will give them lunch himself, as it is necessary that something should be provided.

Bob had to be reminded that it was the Bakers, not the McKergows, who were organising the wedding. "I am rather surprised," she told Bob in her letter of April 10, "that you discussed the luncheon with Dr Reece. I don't see what he has to do with it."

If the Grosvenor Hotel was not going to suit them for the reception after their London wedding at St Peter's in nearby Eaton Square, neither it seemed would the Buckingham Palace Hotel in Buckingham Palace Road, which would charge them three guineas for the hire of the Reception Room, without wine. They would only have to pay ten shillings and sixpence for the room at The Grosvenor over Victoria Station with wine, and hire of a one-horse brougham would cost them £1 10s.

Although Madge was happy to leave the furnishing of the Grange to Bob and his father, she naturally pitched in every now and again with good feminine advice.

> Be careful what you buy. I don't think we want any more heavy chairs in the drawing room.
>
> Fred had a bad accident the other day. He was driving the young horse in the cart and met Colonel Cardwell and his daughter riding on valuable horses. Just as he got inside them, 'Tommy' shied right into them, the shaft sticking in Col Cardwell's horse which died in the night.
>
> Geaver and Maude suppose we are having the wedding in town so that the Prince of Wales can come; aren't they idiots!

Bob saw no reason not to continue his social life at its usual pace, while at the same time giving his fullest attention to tying up every last detail in arrangements for the Great Day.

> Just a line before I go to market… Dick [who was also about to get married] is giving a farewell dinner to his college chums and groomsmen… It will be rather a lively do, I know.
>
> I spoke to the Rector about marrying us yesterday. He has made a note in his diary so as to have nothing on… I am going to Sale's to dinner tomorrow night. Sale is very upset about his pew. I believe the Rector was on my track about them sitting there (in our pew). I would not budge. Well ta-ta sweetheart. Get rid of that cold. (April 10, 1894)

Madge was making plans for the days that followed the wedding, and wanted to make sure that Bob fell in with them.

> You will be pleased to hear that I have decided to have my going-away dress made at one of the best shops in Eastbourne (Plummer and Lawford). I got the enclosed patterns there yesterday for the travelling dress. I prefer the tweed to the covert coating and it is much better cloth. Please give me your opinion. I feel I must worry you about it, as if I get it and you don't like it, you will make a fuss and it will be money wasted.

Male attire was Bob's concern. It must be in fashion.

> I am very sorry to hear Fred has had such an accident. Will he have to pay damages? As under the circumstances they might make it rather hot for him, but I believe Col Cardwell is a very good sort. Now mind you don't ride behind him, there's a good girl.
>
> It is quite unnecessary for Fred to have a frock coat, an ordinary black tail coat is all right. But tell him to have it made in a rough kind of black cloth, same as my frock coat, and to have the tails cut a good length as they are wearing them like that now. (April 12)

The Guv and his son, 1875.

Bob and his step-sister Harriet Laing, 1886.

Downing May boat 1891.
Sydney Sussex bumped.
Bob is at No. 5.

Jeanie (Madge) Baker 1893.

A tennis party at Shermanbury Rectory in 1895 - the only photo we have of the married couple before any children arrived. In the front row is Bob, the Reverend Dick Hunt and Dick Reece. Madge is at the end of the second row, behind Bob.

Bob and his first child Doris, 1896. (Not forgetting the bicycle.)

Madge, Doris and Dudley, 1901 in the 'phaetonised' carriage.

In front of Twineham in the four-in-hand, 1902. This part of the house was pulled down in 1909.

The dog-cart with tandem horses. William Worsfold was the coachman.

The return of the four-in-hand, 1902. The groom has alerted
the maid by blowing a call on the posthorn.

A church parade at the 1902 Yeomanry camp at Lewes. Obviously no attempt to conceal the pristine white tents.

The Yeomanry in front of Twineham Grange.

Officers in B Squadron Sussex Imperial Yeomanry. All good Southdown men.
Bob, Goldfinch, Brand, Whitfeld, Ridsdale.

Madge in 1904. A leader of
society at 2 Eastern Terrace.

Telscombe 1906. Madge is on her
grey with the Southdown Hunt.

Southdown Hunt.

Wife of M.F.H., having temporarily lost the Whisperer, to other Lady who has just ridden across a field of young grass to ask directions of a Farmer. "Did he tell you where to go?" Other Lady: "Yes he did. And if you go over he'll tell YOU, too!"

After and with apologies to
G.D.Armour.

Madge is the one on the grey. Not all farmers were jovial.

The Southdown at a meet at Framfield village.

The collecting ring at the Southdown Hunt point-to-point, 1907.

The first fence.

Yeoman's jockey being disqualified by the Stewards for going the wrong side of a flag.

A meet of the Twineham and Colwood Beagles. Kass Seth-Smith, Dudley, John with West, Kennelman.

Preston Park polo in 1908. Bob is on the left.

And the same applied to what Madge wore to go away in.

> My cough is like a nutmeg grater this morning. I got hold of this cold push-
> ing that beastly mowing machine and then not changing after…
> I like the tweed pattern but the other is like a duster. I should think if
> you get the tweed cut plain and sporting, it will look very well indeed.
> Please send me patterns of the other dress if you have time.

Isaac Baker of Wilmington, Madge's father, under pressure from his daughter,
changed his mind about feeding the McKergow family before the church service,
but only agreed to do so on his own terms. "Father was here yesterday," Madge
told Bob on April 14.

> He is willing to give the luncheon as you think it is necessary. But he won't
> be there himself, as he says he shouldn't be able to stand it. He is afraid of
> fainting, so he is going to keep quiet until it is all over. Charles can enter-
> tain them at luncheon.
> What have you done with the pattern? I believe I asked you to let me
> have it back before I went to Town… I shall hope to see you on Wednesday.
> Don't look like a 'boiled owl' from your dinner, and cold, or I shan't have
> you for my groomsman.

It was for the wedding of his friend Dick Reece for which Bob hoped his cold
and cough would be better. He was nursing himself for the occasion. He would
meet up with Madge at the church. He was sorry to hear that her father thought
he would not be well enough to attend their pre-nuptial lunch. "He and Mrs B
must come over here during May and see the gov, and have a good look round."

From Madge's letter of April 14 it looks as if her father's 'illness' was a sub-
terfuge for opting out of the lunch which he had never considered necessary or
desirable, and that Bob had taken his decision in good part. Sensibly both sides
were taking the wedding, and the preparations for it, with plenty of good-
humoured give-and-take. "I am glad to say I feel none the worse for my day's dis-
sipation," wrote Madge, with reference presumably to the junketing at the Dick
Reece–Ada Perkins wedding

> Cis has some lovely ideas for a wedding dress for me. I will tell you all
> about it when I write on Saturday. Cis suggests that the bridesmaids' dress-
> es should be cream crepon trimmed with a light blue moire, with forget-
> me-nots and lilies of the valley, which I think would be lovely.

When Bob wrote to Madge about attending 'the girls' sale', he must have been
referring to Harriet and Alice Laing auctioning off some of their surplus furniture. He bid for one of their Sheraton chairs, which he called 'Sheridan', but it
went for a higher sum than expected. Madge wrote back to say she did not know
he wanted Harriet's chair, she had never seen it. The matter of what, and how
many, chairs went into the drawing room at the Grange was still unresolved.

And so was the matter of what door the two of them should make their exit from, under a shower of confetti, at the end of the reception. "The hotel where we are married must have a second entrance, as I pointedly refuse to come out of the main entrance of any hotel in London," reiterated Bob on April 20. Why? "I don't think it matters about having a private entrance to the hotel, darling," replied Madge the next day. "Don't make such a fuss about it, because I think the Grosvenor Hotel is decidedly the best hotel to have it from." What mattered was how she was going to look as she *entered* the door of the place where they were to be made man and wife. Bob was paying for the material, so it was only right, she thought, that he should approve what was made out of it.

> The wedding dress is to be of white Liberty satin with train (from shoulders) and sleeves of brocade with a chiffon sash. It will be a lovely dress and I feel sure you will like it. We have bought the material of the evening cloak at Liberty's, a lovely shade of green cloth with velvet cloak to match. I have also a lovely theatre jacket and material for a pale green silk tea gown. I am having a long tweed (grey, mixture) coat made at Lewis's in Oxford St for travelling, strapped seams and large buttons. I think I am very lucky in getting such jolly things, and I only hope they will please you.
>
> I haven't brought more money with me than I shall require… Will you let me have £2 10 so that I can get the material. We are going to a concert this evening to hear the Begum Amahadee sing.

The Begum, it appeared, was a 'very beautiful eastern woman' who did not have much of a voice but had married the son of the vicar of the church in South Hampstead where she was staying.

Bob's observations on Madge's proposed trousseau showed an acquaintance with the world of *haute couture* which probably surprised her.

> I should think the wedding dress will be very pretty, but a train from the shoulders will be rather heavy on you I should imagine. Don't overload yourself as, remember, you are a youthful bride. The tea gowns etc are very nice but the coat is not what you want. You want a smooth coat with big buttons for driving, not a tweed.
>
> My dear girl, I am not going to make a fuss about being married from the Grosvenor even if there is not a private entrance, because they seem to know most about weddings.
>
> I suppose you are coming to Dunkeld [House] on Tuesday week in time for the performance. There are a tremendous lot of tickets sold, nearly all the reserved seats are gone.

Whatever changes Madge made to her own dress to meet Bob's comments, there was no question of altering what her bridesmaids were going to wear. That was settled once and for all.

54

The bridesmaids' dresses are to be white china silk with light blue moire yokes and sashes, leghorn hats with forget-me-nots. The invitation cards have been ordered at Parkyns and Gotto's, you really don't give us credit for doing anything right dear. (April 24)

Not at all. His views on the difference between a hotel's back and front door were worth expressing, should anyone find them relevant. I imagine that was the spirit in which he gave them, and it little worried him that anyone should take it otherwise. He was irked however when his best man saw fit to meddle in what the bridegroom wore.

Yesterday afternoon a cab drove up with a lady and gentleman inside, so I went down into the smoke room. He said, 'Excuse me the liberty I have taken, but I am Dr Reece's tailor. He told me you were about to get married, and I called to see if you will give me an order.'! I said I was not going to have a new wedding rig-out.

That, however, was not the prime purpose of the tailor's visit. Dick Reece liked the cut and style of Bob's suits, and wanted what his tailor made for him to be of the same standard and design, and in similar material.

He came to find out different patterns, as he wanted to see all my clothes, breeches, hunting coat, in fact all the loud things I have got. I told him his class of goods would not suit me, as they were not pronounced enough. He wanted to make me a trial pair of breeches. As I said, Huntsman of London was making for me. I had enough. But I had to give him an order for a trial pair to be made in a hurry first, to see if he can do it.

It was natural that he should be on his own in the run-up to his marriage, but time never hung on his hands. "I am not at all alone," he assured Madge on April 25, "I have got more invites this week than I can go to."

People are very good to me when they know I am alone. I was going to play tennis today at Knowles; tomorrow dinner at Jago's; Thursday dinner at Sale's or supper at the Rectory, I don't know which. Friday rehearse.
I hope you are not fagging yourself out up in Town, and will look like a wet rag at the theatricals. I want you to look very nice that night, as all B.H.[Burgess Hill] will be there. We have already taken £18 in reserved seats.

Apart from tiring himself out on the hunting field and on the village hall stage, he had to continue to entertain his family.

Mother and Alice came over to lunch yesterday and I gave them as good a lunch as I could...
Mother is awfully keen about the wedding and drawing room but, poor

old lady, tears come into her eyes when she begins to talk about it. The night of the theatricals is not till Wednesday, as Tuesday night is the only charity night. You see we shall want you to stay till Friday or Saturday, as we must go to Brighton together... We are going into pianos thick when you come, as we want that in next after the carpet.

The gov expressed a wish to the mater that the 'Perth Stuarts' might be asked to the wedding. I am sure they would not come... Alice and the mater had the most wonderful list, but I told them we were only going to have a family wedding.

While Bob fancied himself primarily as a stage performer, Madge saw the pulling power of having him perform his comic song act on her concert platforms.

I am going to sing at a concert here on Whitmonday, and Mr Aston has asked me if you would favour them with 2 comic songs, Chevalier's he would like. There is 'Mother's Tea' before the concert, but you need not come to that... I hope the theatricals will pass alright. I shall glare at you and make you nervous.

Bob was determined not to be up-staged.

I shall be very pleased to sing two songs at the concert if you like, but what am I to sing? Will *Little Nipper* do? or do they know all of them? I certainly am getting a bit mixed about dresses... Hope you will be blooming on Wednesday,

Madge told him she had heard from Alice that she or someone would meet the train at Burgess Hill on Wednesday. "It rains hard - the Aunt says it is beautiful weather for young ducks, but as I am not a 'young duck' I don't enjoy it."

Bob told Madge on April 29 not to have their banns of marriage 'put up' at St Peter's Eaton Square next Sunday, "as that will leave five Sundays to be asked in, and we only want four. Besides, if I am not in the parish of St Peter's, it would not be legal."

He had a lot on his mind, and being roused from his after-lunch siesta did nothing to calm it.

Stanford came down this afternoon and disturbed my sweet slumbers to tell me that gipsies were pulling my hedge out to light their fire, so I promptly told them to shift. Stanford was making a fence down by the road. Why in the name of goodness he should break the Sabbath I don't know. (May 6, 1894)

After Madge kept her promise to attend Bob's 'theatricals' on Wednesday, hopefully without making him too nervous with her glaring, Bob returned the compliment by going over to Polegate to take part in Madge's concert. She asked him to bring the sheet music of *Little Nipper* and *It Ain't Exactly* "along with more songs for encore".

Bob had to stay over for the concert. It was a period when gentlemen considered it beneath their dignity to do their own packing, and had to suffer the consequences. Madge was obliged to apologise for the packer's shortcomings.

> The Aunt is very sorry but she forgot to put your shaving brush in, and also your gloves which I am sending now. I hope you had another one, or you must look like a Burgess Hill stage 'bailiff'.

The time had come to think about where they should go for their honeymoon. Bob suggested Monmouthshire. Madge thought it seemed a very interesting county, "but perhaps you think it is a little too far from Town [London] for us".

Bob was grateful for the prompt return of what Aunt Maria had omitted from his over-night bag, and showed his concern for the deteriorating health of his father.

> I am glad you sent me my shaving brush, as I only had an old one to go on with. I have lost a Sussex calf this morning, and the colt has had to have a tube put down his throat, or else he would have been choked on Sunday...
>
> The gov has been in an awful state. He told the mater he should not go to my wedding, when the mater jumped at him. I believe he is much better the last day or two. I should imagine, by the time I am married, he will be very ill and unable to go anywhere. It really is most serious to be in such a state. Dunkeld is to be let, which I think is a good thing. It was in last week's *Times*... I gave the gov beans on Monday, which I think did him good,

If Bob and Madge were to go on singing music hall songs, they would have to have a pianoforte to sing them to. Madge was bent on having one moved into the Grange before they did.

> Charles tells me that he has been making enquiries about pianos at E.B.[?] of Shoosmith, the man he was telling you of. It would be nice if we could have it from there, as they are well known as very genuine people and charge low prices.

Dick Reece's wedding present to them took the form of a hideous ram's-head table centre. It consisted of a stuffed ram's head mounted on a silver base, with silver smoker's requisites hung around it. It was very popular in military messes in Scotland. Madge told Bob 'the boys' admired it very much.

May 20 was a very important day for Madge, and Bob needed no reminding.

> I wish you very many happy returns of the day, sweetheart, and may your future be as happy or happier as your past. I shall at any rate be able to say my girl is eighteen tomorrow. I think Moyle is extremely rude not to come to his cousin's wedding... I should cut him dead as I consider he is a cad.

I have been to a school meeting this morning. Stanford and his man have been thrown out of a cart and cut about rather. They are running over the county for Willie to take the groom's place *pro tem*.

Well goodbye my love. I hope you will have a happy day tomorrow (sweet 18). With love and some to the Aunt. (May 19, 1894)

Back came swift acknowledgement from the Sweet Eighteen.

Thanks very much for all your good wishes. I am sure I am looking forward to their fulfilment. Old Mrs Godley sent me a birthday card today. Mrs Fears is going to make me two dusters. She says she feels she must do as much for me as possible, so she wants to wash and iron the dusters before I have them.

The run-up to the wedding was gathering momentum. Getting the Grange ship-shape in time for their moving in, would mean everyone concentrating on the main chance, with as few purely social distractions as possible. "I cannot fix the day for you to come over yet," Bob told Madge on the 20th, "as we do not know when the drawing room will be in a finished state. We have got the music waggon, or rather Akehurst has it. I think it is a very handsome one. The cosy corner is finished."

Bob's mind was reaching out to life after his marriage on June 6, when his, at any rate, would take up where it had left off, and he had to fulfil engagements made as a bachelor - theatricals, hunting, cricket et al. Would the social round continue unchanged, when there was a Mistress as well as a Master of Twineham Grange? Madge trusted it would, but hoped that Bob would understand that she would prefer to be eased into playing her part, rather than plunged.

The day after her birthday Madge was dismayed to receive a letter from her husband-to-be telling her:

I want to be home by June 26 for the cricket match here on the 27th if we can. What do you think? I've got to go to London to meet Bunny etc.

Madge was not amused.

I would rather do anything than come back [from their honeymoon] to the cricket match, as I suppose it is Mr Stevens's team you want to get back for. I thought you said you were going to be so shy and go in at the back door, and not to be seen for a week. I wasn't so shy as that; but I don't care about being waltzed into a cricket match directly.

Becoming assimilated into the McKergow clan, and Bob's circle of friends, would take time. But first of all it was a matter of making sure the Great Day ran smoothly, and that was also taking time - for both of them. Bob kept Madge informed of what he was managing to arrange,

Bunny and I have had a hard day in town. We have been to 8 hotels to find some rooms for the night before the wedding, and have at last succeeded to get two rooms for the night before and a promise of two rooms for us at Keizers Hotel [De Keyser's Hotel, a huge building on the east end of the Embankment] if the people leave. So we have our work cut out if we cannot procure rooms there. Bunny is going to try the Euston [over the railway station]. London is very full and Derby Day [June 3] makes it worse… I have also booked 2 stalls at the Savoy for [Gilbert and Sullivan's comic opera] *Utopia* - good seats.

I have looked out a route and trains for Devonshire [now replacing Monmouthshire for the honeymoon?] which I will show you when you come over.

Madge could not but be appreciative of the hard work he was putting into finalising what they would do on their wedding day, but was still critical of what he was proposing they should do after it. In her letter to him on May 26 she said she was sorry he had so much bother with hotels,

My dressing bag from Grandfather and Grandmother is very nice indeed. I feel quite 'a duchess' already. I don't think much of your idea of getting back for haying. Why, only the letter before you talked of being away until 26th. You can't have much haying to do, and I should think Mr Gander would look after that for you. And please don't go to Devon, just where the Reeces have gone. Let us appear to have an idea of our own.

I am quite tired of seeing anything in the dress line. I have had 8 new ones; that is a dress for every day and 2 for Sundays.

Bob managed to book a sitting room and a bedroom for them to spend their first night at De Keyser's Hotel. "I am afraid you will not like it," he told Madge, "but I have tried all the other hotels." In this same letter of May 27 he told her the Grange drawing room now looked more furnished, and that at nine o'clock the next day the rest of the furniture was coming in. "The gov went in and said it was very nice yesterday." The 67-year-old parent was obviously his own self again. And surely she did not want him to start all over again finding somewhere to spend their honeymoon?

I cannot see, my dear girl, what difference it make if Dick Reece goes to Devonshire, as we are not gong to the same part at all, and Scotland is ghastly cold. The Wye is pretty, but it wants good weather for boating on a river.

By May 31 Madge had been won round to the idea of honeymooning in the West Country.

Mr Farnell says he thinks we are very wise to go to Devon instead of Scotland. Don't forget the PIANO and [my] suggestions of borrowing some money from Harriet. I thought I would just make your respected parent say he was coming to the wedding. He is now 'ready at any time'. Charles took the name of the champagne last night.

Bob was busy gathering in the wedding presents. "I am just off to Burgess Hill to get three wedding presents waiting at the station for me," he told Madge on the last day of May 1894. He also picked up some words of wisdom regarding the state of matrimony from his spiritual adviser.

> I have had to spend hours at the church regards the Restoration etc this morning. This, I suppose, will be the last letter but one, as I shall write one on Sunday. The Rector gave me quite a little sermon this morning at the church. He said he hoped I did not mind as he always did to those he married. He is a good sport.
>
> I am going to write to Dick tonight and thank him for the ram's head.

Madge did her best to taunt Bob with accounts of her growing mountain of presents - more than him - but he could not have failed to delight in her girlish glee.

> I feel so excited today, for I have had such lovely presents since I saw you last, 35 in number altogether. I have had another lovely fern pot and a very handsome vase... The Trangmars have sent me 6 silver fern pots for the dining table which are simply glorious... You don't seem to be getting as many presents as I do. (June 2, 1894)

What did not meet with his approval was Madge wanting to be photographed with him in their wedding clothes.

> I should so like to have my photo taken with you on the day. Couldn't we drive straight from the church to some studio and then on to the reception? It is very often done, and I should so like it if you could manage it darling. Dear Mr Bunny [Vincent] would see about it if you wrote to him at once.
>
> I want to know all about the 'little sermon' when I see you... I am afraid tomorrow will be a busy day as we have people coming who couldn't be here today. Ta-ta my darling - only one more letter from me. (June 2, 1894)

Bob tackled both matters - the presents and the photography - in his letter of June 3.

> I am glad to hear you have such lovely presents... I have also received some very nice presents on Friday and Saturday. I have altogether got 19 presents and there are some on the way that I know about. Turner has sent me a very handsome lamp and also the Arbers, so we are quite set up for lamps.

Now I think it is about time you got married, if you make such proposals about being photographed. I think it would be hardly the thing for you not to be there, to receive the congratulations of your relations and friends, but to go waltzing all the way to Regent Street. Why, we should take the whole time the reception lasted before we got back, and I cannot think why you cannot be photographed some time after, other people are. I simply hate the idea myself, as it seems to me treating the whole thing as a fancy dress ball or private theatricals. I would much rather not be photographed.

Bob was irritated too by the behaviour of his mother's Laing relations, but pleasantly surprised at his father's.

I have asked George and Blanche (Laing) to lunch with me at the Langham [Hotel, in Portland Place], as they are coming up from Nottingham on the day of the wedding, which I think a mad idea. The gov came over on Saturday and was very nice to me. He gave me a good cheque for a present, and told me he would have made it larger if he had not been hard up. I never asked him for it which was rather extraordinary. (June 3, 1894)

It was up to Bob to tighten up the drill for everyone who would be on parade at the church - before, during and after it. It all had to go like clockwork, like a fully rehearsed play.

Is Charles or Turner going to take the other bridesmaid down the church? Charles will have his work cut out to send people off in their carriages, as some order must be kept. Mrs Baker must be sure to leave the church in the next carriage after the bridesmaids… Bunny will be at the church to give Charles a hand, or I suppose he ought to go with his bridesmaid which is rather a bother, but George could help Charles, I mean your brother… Mind bring a small hat for coach driving that will not blow off.
I am your affec. Bob

Miss Jane Baker - Jeanie, Madge - wrote her last letter to the man she was about to marry on June 4, 1894, with only two days to go:

I have now received 40 presents; how many have you got?… It is past seven and I have not yet commenced to pack and I feel perfectly tired out but I shall do my best to look blooming tomorrow. We are going up by the 12.15 and shall expect you at Hampstead at about 5 o'clock… I am looking forward to seeing you tomorrow very much. I do so want my photo taken with you, and I do hope you have been able to arrange it. It seems hardly true that our wedding day is so near.

Ta-ta my darling
yr ever loving Madgie

I have no account of my father and mother's wedding at St Peter's, Eaton Square on June 6, 1894, nor of the reception in the Grosvenor Hotel at Victoria Station - both buildings stand in 1999, though the famous church was badly damaged by a fire a few years ago and rebuilt.

There is no record of the honeymoon, and no photographs of it or the wedding.

Why Bob, who loved being photographed, was so opposed to wedding photos is a mystery. He might have agreed if a garden had been available, but the idea of posing in the street, or at the church door, would not have been acceptable to him. The socially correct way to have wedding photographs taken had evidently not been decided in 1894.

By having the wedding in London, Bob avoided having to ask all the Polegate and Burgess Hill people he did not like. It must have been a great disappointment to the locals who had looked on nervously, as the dashing stranger claimed the local beauty. Years later the correspondent to a magazine wrote of "the lovely lady whom I used to regard (in the pew in front of me in church) with awe and wonder. I can recollect feeling envious, on one bright summer's morning, of her fiancé, securely ensconced beside her, while on his right hand sat Miss Mockett."

Although very little planning had been done, the honeymoon was spent in North Devon and included plenty of driving in various conveyances, including a four-in-hand. They returned, with a good stack of photographs of the beauty spots, to Twineham Grange - maybe, or maybe not, in time for that cricket match in the Park.

~ 5 ~
Sussex Master of Foxhounds

Twineham Grange was a red brick, Victorian house with sash windows. In earlier days there was no proper road to it, but later owners laid out a broad, gravelled entrance to the garden and an impressive carriage sweep in front of the house. From there, looking South, the wooded Weald concealed any farm houses and buildings that might have interfered with the view over the trees to the bare Downs. It was more likely that the Victorian stable block really clinched the deal, as it was worthy of a more important residence. Two excellent boxes and stalls for six horses, coach houses for four carriages, a pitch pine lined tack room, the usual arrangements for straw and feed, and a groom's flat surmounted by a clock striking the hours.

About 220 acres of heavy clay land was taken in hand and renamed Twineham Grange Farm. The whole operation was generously financed by Robert McKergow. He bought the property for a figure not listed in the accounts, put up a further £389-6-0 as capital, £1-9-6 for insurance and a cash float for £50. Each month he provided a further £100, and put in a bit more if the bank balance went into the red. The accounts were intended to relate to the farm only, but trying to separate the outgoings under different headings proved a waste of time, and the book included all expenditure, such as gardeners' wages, grooms' wages, hunt subscriptions and the like. With very little income being generated by the farm, it is no surprise that the losses accumulated to the alarming figure revealed in the letters. As Bob was going to get married in the near future, his father evidently decided there was no alternative but to continue paying up.

Going back to September 1892, the first purchases were as follows:

Iron Plough	£5.3.6
Iron Cultivator and Horse Rake	£5.6.0
Light Spring Cart	£13.0.0
Bay Horse (Boxer)	£43.0.0
Brown Mare (Diamond)	£41.0.0
65 ewes @ 35/- per head	£113.15.0
2 rams @ 2.20 each	£4.4.0
Cart	£6.1.0

Breeding sheep were unlikely to be profitable but Bob was probably advised that a flock would improve the fertility of a farm in poor heart and, in any case, he would have found it difficult to omit sheep after being a pupil in East Sussex. Ellman of Glynde had made Southdowns famous a century earlier and Squire Pitcher, with many others, made it a matter of honour to keep promoting the breed on home ground.

Bob was continually annoyed by the men not doing enough when he was away, and the famous written instructions did not always work. It turned out that the foreman, Matthews, could not read, and had to ask others what the notes said. Very regretfully, as he admired him immensely, Bob asked Matthews to go back to being head carter, and brought in Mockford as foreman. A few years later John Sayers moved up from being a carter to foreman - another great character. Matthews eventually retired on the farm at age 85 having started, as he put it, 'serious work' aged seven. He died at 92. John Sayers, incidentally, nearly missed out on his wedding to Sabina. They had fixed a date in April 1893 with Molyneux, the Rector, who collapsed with an illness from which he died two days before the wedding. Bob called in Jack Hunt of Shermanbury to officiate for his employee, and all was well.

The letters illustrate very well the big differences that existed between parishes. Polegate had adopted all the activities associated with the village church in the 20th century: big Sunday School with lay teachers, working party for the London poor, services on Fridays in Lent, special music for Christmas, choir augmented with ladies from the congregation for festivals, and the Christmas tree - a focus for the church decorations. The clergymen who led the way there were criticised for eccentricity, but must be ranked as very creditable leaders, judging by the extent of the activities.

Twineham Church scored nothing in comparison. The newcomers to the parish wanted reform, but had no hope of altering anything faced with an alcoholic rector in failing health who had been there for 30 years. Parish organisation, as it existed in the mid-nineteenth century, depended more on the personalities involved than on formal organisation.

The Rector could be very dominant, but if the churchwardens (the Vestry) really exerted their authority, they would win the argument. The Rector of Hurstpierpoint, a wealthy and influential man, tried for years to have extra candles on the altar. The churchwardens always took them off. As the Church had responsibility for the Poor Law, the workhouse, repair of the roads and any other civil matter that cropped up, the churchwardens were very powerful figures, and usually had their own pew in church. After the Rector and churchwardens, came the non-commissioned officer of the parish - the parish clerk. He collected the church rates, employed the cleaner of the church building, sometimes took charge of the registers, tolled the bell, was often the organiser of the band and men's choir. During services he sat next to the Rector in the three-decker pulpit, and shouted out the responses required by Morning Prayer. He would also lead the chanting of the Psalms of David that were sung in a metrical version. Hymn books were not used. After the rector's lengthy sermons, the congregation wandered out into the churchyard, where the qualifying poor received their relief under the disapproving gaze of the farmers who had, of course, contributed the money through the rating system.

The Squire was always an unknown quantity. He could be genial, indifferent, or downright interfering. So the government of the parish depended on how these strands of authority got on with each other. As far as I know Twineham was lucky in being reasonably well served over the years, but the church building was in need of a great deal of repair when the Rector died in 1893. Bob McKergow, Davidson and Paget Davies had much more than repairs in mind. By Christmas they had put in place the bulk of the physical and liturgical changes. The antique reredos looked suitably Tudor, a new altar table, altar frontal and pulpit falls were in position, a stained-glass east window by Kempe looked down on a robed choir of men and boys.

Incidentally, the choir bowed to the altar as they processed to take their places. It is surprising that cries of 'Popery' were not heard, particularly as three-branch candlesticks appeared on the reredos. Bob and the rector were in no mood for half measures. It was a good moment for the Church to establish a new identity, since in 1894 it lost all the civil responsibilities to the new Parish Councils. Not surprisingly, Bob was elected chairman at the first meeting of the new body in December 1894. The parish clerk had progressively less to do, and virtually ceased to operate as such by 1921. There is no doubt that the changes put the Rector in a stronger position although, for peace to reign, clergy and churchwardens needed to be in agreement. The laity were given a voice when Parochial Church Councils were initiated in 1920, but it was many years before the old system of authority could be seriously challenged.

Sport provided a rural activity that changed for the worse in the years following the 1890s. All the memoirs of the mid-nineteenth century onwards make the point that most farmers looked forward to their shooting parties. The letters show why: partridges, and to some extent pheasants, were plentiful. Madge reported that her brother Charles Baker and friend were up early in the first day of the partridge shooting season, and had eight and a half brace in the bag by breakfast time.

It is puzzling, however, that the landowners did not reserve such good sport for themselves. Obviously they did not, as all the references to shooting in the Polegate and Grovebridge areas involve tenant farmers. After his marriage, Bob took the partridge shooting over a wide acreage, although it is not known if he rented it from the landlords or the tenants. The point of interest (and regret) is that numbers of partridge had gone down by the 1920s and 1930s to such an extent that shooting parties were no longer worth organising. The reasons are not apparent, as farming routines had remained largely unchanged in the intervening years. There were no herbicides or pesticides, fertiliser use was negligible and mechanisation had only got as far as one Fordson tractor per farm, at most.

Nevertheless there was more interest in being punctual. Haymaking rarely clashed with harvesting and, given good weather, the last sheaves could be stacked by the first week in September. In earlier years farmers had to be more relaxed about timing their operations. If corn was fit to be cut they did not mind making a start on that, and then going back to cutting the last of the grass fields for hay. This would suit the partridges very well, providing cover and plenty of seeds to feed on. Certainly the number of coveys of well-grown birds that provided the shooting on the first day of the season suggests that the early broods were successfully reared. When the partridges became scarce, late broods predominated. Large scale mechanisation and modern farming methods, admirable in themselves, subsequently virtually eliminated the game birds and hares from much of the Weald.

On the domestic scene there is no doubt that Madge found Twineham Grange dull after leaving all her relations behind, and without the stimulus of Eastbourne just one stop down the railway. The big houses were friendly but occupied by fairly senior citizens. The Hunts at Shermanbury Rectory kept up a flow of invitations to tennis in the summer, and in the winter there were visits to London theatres. Bob and Madge always stayed at the Grosvenor Hotel, Victoria, as the floor valets and ladies' maids became almost old friends. The personal service supplied by the station hotels comes over as a big factor in their popularity. Visiting the well-recommended plays and musical productions was not without hazard. Prostitutes gathered on the pavement outside the theatres, and abused the fine ladies when they emerged. So the 'fair sex" of the party stayed in the foyer, while the men scoured the streets for cabs to come to the theatre, where the ladies could embark under cover.

Madge really established herself when Doris was born in March 1895 and Dudley in February 1898. She took a much closer role in bringing up the children than many mothers in similar circumstances. Bob's responsibilities changed as well. The 'Gov' died in 1897, which made Bob the chairman of Findlater Mackie & Co. There was a managing director to look after the detail, but the new responsibilities involved more frequent visits to the office and less time on the farm. There were very significant compensations in the form of the chairman's fees and expenses. Smarter carriages were acquired, including a coach, a bigger stud of horses and improved livery for the coachmen.

About this time ladies and gentlemen of fashion took up cycling as a form of recreation. A bicycle cost far too much for the working man at that stage, so the cycling world was split into two populations. The well off who fitted a gentle summer ride into the general social programme, and the serious amateur and professional racing cyclists. A weekly journal *The Cycling World Illustrated*, described as a Journal de Luxe, was launched in 1896 to cater primarily for the first group. Lady cyclists had to be both beautiful and, if possible, titled to get noticed, it seems. The Countess of Mayo qualified on both counts in the July issue. Humber, the cycle manufacturers, sponsored a club in London. To quote from *Cycling World*, "most people will agree that the great attraction of the Trafalgar Bicycle Club is the fine grounds, where excellent arrangements have been made not only for cycling, but for lawn tennis, archery, croquet, badminton and cycle polo... A number of competent instructors are always at the service of members...."

The Rector of Bolney, the Reverend R.C. MacLeod, had the idea of turning an honest penny by composing and photographing a sort of strip cartoon of updated

Nursery Rhymes adapted to the bicycling era. Bob and Madge posed for him, and featured in the journal. Each line of verse had its accompanying photo - with bicycle.

"Where are you going to, my pretty maid?"
"I am going a' milking, sir," she said
"Can I come with you, my pretty maid?"
"Shall I marry you, my pretty maid?"
"What is your fortune, my pretty maid?"
"My face and a bicycle, sir," she said
"Then I can't marry you, my pretty maid."
"Nobody axed you, sir," she said.

Another series had Bob more tastefully costumed in smock, floppy hat and gaiters; Madge was never convincing as a milkmaid!

Just before the end of the Boer war in 1901, a new Yeomanry Regiment was raised in Sussex. Bob lost no time in being gazetted, yet again, as Second Lieutenant in the Imperial Sussex Yeomanry. It turned out socially to have been a very good move. Many of the landowners joined, and the regiment was commanded by Lt-Col the Lord Leconfield, ex-Life Guards and Lord Lieutenant of the County. His Lordship was a quiet, rather introverted character. Bob, being the exact opposite, hit it off with his CO immediately and was lined up as a good man to give responsibilities to in future.

The first camp of the regiment was at Arundel by invitation of the Duke of Norfolk; the following year they went to the Dripping Pan, Lewes. The camp was laid out in the open without any attempt at concealment, in fact the more dazzlingly white the bell tents the better. Regimental Sergeant Major Quigly, also ex-Life Guards, ensured that everyone was well and truly sorted out.

The officers in Bob's squadron were the Hon Charles Brand, Master of the Southdown Foxhounds, brother of Viscount Hampden of Glynde; George Whitfeld who was to command one of the Yeomanry Regiments in the 1914-18 war; and Arthur Ridsdale, a splendidly eccentric sportsman. Arthur had left instructions in his will that he should be buried, wrapped in a blanket, next to his favourite dog in the orchard. He was no churchman, but had to turn out for Morning Prayer when he stayed the week-end at Twineham Grange. When Bob tolled the bell urgently for the service to start, Arthur's loud interjection of "Jockeys up!" brought immediate "shushing" by the family, but he could never be quelled for long.

When in 1903, after 22 years, Charles Brand retired from the mastership of the Southdown Hunt, he proposed to the committee that Bob McKergow should take over.

There was never much doubt that Bob would jump at the opportunity to become Master of the Hunt he knew particularly well. It was not totally plain sailing as the country was short of foxes following a protracted outbreak of mange but, as everyone knew of the problem, the Master could not be held responsible for coverts not holding foxes. Nobody could say an ill word about the hounds which were a bitch pack of forty and a half couple, but Bob changed the previous policy to include dog hounds.

Bob's term as Master of the Southdown Hunt began on September 14, 1903 with a 6 am cub hunting meet at Glynde Rough where they found two brace, followed by one cub at Laceys Holt. On the 18th, meeting at Newick Park, they found two brace at the first draw, followed by another and then the small covert below Gyps Wood produced one more fox which they killed. Two foxes were then run to ground on keeper Kenward's territory and on Whitehead's. The keepers were named as they were entitled to payments of 'finds' by the hunt, usually at the rate of ten shillings for a find in their coverts. As they would have been earning less than one pound a week, this was a useful present. A keeper could be put in a difficult position if his employer was primarily a shooting man wanting foxes disposed of on the quiet, while professing loyalty to the Master and his hunt. If the keeper managed to please both sides, he was certainly worth a tip.

The cub hunting season ended on October 30. The Master was able to report finding forty seven and a half brace of foxes and killing seven and a half brace in 18 days hunting. Mangey foxes were found at eight sites.

The opening meet was held at the Kennels, Ringmer, on November 2. It was a day of two good runs, and the horses were dead beat at the end of it. The rest of the season which finished on March 30, 1904, was not very remarkable, but the account which Bob wrote in the Hunt Diary for that last day showed it to be a thoroughly enjoyable one.

> Drew Northland Pits, King's Wood, Scales, Hannington, Sayer's Common blank. Found in hedgerow on Mr Laurence Smith's; ran him to Poynings through Wick and Holmbush Pondtail to Newtimber through and over the hill by Holt, ran over Railway, nearly lost the pack, past Pangdean Holt to Stanmer wall where we lost him. This fox ran about an eight mile point and very fast on the hill. Drew Stamner blank and then on to Tenantry Gorse where we found a brace; one went away to nearly Clayton then turned under hill and ran side hill to Westmeston, sunk the hill and through Middleton Coverts, where we whipped off after a good day.

After they met at The Star at Piltdown on February 8, 1905, they found at High Wood and got away at once over the road to Fletching Village on to Sheffield Park, nearly to the Sheffield Arms right handed to Scailes, Fletching right handed back to where they found him; a brace got away.

> But Sam stuck to the hunted fox and killed him in the Burstow Country. Mixed pack hunted all through these woods beautifully and although other foxes were on foot, never left hunted fox. We were actually running 2 hours & 20 minutes, the last 20 minutes in the covert where we killed him - other foxes being viewed. The best woodland hunt of the season so far. Found again at Fairhazel and lost him at once. Found at Rocks, ran over to Fairhazel, back to Rocks to ground, could do little with him. I think he

went to ground in the Rocks by the pond.

A good day.

Ten days before Christmas 1905 they met at Pyecombe and drew Giles, found and ran to the Holt. They put any number of foxes up but there was no scent so gave it up. But then on their way to Sayers Common a fox ran across the road from Pondtail to Cakes Wood, and the pack broke away, on to Clayton and over the line above Hassocks Station away to High Chimneys Farm, Burgess Hill over the road to One O'clock Farm, over Ditchling Common to West Wood, over the road to Lashmans, Mercers Shaw, Sedgebrook to the Wilderness by General Leigh Pemberton's Coverts, to Anchor Wood in Burston Wood.

> Then my horse Bulldog was done. Hounds then ran south to Wivelsden Farm and Sedgebrook where they stopped them. We ran for 2 hours 50 minutes. Hunt horses done right up. We covered something like 14 miles of country. This was one of the best hunts I ever had with the Southdown Hunt. We went home by train from Haywards Heath.

But for Bob there was more to be had from being a member of the hunt than days in the saddle cantering across the fields. He greatly enjoyed attending, and now, as Master, presiding over, the Puppy Shows the hunt held every summer and making a jokey speech at the luncheon.

At his first Puppy Show as Master he said he hoped those who had been walking puppies would continue to do so. Moreover he suggested that they would find walking two puppies much better than walking one - and everyone laughed when he added that they were told that every year but no-one seemed to pay much attention to it.

It was the occasion to take a look back at the last season. He called it 'fairly successful', having accounted for twenty three and a half brace of foxes and run fourteen brace to ground. He thought that was fairly creditable (Hear, hear). Mange was still affecting foxes on the east side, he said, but there were plenty on the west side, and they hoped for good sport next season.

In fact the fox population increased, and subsequent seasons were an improvement. Bob contributed to this by extensive hound showing which did much to promote the name of the Southdown Hunt. He tried to link up with the legendary Frank Gillard by introducing the blood of Belvoir Dasher, followed by Oakley Sailor, Atherston Villager and Cleveland Dashwood.

It was the link that gave the Southdown Hunt its special position in the history of British foxhunting, as anyone will know who has read the copiously illustrated booklet *Three Hundred Years of Hunting in Surrey and Sussex* published by Sotheby's of Billinghurst.

By the mid- to late-17th century, hunting wild deer was becoming impracticable in lowland areas and someone hit on the idea of hunting fox. Who started it? A claim can be made for the Charlton Hunt. Hounds entered to fox were kennelled at Charlton, Sussex in the second half of the 17th century. The first Masters were the Duke of Monmouth, Charles II's eldest natural son, and Lord Grey of Uppark. It is thought that the first Duke of Richmond bought the Goodwood Estate in 1695 because of its proximity to Charlton, and his son became Master in 1728. The Charlton Hunt then entered a period of great success, largely due to the skills of Tom Johnson, the huntsman. After his death in 1744 a fine memorial was placed in Singleton Church. The death of the duke in 1750 marked the end of the hunt as a centre of fashion. It is thought the hounds were put down in 1820 when signs of rabies appeared.

Foxhunting was also getting established nearer London. The Sotheby's publication gives an entertaining insight into the early days:

> While the Duke of Monmouth and his successors disported themselves from Charlton in Sussex, in 1735 the Duke of Grafton persuaded his friend Lord Onslow to keep a pack at his seat Lovells Grove, to hunt the country round Croydon, which consisted of rolling chalk hills not dissimilar to the country of the South Downs round Goodwood.
>
> Having set up the establishment, his Grace found the most tedious part of the operation was the journey from Suffolk, having to cope with the dilatoriness of the Thames Watermen and the delays, which must have been very long, that they caused to his progress! Thus he is reported to have initiated the Bill through Parliament, which eventually led to the building of Westminster Bridge, although it cannot have been completed until many years after his Grace ceased hunting South of the Thames.
>
> At that time foxes were somewhat scarce throughout Great Britain, especially near London, so he charged his deer keepers on his Northants estates to send foxes to London in the venison cart, for onward routing to Surrey the day following the delivery of venison to Leadenhall Market.
>
> The fox had become rare in the 17th century and had not the great estates, such as Belvoir, switched their hunting activities from deer to fox, finding it a quarry giving better sport partly due to the opening of the countryside through the Enclosure Acts, the fox might have become extinct by the end of the century.
>
> The next recorded hounds to hunt this part of Surrey were those of Mr Godsall who, in 1750, set out to entertain the City merchants somewhat nearer London, and who hunted the country round Peckham Rye, Forest Hill and Sydenham, with hounds kennelled in Mr Dudin's wharf at Bermondsey. Most of this was common land and suited the aspirations of the merchant adventurers and commodity brokers, dealing in such things as sugar and tea, and who found it necessary to be 'back on Change' by 4pm every day. Mr Godsall is reported not to have drawn for a fox after 1 o'clock in the afternoon to enable the field to get back to their money making activities [shades of today's 'yuppie'!]
>
> Mr Dudin, who owned the wharf, is said to have succeeded Mr Godsall as Master and Mr Dudin's sons were certainly known to have been hunting with the old Surrey up to 1870.
>
> By 1800 the country north of Croydon was beginning to get somewhat

congested and built up, so that Croydon became the Melton of the South. Hunting people hacked to Croydon where they put up their horses in livery stables to allow them a respite, while they themselves went in to a hearty breakfast before hacking on to the nearby meets. The centre of all their activity was the Greyhound at Croydon.

The great classic comic novel of hunting, R S Surtees's *Handley Cross* or *Mr Jorrocks's Hunt* (1854), is a fictional source that accurately depicts the development of foxhunting at the more rustic level.

The farmers of the Vale of Sheepwash originally hunted hares [he said]. The hounds at first were of that primitive sort, upon which modern sportsmen look down with contempt. Few in number, uneven in size, and ill matched in speed, they were trencher-fed all the year round, and upon any particular morning that was fixed on for a hunt, each man might be seen wending his way to the meet followed by his dog, or bringing him along in a string. ['trencher-fed' meant unkennelled or left at farm houses or cottages]

There was Invincible Tom and Invincible Towler, Invincible Jack, and Invincible Jowler.

Day would hardly have dawned ere the long poled sportsmen assembled with their hounds. Then they would trail up to puss (the hare). Tipler would give the first intimation of her erratic wanderings o'er the dewey mead. Then it was 'Well done Tipler! Ah, what a dog he is!' Then Mountain would throw his tongue, and flinging a pace or two in advance would assume the lead. 'Well done, Mountain! Mountain for ever' would be the cry… 'Hoop! Hoop! Hoop! There she goes!'…. what a panic ensues! Puss lays her long ears upon her back, and starts for the hill with the fleetness of the wind. The pack with more noise then speed, strain every nerve, and the further they go the further they are left behind" [and so on - puss escapes by hiding in a stone wall!]

The next step, said Surtees, was getting a boy to collect the hounds before hunting, and then some farmers began to ride. Foremost among these was Michael Hardy who seemed a natural leader and became the unofficial master. In the course of time hounds were fitted up on his farm. "They were then called foxhounds." Good times followed, but all went sour after Michael Hardy's decease.

"Who now was to take the hounds? was the universal enquiry, which no-one could answer." Many packs were to ask the same question then (mid-nineteenth century) and subsequently!

The Handley Cross Hunt induced a cockney tea merchant, John Jorrocks by name, to uproot himself from London and become their Master. Surtees then launched on his lengthy exploration of the comic possibilities of a corpulent cockney holding forth on his favourite topic of hunting, getting himself into embarrassing situations and battling with his illiterate huntsman, James Pigg. The book was so widely read that the favourite quotations became common currency among the hunting fraternity. Here is one of them, delivered by Jorrocks during his speech to cheering crowds after his arrival at Handley Cross: " 'Untin, as I have often said, is the sport of Kings - the image of war without its guilt, and only five-and-twenty percent of its danger." To a considerable degree this is what appealed to the young bloods. The excitement of a cavalry charge without an enemy responding with shot and shell.

To the late Victorian Masters of Hounds, Jorrocks was entertainment laced with self-satisfaction. "By Jove!" they might have said to themselves. "We certainly do things better nowadays. The Masters round here are real landowners, the hunt servants are educated and sober and we are all really well mounted. What progress!"

The great Leicestershire and Midland packs led the way and were much written up. Bradley's *Hunting Reminiscences of Frank Gillard* 1860-1896 is a useful source of information on what went on in the leading packs. Gillard was taken on by the Duke of Rutland to hunt his hounds, the Belvoir, in 1870. It was one of the most responsible jobs of its kind in the country. They hunted five days a week and had 67 couple of hounds in kennel, more than the strength of the usual pack. The huntsman was equivalent to a departmental head combining many of the responsibilities of the conventional master with those of a huntsman in charge of kennels. The relationship with the Duke of Rutland was a bit like the prime minister with the monarch. In Victorian times the prime minister sent a daily handwritten account of his doings in and out of Parliament to the Queen by special messenger. Similarly Gillard wrote an account of each day's hunting for the duke's benefit the same evening. Gillard had his own ideas on hound breeding but would undoubtedly have had to defer to the duke's wishes. To quote the author, "Few things interested the Duke more than a chat with his huntsman about hounds in the Sanctum at the kennels known as The Duke's Room where the celebrated sires and favourites of his pack were drawn for inspection, and he would dwell long in silent contemplation on their beautiful symmetry and colour. A corner of this room at the Kennels was railed off so that the hounds should not touch the noble master's gouty leg, aggravated by severe accidents in the field."

The amount of money spent on hunting by the leading packs was extraordinary. Gillard recalled that the whippers-in to the Barton Hunt had three or four horses a day to ride and each one cost around 300 guineas a piece. They were so fresh that the men could hardly control them. Incidentally Bob only once paid 200 guineas for a horse up to about 1910, and generally paid nearer 100 guineas for a good weight-carrying hunter.

Nevertheless, in Frank Gillard the Belvoir had an exceptionally talented man whose reputation brought a procession of hunting men to the Belvoir Kennels. In one month during the summer it was said that 25 masters of hounds visited the establishment.

By late Victorian times the foxhunting year had settled into its routine. The season opened with cub hunting in late August or early September. The object was to identify which coverts held foxes, to cull some of the cubs and to get the young hounds 'entered' to the scent of fox and, in due course, become relentless pursuers of the quarry. It was an informal affair; the first meets were timed for

6.30 am, nobody dressed up in 'pink' except the hunt servants and, as it was not practicable to ride across country owing to the hard ground and harvesting operations, hounds were held up in the coverts to do their hunting at close quarters. Everyone went home during the morning.

The meets became progressively later until the big occasion of the opening meet in November. This is when the new coats, boots, breeches were on show and the really serious hunting began. The Hunt Ball took place in January and the Point-to-Point in March or April. The season finished some time in April although the enthusiasts always hoped it would be possible to spill over into May.

The hound puppies, that had been walked at farms and estates during the winter, were adjudicated, as seen, at the Puppy Show in June, and the 'walkers' entertained to lunch, so bringing to an end the hunting year.

In regional Hound shows the Southdown had numerous placings; and then at Peterborough, the peak of hound showing, Bob won with a dog hound and also with Southdown Hamish in the brood bitches section. Tempest and Telltale also won the couples some years after he had retired from the mastership.

The hounds were the real love of the true foxhunter. A wealthy few could actually aspire to own their personal pack and hunt them over a block of county prised out of the hands of other hunts. For the titled landowners with vast estates this had always been easy and by the early twentieth century they had their heyday. Lord Leconfield's Hounds hunted six days a week, Viscount Cowdray's family created their own hunt next door at Midhurst and the Marquess of Abergavenny reigned long and successfully in charge of the Eridge on the Kent border. The local hunting people seemed quite happy with these personal fiefdoms but must have been a bit envious at times of committee-run hunts that had to take some cognizance of local opinion. These elected masters could be held responsible for everything that happened or failed to happen. "Hunt servants not up with their hounds." "The Master never should have engaged them" or "the Master is too mean to buy decent horses" "Too few foxes killed" "The Master's hound breeding policy is a disaster" "Too many farmers objecting to the hunt crossing their land" "The Master is not looking after his farmers properly" - and so on. The other side of the coin was the high social position that the successful master enjoyed. It was said he was almost equal in esteem to the local MP and received only slightly fewer anonymous letters!

The Southdown Hunt must have been quite an easy one to run, as the principal members were also in the Yeomanry together, and some of them were involved in the Polo Club as well. It was a group made up of landowners and gentlemen of independent means (so called) who could fill their time as they wished.

William Wood made it plain that the farmers did not take part to any great extent in hunting. Up to a point he was right but quite a number turned out occasionally to remind potential horse buyers that they should not be looking far afield for their mounts. There was a large turnover of horses and farmers with a good reputation made money. Isaac Baker did not hunt, but in one of her letters Madge said that for a short while only the milk float horse was left on the farm. Everything else had been sold.

Being part of the Southdown Hunt was also a good means of collecting orders by tailors, bootmakers and others who never made the social mistake of actually canvassing for custom. Mr Thorowgood of Dutton and Thorowgood, Bootmakers of Castle Square, Brighton was easily the best known tradesman of the period, although he ought not to be labelled as such since he was a leading member of the hunt. Still, he was glad to do business with regular customers at any time, and was pleased at the start of one cubbing season to have Bob calling out, "I want the hunt servants to have new boots for the opening meet; I will send them down to be measured." To Thorowgood's surprise, when the men turned up they had other ideas. "We think our boots are good enough," they said. "Can you make us shoes instead?" Thorowgood was not sure how he would stand with the master if the deception was discovered but eventually agreed, and the men were able to cut a dash with the girls in their bespoke footwear. The master paid up and asked no questions.

It had been obvious from the start that Bob could not go on living at Twineham during the hunting season since the Southdown Kennels were at Ringmer, east of Lewes, and the country extended north and west of that point, as well as west to Twineham. He rented a house {and presumably stables) for the first year and kept a close watch on houses in Brighton coming up for sale.

The estate agents (Jenner & Dell and Wilkinson, Son & Welch) came up with something that was clearly "interesting". They announced they were offering for auction on 28th January 1904 the valuable, Well-Built, choicely situated, FREE-HOLD MARINE MANSION known as No.2 Eastern Terrace, Kemp Town, Brighton together with Excellent Stabling. In the Particulars they could hardly contain their enthusiasm. "This commanding Mansion is of handsome elevation and is well situate on the East Cliff, within ten minutes' walk of Kemp Town Railway Station, occupying one of the finest positions on the whole Sea Front of Brighton, directly facing the Sea, commanding unrivalled Views of the Channel and overlooking the Madeira Promenade and Lawns. The Property is unique in many respects, the Reception Rooms and Principal Bedrooms being of particularly fine proportions.

"The Mansion throughout is in complete decorative repair, Electric Light is installed and no expense has been spared by the Owner in making the House most complete in every detail."

The accommodation comprised (a favourite word)

On the Top Floor	Four Bedrooms
On the Third Floor	Three Bedrooms
On the Second Floor	Three Superior Bedrooms (one of them with an enamelled iron Roman Bath with hot and cold water supplies and nickel taps)
On First Floor	One Fine Principal Bedroom. EXCEEDINGLY HANDSOME DRAWING ROOM
On Ground Floor	NOBLE DINING ROOM.

FINELY PROPORTIONED BILLIARD
ROOM

In the Basement there
are commodious

DOMESTIC OFFICES including CAPITAL
HOUSEKEEPER'S ROOM, SERVANTS'
HALL, BUTLER'S PANTRY and
EXCELLENT KITCHEN.

Two men-servants' bedrooms could be reached from there but they could be included in the Stable accommodation. The Stables themselves consisted of four stalls and a large loose box, a coach house and living rooms over.

Here was a house that would be an excellent base for the family. The decision was to buy it, preferably before the auction. Bob only just did the deal in time; £310 was paid as deposit three days before the auction. The purchase was completed on April 9, 1904 by the payment of the balance of £2,965, including some furniture, carpets and curtains.

Bob was much too busy to take on the fitting out of the house and delegated all decisions to Madge. She thoroughly enjoyed herself. All heavy Victorian furniture was banned. The eighteenth-century style would be just right for the house. Her adviser on how to proceed was C.H. Fox, Dealer in Antique Furniture and Works of Art, based at 13 Ship Street, Brighton. A quick look round and he had suggestions to make. The dining room was indeed handsome and would set off two Sheraton sideboards to perfection. If madam wished he would have them for her inspection next week. Such a room needed a top quality set of dining chairs - he favoured Sheraton again and a set of eight at minimum. Madam could see them at the same time. Madge found it all so easy, and the furniture was absolutely right when it came. He was so quick too, that he earned the name of 'Foxy Wizard' and finished up by supplying most of the better furniture for the residence. He probably failed to mention that some of the pieces were 'reproductions'.

The Edwardian decade saw Brighton recover its reputation, briefly as it happened, as the resort of the fashionable and well born. At the top of the tree came King Edward VII who was an occasional visitor to the house of his sister the Princess Royal. The leaders of Brighton Society could not aspire to mix with royalty but the right tone was set.

The King's morning ride along the front did allow the men of fashion a moment of glory. The technique was to guess correctly the time of His Majesty's departure and the direction he would take. They would then ride out in advance and hope to meet him as they returned towards home. As they approached the royal party their top hats would be swept off in an expansive salute, the crown touching the knee. At the same time performing a smart 'Eyes Right' turn of the head. This was a worrying moment. Would the King nod or not? It did not really make any difference. They would be certain to remark off-handedly to their wives, "We met the King this morning. He of course acknowledged our salute."

Madge soon built up a reputation for distinguished entertaining at 2 Eastern Terrace.

The menu quoted below was for a formal dinner entertaining the Brighton and County Polo club, which Bob had helped to found in 1903:

Hors d'Oeuvres
Mock Turtle Soup
Boiled Salmon
Sweetbreads
Saddle of Lamb
Quails

~

Baba, Wine Jelly
Cheese Straws
Ice Pudding

~

Dessert

Having the stables almost attached to the house helped the evening along. When the ladies withdrew after dinner the gentlemen could stroll through a covered way, shod in what Betjeman calls 'indoor pumps', and admire the polo ponies in their stalls. Bob did a bit of showing so the guests would have to hear how the successes were achieved and the trophies won.

Madge specialised in her musical soirees, and invitations to formal tea parties in the EXCEEDINGLY HANDSOME DRAWING ROOM were also coveted. To one of these came Siegfried Sassoon in his early days as a member of the Southdown Hunt, 'immortalised', as they say, in his first flourish of autobiography.

Siegfried Sassoon, poet and author, was to make his reputation in the years of the Great War as one of the important voices expressing consuming grief and frustration at the wholesale slaughter of young men in the trenches on the Western Front.

It must have taken his public by surprise when he published his *Memoirs of a Fox-Hunting Man* in 1928. Unexpected or not, the book promptly sold out and the publisher churned out six impressions between September and November. In 1930 *Memoirs of an Infantry Officer* followed. Sassoon admitted to going to 'London', but everywhere else and everybody else is given a fictitious name. This allowed him to put incidents in any order he liked and to be very critical of some of the characters. It must be doubtful, in fact, whether he could get away today with describing a Master of Hounds as a drunkard and unsporting, when those in the locality would have been quite aware of who he was writing about. The *Infantry Officer* is much more straight autobiography. It would have been absurd to try to conceal the places that every serving soldier would know intimately.

Sassoon would not have expected to find his *Memoirs* in print and on the booksellers shelves 60 years or so later, but it is a remarkable tribute to him to have produced a minor classic from what, on the face of it, is unpromising material. To add to his laurels, a contributor to a broadsheet newspaper in 1993 named *Sherston's Progress,* the third in his semi-autobiographical excursions, as one of the 20 best novels of the 20th century. It hardly comes into the category of a novel but deserves inclusion. Sassoon himself modestly wrote of "a modicum of mental ability in the writing of these Memoirs".

As a boy he had learnt to ride a pony and had become a good enough rider to enjoy the occasional outing with the hounds, but as he lived in a 'deprived district' that was not regularly hunted by any pack, he had to decide which of the accessible ones to attach himself to. The Ringwell (Southdown) seemed to offer the most 'exhilarating' atmosphere. He became a subscriber. Arthur Ridsdale was delighted to have a recruit to talk to, and told Madge there was a new young chap who would be immensely impressed to come to Eastern Terrace and be entertained by the Master's wife. So the day came when Arthur and Siegfried Sassoon were both taking a delicate tea with Madge. Sassoon could never meet strangers at close quarters without twitching and squirming with shyness. On this occasion his gyrations in an easy chair dislodged the tea plate which broke in half. Hoping to cover up the disaster, he tried to hide the bits of plate down the side of the chair.

Inevitably Arthur Ridsdale spotted him and called out, "I say Sassoon, this is too bad. I get you an invitation to tea with Mrs McKergow and you do nothing but break her plates!" Arthur was quickly squashed, but Siegfried probably took a long time to recover his equanimity.

Sassoon gives a clue as to how the *Memoirs* came to be written in the book itself. The first eight parts or chapters are on the theme of Hunting; the last two have the author as a military man at the start of the 1914-1918 war. At an Officers' Training Camp, says Sassoon, he shared a bedroom with a young Sandhurst trained recruit. He was a friendly and unassuming character, and they talked about the course and their peacetime activities. "I talked to him about foxhunting which never failed to interest him. He had hunted very little, but regarded it as immensely important and much of the material of these Memoirs became familiar to him through our conversations in the hut. I used to read him Stephen's letters from the Front, which were long and full of amusing references to the sport that for him symbolised everything enjoyable which the War had interrupted and put an end to". 'Stephen' was in fact Gordon Harbord of East Hoathly Vicarage.

'Our conversations' is the phrase that describes perfectly the author's methods. He artfully chats away informally on his accident-prone progression from pony riding boy to a baffled youth introduced to the hunting field, bringing in incidentals of countryside, weather and the characters of horse and human kind as he goes. Over time his experiences convert him into a fully fledged member of the hunt capable of winning the Colonels's Cup at the Southdown Point-to-Point.

Bob had no trouble in putting names to many of the characters in Siegfried Sassoon's *Memoirs*. Arthur Ridsdale was there of course, George Whitfeld and Kennedy Megaw (the Hunt Secretary). Gordon Harbord's death in action while Sassoon was still training was hard to accept. So by the end of the book the carefree world of cricket in the summer and hunting in the winter gave way to the front line in France.

In the next volume of the *Memoirs,* Sassoon took up the story from 1916 when he was serving with the Flintshires (Royal Welsh Fusiliers). The theme was growing disgust at the slaughter that he was now experiencing at first hand. He could best express himself through his poetry and published a collection in 1917. The title *The Old Huntsman and Other Poems* was a bit naughty. It was guaranteed to be bought by the sporting fraternity in the expectation of getting some light relief from the war. Arthur Ridsdale thought so; he sent Bob a copy inscribed "Memories of old days by our mutual friend Sigismund [sic] Sassoon. Wishing you all good luck". Of course it was not hunting memories. The first poem was genuinely about an old huntsman in reduced circumstances. Most of the remaining 71 pieces were thoughts on War and were far from cheerful.

Sassoon went on to take his protest much further. He published a Statement calling for both sides to cease fighting. His friends realised that he was heading for dismissal from the army and might be incarcerated in a mental hospital against his will. Fortunately he agreed to apply to a Medical Board and be classed as an officer suffering from shell shock. As he arrived at the specialist Hospital he ended these pages of biography with the words "this volume can conveniently be concluded".

By extraordinary coincidence Wilfred Owen, now recognised by many as the 'best' of the war poets, was also under treatment at the hospital, and it is thought Owen was helped by Sassoon - the far more experienced writer.

Both men returned to service. Wilfred Owen was killed just before the Armistice; Sassoon came through and continued to send his regimental Christmas cards to his hunting friends. After the war he befriended Stephen Tennant, described as the 'brightest of bright young things'. At the week-end house parties Sassoon was thrown in with members of the Bloomsbury group, the Sitwells and others in the literary social swim. Then, amid much rancour, he broke off his relationship with Tennant, which left him alone and depressed. He is supposed to have blurted out to Virginia Woolf, "I sometimes wish I were back among those brainless fox-hunters again!" It would be wrong to leave Siegfried Sassoon in that mood. Much better to quote the line from Henry V with which he introduced his foxhunting memoirs, "This happy breed of men, this little world."

The Southdown Hunt Point-to-Point was organised at different sites year by year for the convenience of the members entering horses for the races and the spectators. The owners who lived miles away had to arrange for a groom to ride the horse to a friend's farm the day before and complete the journey on the day of the meeting. In 1907 Bob arranged the Point-to-Point at one of the most difficult points to get to, namely Wapses Farm, Twineham. It was not only at the extreme north-west tip of the Southdown country but stood well away from the public road from Albourne to Henfield. The local papers brought their best writing to bear on the event. One was brief. "The attendance at the annual Point-to-Point races of the Southdown Hunt near Twineham Grange, the residence of Mr R McKergow MFH, on Saturday was as big as ever, although the members of the committee had announced their intention of putting a stop to the betting which had proved so great a bar to the enjoyment of visitors at some of the Southdown meetings last year because of the 'Welshing'. Free of the rough element Saturday's meeting proved to be most enjoyable; the fields were large and the weather delightful."

The *Sussex Daily News* went to greater descriptive lengths.

Twineham Brook was in full flood on Saturday. This brook is well known to hunting men. The Southdown Hunt Point-to-Point Races were held on that day at Wapses Farm (Mr Beard, farmer) close to the famous brook. The weather overhead was glorious, but the brook after the deluge of the previous day assumed the dignity of a river, and was even deeper and broader than some rivers. The sun shone brilliantly. A breeze licked up much of the superfluity of water, but there was still the flooded brook and the water-logged land, and the Sussex mud would have been creditable to the county in its 'palmy' days. Every road led to Twineham. It was a merry business getting to Wapses. It is about the most distant spot from a railway station in those parts. The particular part of Twineham that accommodates Wapses had first to be located and then there was a long narrow farm road to negotiate, about half a mile of it, churned up by the invasion of horses, traps and motor-cars. The attendance was great. Policemen directed traffic in accustomed places. Sometimes a motor-car would 'jib' in the narrow road. It was a day when one could see motor-car wheels revolve at fifty miles an hour speed, while the car declined to budge an inch. The 'stick in the muds' had literally to be hauled out of the mire and pushed along in the soft places.

However in spite of it all there was a large assembly of equipages of every degree, and hundreds of people horsemen and ladies, cyclists and pedestrians. Wapses was absolutely besieged with the hunting folk and their friends. Under the blue sky luncheon baskets were cheerfully opened. It was like a Derby pic-nic on the hill, and the hunt had a thoroughly good time. Owing to the flooded condition of the district the course had to be altered. The Twineham brook was 25ft wide in many places and even Southdowners could not face such a water jump. The starting point and the winning post were both in the vicinity of the Wapses farmhouse. In the four mile course there were several water jumps, and the going was very heavy.

A number of photographs were taken at the meeting. They showed no roped off paddock or saddling enclosure. The horses were got ready in front of the farm-house among the onlookers. As implied in the report the hedges were entirely unprepared and thin. The runners had to jump sections marked by red and white flags. So it was quite easy to alter the course by sticking the flags in different hedges but a bit confusing for the riders. 'Yeoman' was disqualified in the Heavy Weight Race for going out of the course. Most of the riders wore their normal hunting kit of pink or black coats and top hats. After the racing the motors had to be dragged out and the cyclists had trouble with their tyres, but one of the papers recorded that "primrosing became the homeward pastime".

For the gentry the big occasion was the Hunt Ball at Lewes Town Hall in early January. The care taken to put on a really splendid occasion is well illustrated by the menu for the ball held on January 4, 1907.

The covers had one of two prints of hunting scenes by G. Wright surmounted by a stamped fox's head in gold. The prints measured 2 ³/₄ ins by 2 ins and were extraordinarily good quality in colour and sharpness. The artist's signature was perfectly readable under a lens. In one print the brass buttons on the pink coats were picked out in gold. The menus demonstrated the fine craftmanship that could be called on locally at what would then have been regarded as a suitable price for 'ephemera'. The dinner by Booth & Sons of Brighton was, apart from consomme soup to open proceedings, entirely made up of cold dishes. The first section of Entrees Froides had ten choices, followed by 11 in the next, including unadorned 'Sandwiches de Saumon fumée'. The choice of Sweets (or Dessert as they would have called it) offered nine, followed by Pineapple and Raisins. It is a pity that no wines are listed; they would have been chosen by the Master. The cost of the ticket would have been between £1 and thirty shillings (£1.50) and the committee would expect to make a small profit.

The Committee of the Southdown Hunt must have realised in 1903 that Bob McKergow would not remain with them for many years, but his wish to depart at the end of the 1906/07 season was a disappointment, and the cry went up "Don't go yet!" The compliments flowed in and the *Sussex Daily News* added its quota. "Of his popularity too much could not be said," they said. "Genial in the field and an excellent Master, foxhunting stands first with him as a sport." So Bob gave in and agreed to continue for another season when the hounds would hunt seven days a fortnight instead of four days a week. Cubbing would be four days a week and he was guaranteed £1,800 per annum. At the end of April 1908 he wrote up his summary of the season.

> This is the end of my last Season. Misa has taken over hounds. Fred Carroll is to be Huntsman. Ned Farmer is going to the Chiddingfold as Kennel Huntsman. We have had a good Season on the whole but the foxes have not made such good points as in previous years but we have had very fast gallops and some good runs. We have been out 110 days and killed 50 ¹/₂ brace of foxes and run about 30 brace to ground. We have killed a good many foxes with mange and seen several more. I am afraid it is returning to us on the Hills, it will be a serious matter for the SDH if it does. We have a nice entry to leave behind and put on 11 couple of hounds; some nice dog hounds. We have left 49 couple in Kennel. I started with 36 ¹/₂ in 1903.
>
> We had our Point-to-Point Races at Oakwood Farm, Streat. It was a most enjoyable day, no accidents; in fact the best Point-to-Point we have had in my opinion.
>
> George Whitfeld very kindly assisted me and helped make it the success it was. I was away for the month of February. Mr Brand and Mr Campion acted as Field Masters in my absence. The Southdown have not killed 50 ¹/₂ brace of foxes since 1897 when they killed 51 brace. I hope we shall kill more next season as the county is well stocked except in far East part.

Bob lost no time in joining up with the Crawley and Horsham Hunt again and was given a special welcome by Colonel Godman, the Master, when he officiated as Judge at the Point-to-Point in April 1908. At the Farmers Luncheon Col Godman said he was glad to see Lord Leconfield and their old friend Mr R.W. McKergow with them that day and, referring to the fact that Mr McKergow had given up the Mastership of the Southdown Hunt, he declared that their loss was the gain of the Crawley and Horsham Hunt. They were glad to have him back with them again as a good old "Crawler" (laughter and applause).

The McKergow family did not return to Twineham Grange from Brighton immediately. Instead in 1909, they pulled most of it down and rebuilt the house to be larger and in, what can be described as, 'Edwardian Tudor' style. The rooms not demolished kept their Victorian windows; the new part was fronted with half-timbering and leaded window panels. Inside the front hall rose to first floor ceiling with galleried corridor and oak staircase. To the east the new dining room took up half the width of the house. The servants' bedrooms were now on the new second floor. The resident Ladies Maid/Dressmaker had her workroom up there with a telephone link to Madge's dressing room. It was evident that Eastern Terrace had expanded their horizons in the field of entertaining.

In 1902 Madge bore a second son whom they called John, making the family two sons and a daughter. It was time for Bob to start thinking about a prep school for his boys, for Dudley anyway. And now they were living in Brighton, preferably somewhere on the south coast.

The Seth-Smiths at Colwood, Bolney, also joined in the decision, as Kenneth Seth-Smith and Dudley had become the best of friends, and it would be ideal for them to board at the same school. Rottingdean School, which was close to Brighton, was among the front runners in all departments and was particularly strong in team games. Although not in Brighton, it was easy to reach, so Dudley and Kenneth started there - in the bottom class - in 1907.

Rottingdean School had been in existence as a cramming establishment since about 1810. James Hewitt bought it in 1863 and changed it into a Preparatory School, which meant he only took boys at about eight years old and 'prepared' them for entry into the Public School system. It was one of the earliest schools of its kind. T H Mason joined Hewitt in 1887 after starting the Preparatory School to Dulwich College. They built a big new school with a large playing field. By 1900 Rottingdean had 61 boys, seven masters, a violin teacher and the inevitable Staff Sergeant to teach 'physical jerks' and small-bore rifle shooting.

They were proud of their high level of good health. It was due, they stated in their prospectus, "to the excellent situation of the school buildings and the wonderfully bracing air of Rottingdean Downs. In fact we would go so far as to say that we do not believe that there is a single preparatory school in England that has a more healthy situation than our own, or which gives its members a better opportunity of retaining or acquiring robust health."

Standards of water supply and drainage were improving rapidly, but prospective parents would remember that schools used to be death traps, with boys at risk from diphtheria epidemics. Schools built outside villages had room for large playing fields and proper sanitary arrangements; the point was worth making. It was as well that the boys were 'robust'. They were kept busy at their games: Association Football, Rugby Football, Cricket, Fives, Racquets, and Small-Bore Rifle Shooting. An enthusiastic master introduced the boys to golf. The annual Sports Day included some serious running as well as Sack Races.

The headmaster started rugger as well as soccer at Rottingdean in 1905 - unusual for prep schools at the time. Feeling, no doubt, that parents might require some kind of explanation from him as to why he had taken this step, and given assurance that it was unlikely that their little darlings would suffer injury from playing so rough a game, he wrote a piece in the school magazine to allay their fears.

> The game was taken up this term with the greatest possible keenness, and after a few weeks practice both forwards and outsiders showed marked improvement in combination and passing; as a rule too the tackling was sound. A boy who had learnt to go 'hard and low' by the time he has left his private school has learnt a very valuable lesson. It may be reassuring to parents to learn that hardly a single game has produced an injury of any sort to the players, and no serious injury whatsoever. A thing that forwards in future years must master, is the art of getting the ball into the second line of the scrum and taking it on with them at their feet. They must learn how to 'wheel' a scrum and break up quickly. Improvement in both these branches of forward play has been observable, but there was hardly the same intelligence shown among the forwards as among the outsiders. Putting one's head down and shoving blindly is not playing football. Forwards must listen to the halves to hear whether they are to heel the ball out and above all keep their eyes open, and halves must help the forwards as far as possible, in telling them when to break up. One thing the outsiders must realise is that the only way to stop a forward rush is to fall on the ball. Houghton and one or two others were the only players who could bring themselves to believe this. A flying kick at the rugger ball is generally fatal to your own chances of success.

They added yet another activity to the curriculum when Robert Baden-Powell published his *Scouting for Boys*, and created the Boy Scout movement, in 1908. The school had a dozen boys in their first troop by 1910, and took part in a parade with other boy scouts on Brighton's Preston Park that year, inspected by Baden Powell - still in army uniform. It is not clear to what extent the founder, a military hero for his defence of Mafeking in the Boer War, intended military values to have a place in his organisation. Probably to a very small extent, apart from a correct turn-out and ability to march in step. He genuinely offered something new in the combination of helping others, and a chance to use the countryside for adventure. To the public, 'Boy Scouts' were a huge joke, and the comic postcard industry took every possible opportunity to poke fun at them. Dudley was sent several for his postcard album.

By any standards, sport was extremely well catered for at Rottingdean, and fully reported in the school magazine. All the more surprising to find a total absence of comment for school work in it, apart from the Classics. It must have come as a fearful shock to a nine-year-old boy, fluent in all the best jokes in *Jorrocks,* to find that Greek and Latin would be the bulk of his fare in the years ahead. No wonder many of them earned the verdict 'Not good at school'. The external examiner in Classics, Alfred H Legat MA, of Oriel College, Oxford wrote of Rottingdean in 1904:

> The Grammar, that sure foundation of Classical work, deserves special commendation for, with scarcely an exception, the marks are over 60 per cent and in the higher forms the average is nearly 70 per cent. The Unprepared Translation is much more successful than has lately been the case, and shows marked improvement in analyses and vocabulary. The Prepared Books, which in the highest forms are this year of exceptional difficulty, reach throughout a high pitch of accuracy in translation and appreciation of subject matter.

Later Legat got down to singling out boys for good work. "In Form VI, Stanford and Pugh receive commendation for every single paper, while Willock is not far behind. He was top of the list in Latin Unseen Vergil and Aeschylus, and did well in Vergil, Greek Grammar and Aeschylus; Anderson in Vergil, Livy and Thucydides. Phillips and Bradley receive mention for Greek and Latin Grammar respectively."

Dudley and Kenneth did not get many mentions. However Dudley received good marks for Latin and English, which does at least give a clue that some other subjects were taught to supplement Classics. On the sports field the two of them were more often in the news. Dudley was in the Shooting VIII representing the school, and Kenneth ended up as Captain of the VIII and a member of first cricket eleven. Dudley's best performance came in football. As goalkeeper he won some praise. Against Windlesham House, Rottingdean were beaten by two goals to one. "The score against us would have been much heavier but for the excellent play of McKergow in goal." St Ronans, Worthing, gave them a much harder time. They were "thrashed soundly by eleven goals to love. Morris was responsible for nine of the eleven goals, and he was one of the fastest and cleverest forwards we have ever seen. Our eleven were rather outclassed, but McKergow played very well in goal, and received his colours after the match." At the end of the term the headmaster reported Dudley "has been a success in goal. He has distinguished himself at times. He is at his best in dealing with overhead shots."

In his last term Dudley won the School Fencing Competition, and sportingly 'retired in favour of Hawkins' in the Boxing final. Being tall with a long reach obviously had its advantages. In 1911 he left Rottingdean to go to his public school, Uppingham. Kenneth Seth-Smith left to go to Charterhouse where, according to Dudley, he concentrated on cricket.

Time out
on
Safari
1911-1912

Kongoni Hash and Claret

The Victorians and Edwardians had a great liking for collecting deceased wild life. Framed collections of butterflies hung on walls, glass cases of birds or animals decorated a corner, mahogany cabinets housed the birds' eggs of earlier days and the hunting man could look forward to accumulating the mounted masks, pads and brushes of foxes that would steadily occupy more and more of the wall space.

It is not surprising that when the exciting riches of East Africa in wild animals became available there was a demand for safaris to secure a good variety of first rate specimens that would impress the neighbours when the taxidermist had performed his miracles on the skins, horns and heads of the 'bag'.

Safaris were organised on package tour lines by agents such as Newland and Tarlton. On these the client was met off the boat by his personal White Hunter who selected the small army of porters and servants needed for the expedition, hired the tents and equipment, provided a selection of ponies to ride, advised on ammunition and then led the outfit to places where a good variety of game could be found. At the proper time the client had to be delivered back to his boat and the specimens crated for despatch to the London taxidermist.

Bob improved on this impersonal process by persuading Martin Seth-Smith to act as White Hunter. Donald and Martin, elder brothers of Dudley's constant companion Kenneth, had been earlier settlers in British East Africa (Kenya) and had developed a sisal growing enterprise.

In the 1890s they were on record as despising the game hunting safaris, saying that what the country needed was investment not short term visitors crisscrossing the country. Why Donald and Martin changed their minds is not revealed, but they would clearly have been under much pressure from friends in England to help them get some good sport. At all events, Martin agreed to Bob's request to head a safari in 1911.

Dick Reece will have greeted the news with total hilarity. It was exactly the sort of activity on Bob's part that brought forth a host of leg pulls.

He established Bob as a super-hero, braving unknown perils, and at the mercy of fierce cannibals. Dick and the Cambridge friends carried their foolery to extraordinary lengths. A send-off dinner was organised at the Ritz Hotel, Piccadilly.

Dick sketched a caricature on the front of the menu folder and wrote out a 'cod' menu inside.

VIANDES
Oeufs d'Autruche
Consomme au Missionair
Truites de Twineham au Crocodile
Sauce de la mer Rouge
Pie d'Elephant Farcie
Loin of Lion
Cactus Bouii Ignames Frites
Tête de Sanglier
Sauce Robert au Pochon
Capon de Mombassa
Salade des Palmiers
Paon en Deuil
Souffle Glace Uganda
Bombe McKergow

DESSERT
Café Noir

The wine list he proposed was serious - and then some!

VINS

PUNCH
MOSELLE   Grunhauser Maximum 1884
HOCK   Steinberg Cabinet 1868
SHERRY   "Tio Pepe"
Vino de Pasto (bottled 1875)

CHAMPAGNES   Cliequot (Veuve)
Vin Rose 1898
Pol Roger
Cuvee de Reserve 1898
PORT   Cockburn's 1847
Dows 1863
MADEIRA   Vintage Sercial 1850
CLARET   Chateau Latour
1er Grand Vin 1874
COGNAC   Raynal's 1820

The Ritz Hotel have kindly reconstructed the wine list into current vintages and then costed them. There are reservations about the age of the wines, but assuming they are drinkable the Moselle, Grunhauser maximum at 27 years old would be translated to Grunhauser maximum 1969, and priced now at £70 a bottle. Today's price per shot of 91-year-old Raynal's Cognac would be £75; 37-year-old Chateau Latour claret £900 a bottle; Cockburn's 64-year-old, and Dow's 48-year-old, port £400 a bottle serving five; 13-year-old Veuve Clicquot champagne £150 a bottle; 13-year-old Pol Roger champagne £120; 43-year-old Steinberg Cabinet hock £90.

The total list would cost today something in excess of £500 per person. Even accepting that the list includes some of the top products of the time, it is difficult to envisage the party paying more than a pound or so a head for the privilege of drinking them.

Ready to move off.

It is to be hoped that the farewell, pre-safari dinner at the Ritz in fact took place with something resembling Dick Reece's jokey menu. Be that as it may, after a few days of final arrangements, Bob was ready to set off.

The route taken by travellers to East Africa was by rail to Dover where they transferred to the ferry, and then by the overnight train to Marseilles to board the ship that would take them to the east coast of Africa.

Bob joined the Boat Train at Victoria Station on October 12, 1911. He must have been an impressive sight striding down the platform, followed by two or three porters with barrows piled with luggage. He had several cases of clothes including riding boots and breeches, a shot gun and two rifles in their cases, a crate of tinned goodies from Fortnum & Mason and boxes of medical supplies, dental instruments and hair cutting clippers that might be needed to keep the safari neat and healthy. His progress down the platform was impeded by sobbing women clinging to their husbands, fiances or other close relatives who were about to set off to make their fortunes in British East Africa. The settlers did not face big physical dangers, but it was by no means certain that they would be sufficiently successful in the short term to be able to summon the ladies to join them.

The ferry crossing from Dover went smoothly, although they noticed the body of a drowned fisherman floating past as they left the port. The French train delivered the passengers to Marseilles on October 13, where the Union Castle steamer SS Carisbrook Castle waited for them.

At this point Bob started writing a diary, and kept it going until January 20, 1912, when he set foot in Twineham again.

October 13, 1911

We experienced some difficulty in getting out of the harbour and although we had 3 tugs to help us we knocked against the swinging bridge. We have over 100 passengers on board of which 54 are for Mombassa, this includes only first class passengers. We have some cattle for BEA for stocking farms, also a number of falcons and dogs of various breeds which howl at night and disturb all the passengers on the promenade deck. This boat has a new crew from Captain downwards.

October 15
Arrived at Naples. The Captain announced that passengers would be allowed to land so, after lunch, we went ashore in a row boat and procured a guide who spoke English. He told us this was the first English ship to land passengers for 5 weeks owing to a cholera scare. I am not at all surprised they have these outbreaks at Naples as the condition of the streets is awful - no refuse is ever swept up. The guide had to join his regiment the next day for Home Defence. (Italy and Turkey were at war). On our arrival in the Harbour we saw troop ships leaving for Tripoli, amidst cheers and firing of guns.

We had a calm night, but the howling of hounds and dogs in the night disturbed us very much.

The barber with Biltong drying in the background.

October 16
The English passengers hope to be allowed to land at Port Said, unless the authorities consider us an infected ship. We hope to arrive at Port Said on Thursday. I find much amusement in hearing our Ship's Officers talk to the officials at different Ports, they don't know the language but seem to get through all right by shouting at them.

I think our Captain is a very nice man… but this Line is on the make and does not allow enough staff for the number of passengers on board; the ship is full.

October 18
We had a terrible stormy night, hardly any passengers to lunch or dinner, in fact nearly the whole lot went down with sea-sickness; I kept about all the time and enjoyed my meals. We had an awful tossing about at night.

I am afraid we shall not be allowed to land at Port Said tomorrow.

October 19
We arrived at Port Said and came to anchor about 1.30 and coal was carried aboard by a villainous crowd, about 900 tons. We turned in, all coal dust, at 11 o'clock and I slept till 7 o'clock. Port Said is a beastly place, the Port Authorities will not let us land, as we have a suspected case of Cholera on board.

The whole crew are sick of this job of moving cargo about which has been so badly packed that it has to be handled twice over. No labourers can come on board to help or work the donkey.

The passengers were very sick last night and swear they will never come this way again. The charge for Reuter's wire this morning was 1/- for a few lines. We know that Winston Churchill has been made Secretary for Ireland!!

Bob with his gun bearers and groom. Note the head gun bearer in his top hat.

October 21

We left Port Said at 3.30 and came through the canal during the night. We arrived this morning at Suez; again no-one is allowed to land and the people for Port Said and Suez were got up at 5 o'clock and told to parade before the Port Doctor. I was awakened at 4.30 by hearing those black devils talking like a lot of parrots on their sailing barges which were to take these people away.

We are kept in at every Port owing to this Cholera.

People have now started wearing white clothes and sun hats. I was most anxious to obtain some really thin clothes at one of the places, but they will not let the people aboard to sell them to us. This journey is very monotonous, hanging about and everybody is grousing.

October 23

We shall not arrive at Port Sudan until daylight as the Captain says it is no use as we have a lot of cargo to get rid of.

We have had a nasty rollable night, and last night several people left their port holes open and the sea came in and flooded their cabins badly.

I always understood the Red Sea was very calm and no breeze, but it is not so, we have quite a big sea running today.

October 24

We arrived at daylight at Port Sudan; after breakfast we went ashore to purchase thinner clothes from the Greek store. They are real swindlers these store keepers. We were told the ship would leave at 4.0 pm but it did not do so. We had a 13 ton boiler in the bottom of the hold, which they attempted to get out with the ship's crane, which would not hold it. The whole thing gave way and the boiler went to the bottom smashing up most things and very nearly killing some natives. This delayed us until 2.0 am this morning when we left.

I never knew nor saw such a place as Port Sudan. Very fine docks but poor habitations and tents; I cannot understand how they ever get a white man to stay there.

October 25

We are now two days behind time, and we cannot see the Captain will make it up, I cannot see how he is going to. Wait till I get home and I will wake this company up. Everybody is on the growl. They have even got cargo in the berths forward and were running about collecting it, a few cases here and there, it really is most disgraceful. We might be an ordinary tramp steamer.

* * * * *

Further delayed by a strike of their stokers, the boat did not arrive at Aden until October 27. Bob was not impressed - "nothing but a barren rock with huge crowds of natives, half naked, begging around the streets."

The passengers were amused by the gun salutes for a visiting Russian Prince, but not by the malodorous cargo being taken on board. "Yesterday they loaded 2 holds with Bombay Duck, which is nothing else but stinking fish, half cured shark which abound at Aden. The smell in the Saloon this morning is enough to make me sick. I should like to see a real good line of English Steamers on this route and knock this line out; they deserve it! The Germans are doing their best."

* * * * *

October 29

We passed Cape Guardafui early this morning. There is no light on this Cape owing to the Somalis having twice killed the light-house men, and at last they have pulled the light-house down, so it has become most dangerous to shipping. The Fifeshire was wrecked at this point some few months back and the crew were afraid to land on shore, although close to, as they would have all been killed by the natives. A cheerful shore to be near. I have had my photos developed by the barber and most of them turned out well. We had a dance on board last night. I had several dances with some very good partners.

October 30

Progress is really dreadful.

The fact is we are going all round the place as no one seems to know the way, so we keep out in the Ocean by night and come in during the day. There are no lights to go by, so it makes it very difficult to navigate. They tried to get up a Concert on board to enliven matters, but not one of these prigs on board would do anything to help.

October 31

Very slow work [500 miles yet to do before reaching Killindini, the Port for Mombasa].

They say there is a possibility that we shall overshoot Mombasa, as it is difficult to find. One of these boats did and went 6 hours down the coast. That would be the limit for all of us!

November 2

We arrived at Mombasa today at 3.45. Martin (Seth-Smith) met me there and I came off with R.J. Cunningham, Mr Scott's White Hunter… went to the Hotel Metropole in Mombasa town, changed and had dinner by 7.30 o'clock. I was dog tired.

We had heard of trouble with the ship's tube boilers and we only just arrived in Mombasa harbour when they burst, fires had to be drawn, and the ship had neither electric light nor fans working all night. A very good thing this did not happen in a storm in the Indian ocean.

November 3

We got up at 6 o'clock and went to the station and saw the Station Master and talked to him nicely as Englishmen, and got him to put us in the first train. They had three trains on Friday, as there were such a lot of people to go up to Nairobi and Uganda.

Mombasa is an interesting town but very hot. The palm trees and flowers were most beautiful, palms 20 feet high. All the trees look in splendid condition. Mombasa is infested with leopards which carry off the dogs and cats in the town and also a native now and then. All the natives have to carry a lamp after dark. We left Mombasa at 12.35. Scott, Cunningham, Martin and myself had a carriage to ourselves and we started on the most interesting journey I have ever made.

November 4

We arrived at Nairobi today. After dinner at Voie and a good night's rest we awoke at day-break and saw beasts from the train. When I woke, Scott had already seen 6 different species. We saw them in hundreds, Kongoni, Thomson's Gazelles, Ostrich, Wildebeste, Steinbuck, Zebra and Giraffe. You really cannot conceive what these vast herds look like on the plains. You can see them away in the distance like huge herds of cattle. We arrived at Nairobi at 12.35, just 28 hours in the train; every convenience is made to feed the passengers etc, but the travelling is very slow, as you go up and down and round curves. The railway is a very fine piece of engineering, and cost 6 millions of money to make.

Having arrived at Nairobi we were met by Martin's savages on the platform, all looking very cheerful. The ponies were outside the Station, held by nearly naked syces. [They then sorted out their luggage and formed up a squad of porters to carry it to Martin's House four and a half miles from Nairobi.]

Martin has quite a nice house, and stables with a courtyard surrounded by Kennels and retainer's shed, cook house etc. The number of people you see about the place now is extraordinary; they hear he is going on safari. There is any amount of buck about here within 100 yards of the house. Also snakes and leopards come round.

November 5

Got up 5.30 and had a hunt with Martin's pack. We found and hunted hare, duiker, steinbuck and bushbuck, returned home at 7.30 for breakfast. We then packed clothes, guns etc all the morning with the aid of Juma, my tent boy. [The arrangements for the safari have to be made the next day. The cook is already engaged.]

November 6

I am riding another pony today on trial. I had a ride on a good pony yesterday, so I am sticking to him. The mule we had to return, as it took 6 men to put the bridle on. We have returned from Nairobi after having arranged food supply, ammunition and porters; we find the amount of stuff to be carried amounts to so much we must have 43 porters, making a total of something like 70 people all told [an underestimate!].

There is trouble up North with a tribe, and the King's African Rifles have been ordered to leave at once for Eldeyo to quell the disturbance, a very bad part of the country to go into at this time of the year!

November 7

[Bob was off colour, and did not feel like going into Nairobi. Martin assembled the safari and returned home in the afternoon.]

Bob suitably mounted.

The costumes of some of the porters are extraordinary - our head gun bearer wears a top hat. The Head man, after having got his porters together, addressed them at great length on the subject of stealing. This man was with Stanley through Africa, and is supposed to be an excellent fellow; Martin does not know him. [Stanley, journalist and explorer who made his name by finding Livingstone, was a ferocious disciplinarian, and the Head man applied a hide whip too frequently in the opinion of Martin and Bob - probably copying Stanley.] I am now most anxious to get off....

November 8

We started from Ruasaka at 4.35 am on Safari and went by the Fort Hall Road to the Blue Posts Bridge where we arrived at 3.30 pm after doing nearly half of the distance in deluge of rain. I shot my first head of game before arriving at Thika. We saw Kongoni from the road, also Zebra, Impalla and Wart Hog all at once. I got my Kongoni at a distance of 244 yards first shot. It was not a very good head, but I saved it as it was my first beast.

November 9

We left the Blue Posts at 7.30 - a very wet morning. The going was very bad all the way, we arrived at Makuyu, Donald Seth-Smith's house at 11.30 and had some lunch; it rained very hard. I shot a brace of partridges on the way, which we had for dinner tonight.

"On November 24th 1911 we left Ketito ar 6.30am."

[The party then went to a shooting box which provided cover for Bob and Martin and room to store saddlery and other equipment. Most of the porters had to sleep in tents that leaked. The weather continued wet and cold. But their cook provided quite lavish dinners.]

Our dinner consisted of Kongoni hash and partridges, some good soup and a bottle of claret. [Bob had shot a wildebeste on the way and the meat had to be collected for the porters. They sent an armed Askari with the men to bring in the meat, who had to carry lamps when it got dark.]

November 11

We have had a most enjoyable day. It rained in torrents all night and we could not start until 9 o'clock when it cleared up. We only had one shower all day and the sun at times was very hot. I wounded a pig and we tracked him for 2 miles; it was interesting work to see the gun bearers working out the trail, but we came upon some Impalla and gave up the pig hunt; I missed my beast, but shortly after we came upon some Kongoni. I wounded one but followed him up and got him and another. We sent the meat back to camp. We then mounted the hills at the back of Kitito, and had the most glorious view I have ever seen; I counted from the top of this hill 84 head of game, and the lights on the far distant hills were simply lovely, in fact this sort of thing is quite as interesting as game shooting.

On the way home we had a funny incident. We came upon 3 Wart Hog and I stalked them. I shot the first stone dead, another much finer boar came in sight and I struck him. He came for me and the gun bearer. I was then standing on the Ant Hill loading. I shouted to Martin, "Look to your right front." Martin was below me and could not see him coming. As I raised my rifle to have another shot, Martin knocked him over stone dead, about 20 yards from me. He had a fine head and was, they think, 12 years old, so the porters had about 70 stone of meat. I have saved his head, and had a knife sheath made today for my hunting knife out of his hide. We set traps for Hyena in the evening: they came at night and took all our bait, but did not catch one.

[On November 16 they had a check up on the bag so far.: 3 Kongoni, 2 Wilde-Beeste, 1 Steinbeck, 1 Thomson's Gazelle, 1 Bush Buck, 4 Wart Hogs, 1 Duiker. Buffalo had not featured so far, and they were determined to rectify the omission.

The next day they sent out a gun bearer to try and locate some, but he could find no trace of any.]

November 17

We climbed about 600 feet over some bad-going for ponies and men. I saw a waterbuck, a fine specimen and stalked him, but he moved. Martin and I got out our glasses to look at the country below, and we both said at the same moment, 'Buffalo!'. We did a great stalk and Cosimoko, my first gun bearer, led us up to within 30 yards of them. They gave one snort and were gone. Martin's second gun-bearer ran hard down the hill, got behind a rock and marked them. I ran as fast as I could, lay on my back, and slid down the rocks till within 200 yards, when I marked the bull. I got a good view lying on my back, and I gave him a shot out of my big gun, and knocked him down. Martin and I then opened a regular fusillade on him to make sure he was a deader. I ran down behind him and he gave a final kick. He was a good bull but not old, and I should think weighed 150 stone.

Great rejoicing of porters who put sprigs of trees on him and shook me by the hand. We then sent for more men and had the head and meat taken back to camp. At camp it was awfully funny, the whole place turned out, shook me by the hand and gave us a war dance. These natives hate a buffalo. They say, "It was a good cartridge that killed him." They have about 1600 lb of meat tonight to eat.

On the way to Maragua Bridge.

[The next few days were successful but Lion did not show up. On November 24 they left Ketito and camped at Maragua Bridge Farm for the night. From there it was a short walk to Fort Hall where the District Commissioner had his HQ and, after some shopping, pressed on to a camp site six miles away - in torrential rain. The following day they went on in the direction of Nyeri and Kikuyu country and, after yet another wet night, got to Nyeri on Novmber 27 where their donkey man was waiting for them with 22 donkeys.]

November 28 - Nyeri

Rained hard when we were packing our kit and left in a deluge. I walked nearly all the distance to Amboni River, our next camp. We arrived at the river at 12.30 and had to wait for the porters. We found the river in full flood, up above a man's waist and the current was running at about 30 miles an hour. Having got a porter across and a rope, we then proceeded to get the horses over. They went over well, and then the porters took hold of the rope and went across, but some of the porters were nearly swept off their legs. The sheep and hounds had to be carried across on men's shoulders. The donkeys then had to be unloaded and we had some difficulty in getting them to go in the water. The last to cross were Martin and myself. Having divested myself of my lower garments and pulled my shirt up round my waist, I went through followed by Martin, who had not divested himself of clothes. He got as far as the middle, stepped on a stone and went under. Luckily we had the rope, otherwise he might have been swept away by the current. Have made big fires for the night and put the horses and donkey in the middle.

[They left the Amboni River at about 7 o'clock, crossed a plain and came on the Naramuru River which again was flooded. Crossed by a fallen tree. Then rode on to inspect the Birngiette River and decided it would be wise to wait until morning to organise the crossing.]

Four of our lady porters.

November 30

I cut down some trees and with the aid of our rope we made quite a good bridge; we got over but had a good deal of difficulty getting the donkeys over. We have marched now for seven days consecutively, and not had one fine day and night.

December 2

We took some porters and gun-bearers with us shooting and, having travelled some three miles from Camp, we heard a porter screaming and saw him running up to us. He said he had seen two lions sitting up. We dismounted at once, took our heavy rifles and went back to find a scared porter who, if he had not had a black face, would have had a very white one. It appears he too walked up to within 20 yards of the lion, who was sitting up behind a bush swinging his tail and looking nasty; the lioness was close and ready to attack. The porter evidently ran away at once and was not quite sure of the place, as all the scrub looks so much alike. I saw the lion disappearing into a ditch place, up and let him have one shot which went over his head. He grunted and galloped off as hard as he could go. I ran forward and got in another shot, but missed again. It was very hard luck to miss the pair, and I was disappointed and so was Martin, also gun bearers and porters.

December 3

I have come to the conclusion we are good doctors, as we have several patients every night, and they certainly get better after our doctoring. We hope to make an early start tomorrow to our next camp about 17 miles away.

December 4

Arrived at No 2 camp on the Gwysa Nykui River at 12 o'clock [After a good afternoon's shooting Bob counted up his safari - 92 men with three ponies, five hounds and 22 donkeys. Some annoyance comes through, after meeting a German sportsman who trumped them with 150 men!]

December 6

[Roaring lions as late as 8 o'clock in the morning gave hope that they could be found in the vicinity.]

From Kitito, to within a few miles of the 'Camp in the swamp' country, one sees no game at all, as it is thickly populated with the Kikuyu people and all game is driven away, as it eats their crops, which consists of a patch of potatoes, some 20 yards square and a similar patch of maize.

When the maize comes out in ear the boys and girls of the family sit by all day to frighten the birds away. They only send them to their neighbours patch and so it continues. A man having no family borrows his neighbours boys for their food. You see numbers of men dressed up in any amount of rings and ornaments, walking about the country with spears mostly in threes and fours; the women stop at home and do the work, also the children.

They are a very civil people but haughty in their manner. We stop most of them and examine their ornaments and spears. In this part of the country you never see a living person, neither are there any native tracks as in other parts. It seems to lead to nowhere, and the funny part is that the game is very wild here and not at all easy to get at. I fancied when I came here I should like to stay in one camp a long time, but I must say I like a change of country since, although so far I have not procured any birds except for the pot, we have bagged a great variety of game: one each of buffalo, waterbuck, roan antelope, steinbeck and oryx, plus kongoni, colobus monkey, grey monkey, zebra, servial cat, impalla, Chandler's Reed buck, Thomson's gazelle, wilde-beest, hyena, duiker and fennic fox.

The buffalow bull.

* * * * *

They killed common species such as kongoni, impalla and zebra for meat, and brought back a number of zebra skins to mount as covers for balustrades, and to put under glass as a table top.

Their break, to take stock of what they had bagged so far, emphasised their failure to get a lion or a rhinoceros. There were eight or nine days left until the march back to Nairobi began, so it was worth putting in some effort to fill the gaps. The men were instructed to report any lion in the vicinity of the camp at once. On December 9 one lioness was seen when she sat up to watch the men on the hill opposite. By the time Bob was guided to a spot from where she could be seen, the lioness was crouching low and Bob's shot missed her. Martin blazed away as she dived into the scrub, without effect. Firing at an indistinct and moving target at 300 yards was obviously most unlikely to result in a kill.

Bob with the Masai women who had driven a hard bargain to get them to help as porters.

Two days later a better opportunity came after Bob himself saw a male lion and two lionesses in the scrub. A plan was made for Bob and Martin to get behind them, and then signal the porters to advance when the lions might move towards the guns. This scheme came unstuck when two other lions strolled past the beaters and growled at them. The beaters and gun bearers had not bargained for this, and set up a fearful row to frighten them away. The lions originally marked went off at speed, and Bob's sharp shooting at 350 yards cut up the dust but left the animals unscathed. That was the end of lion hunting.

The rhinos were plentiful, but a mature male with a good horn never showed up. When the tracks of a group of rhino were seen, the party diverted to follow them. Usually they found cows and calves. Bob thought, in retrospect, they might have had a younger male, but Martin was very definite they had seen nothing worth taking.

On December 19 they left camp and headed for Nairobi on the same route that they had used on the way out.

They found the Birgniette River easy to cross, and were pleased to see their tree bridge still in place. On the 20th they reached the Amboni River and then crossed the Naramura, using the temporary bridge the District Commissioner had put across. On 21st they reached Nyeri and went on to Wambogos, where the young men gave them a dancing display by firelight. Bob commented "a fine lot of young fellows".

The next day they passed through Fort Hall and camped on one of Donald Seth-Smith's farms. It was Blue Posts the next day, and Martin's homestead after that - arriving on Christmas Day. On Boxing Day they got up at 5.30 and went to the meet of the Masara Hounds. Bob commented, "It looked very odd to see the usual pink coats of Master and servants - everything turned out very well. One white man as Whip, and 2nd Whip a black man. The Master hunts his own hounds, which consist largely of drafts from Lord Leconfield's. We found a jackal, but hounds could hardly speak to the line. We soon went home, as our ponies could not take much more."

On the 27th they left for Nairobi with the porters singing and shouting through the town. They were paid off, and the kit taken back to Newland and Tarlton's. Only one tumbler and one fork were unaccounted for. The next day, the final pre-breakfast hunt yielded one kill - almost the only one of the entire trip - and final accounts were settled in the town.

The journey back to Mombasa was spoilt by an attack of food poisoning, and Bob felt very unwell when he arrived. As the hotel could not offer much attention, he asked to be admitted to the hospital for the night, and was well looked after. The next afternoon his friends organised the transfer of his luggage to the ship, and ordered a carriage to take him to the dock the following day, from where he was rowed out to the S.S. *Goorkha* for the voyage home.

The Union Castle Line got some credit for being able to provide a properly run boat on this occasion. They kept to time and had an efficient crew. The passengers were a cheerful crowd, either settler's families coming home for a holiday or big game hunters mulling over their exploits on safari. The children were rather a blight as before, but "they (the adults) really do get up something on this boat to while away the time".

Rifle cleaning.

Bob was clearly getting restless. Also, the news that ships had been foundering in a Bay of Biscay storm did not encourage staying on board. So on January 16 (1912) he decided to leave the boat at Naples. The next day he wrote that "two of us have quite made up our minds to leave the ship"; and with the entry in his diary of January 18 he rounded off his account of his adventurous safari in British East Africa.

January 18, 1912

We arrived off Naples in a bad fog and could not find the pilot and he could not find us. We got in and tied up about 8 o'clock. Having found a train leaving at 1.40 for Paris, we made arrangements to go ashore. We left ship at 12 o'clock, went through customs and saw large bodies of troops embarking for Tripoli, the Italians having hired American liners to convey the troops. [Italy had declared war on Turkey on September 29 1911 and bombarded the Tripoli coast. On November 6 she annexed Tripoli, and three weeks later won a decisive victory there.] We lunched at the station and were seen off by many of the passengers on our boat. We went to Rome, caught a train to Turin, then by Genoa, Mont Cenis, Chambery, Dijon to Paris. We passed through large tracts of country in the South of France under snow. We saw a nice lot of Italy passing through on the train. Arrived in Paris at 11 o'clock at night, slept the night in Paris and left at 8.25 in the morning of January 20, having already spent 40 hours in the train. After a comfortable journey we arrived in London at 3.25 on Saturday afternoon. I left Victoria Station at 4.30 for Twineham, having been away 15 weeks, and had a most enjoyable trip.

* * * * *

During the winter a *Sussex Daily News* reporter "induced Mr McKergow to chat about his trip" - as he put it. "Any trouble with the natives?" was one question that would hardly be put today. "Not the slightest," was the reply. "Generally, they were found to be a good tempered and genial race of people. The native men were very brave and courageous in hunting and took a keen interest in the sport. The native porters and attendants were a ripping lot of fellows. They did their 20 to 30 miles a day carrying loads of up to 60lbs on their heads."

The head gun bearer and some Masai women who were recruited as additional bearers for the final march home.

"What of the future?" Mr McKergow was not optimistic, "Unless more preservation takes place by order of the Government, big game will become extinct in the district, not through the exploits of sportsmen but by the increasing number of settlers who wage daily war upon the wild animals. The advance of the settler means the extermination of the wild beast, or driving it away to impenetrable retreats."

When it came to displaying the heads and other specimens at Twineham Grange, the extended wall area in the new hallway, extending up to first floor ceiling height, took the big heads easily, while the Colobus monkeys were mounted on a suspended branch in the gallery over the front door, in naturalistic poses. Visiting children were thrilled at the display.

Dick Reece will certainly have made plans to celebrate the return of the Triumphant Bobby with another dinner, again at the Ritz (to be given by Bobby, of course). Did it ever come off? Regrettably there is no record one way or the other.

Riding into the Twentieth Century

1901-1947

~ 6 ~
Out with the Hounds and Yeomanry

Twineham Grange in its Edwardian Tudor glory was much admired for miles around and was identified as a useful place for location work by the silent film makers of Hove, who for a short time seemed likely to be building a national cinematograph industry at that unlikely spot. Bob was asked by one of them if they could use the front porch of the house to take a few shots for the film they were making. In one scene the heroine, in historical riding costume, had to emerge from the door and watch her horse being led up by a groom. Hoisted on to the saddle, she then had to be sent on her way - to be immediately stopped out of shot, as she was in no way in control of her mount.

They started to rehearse this scene with Bob as technical adviser. They did not get very far before he was shouting "Stop! Stop! What's that man doing"? He was the groom, they told him. "Not dressed like that he isn't," barked Bob. "No groom of mine would come to the front door without his jacket on, let alone with his braces hanging down." The director, who had evidently seen too many Christmas cards depicting ostlers at an inn, doubtless felt that his adviser was being too fussy, but for the sake of not upsetting any of the hunting fraternity who might happen to see his masterpiece at the local picture house, will have been guided by what Bob had had to say when it came to a 'take'.

Many Masters of Hounds and amateur huntsmen got their first experience of carrying the horn with beagle packs belonging to their schools and colleges, and Bob was one of the lucky ones able to have his own hounds in pre-Cambridge days. He decided to repeat the process for his son Dudley's benefit, built a nice range of authentic hound kennels behind the stables and got together about eight couple of beagles. Dudley hunted the pack, his friend Kenneth Seth-Smith acted as First Whip and his brother John, very much the junior of the outfit, was Second Whip. They called their pack the Twineham and Colwood Beagles which described the area in which they operated - namely the west part of Bolney centred on the Colwood Estate of the Seth-Smiths and all Twineham Parish. The younger members of the garden and stable staff acted as kennelmen and auxiliary whippers-in. They evidently entered into it with a good spirit. One of them in his retirement remarked, "I used to enjoy running with the boys."

103

Dudley was responsible for keeping the breeding records and Hunting Diary. Evidently his beagles had few followers outside the family. Most of the entries which Dudley made in his diary under the heading 'The Field' were confined to "Mother and Miss Mockett". Aunt Maria Mockett had by that time given up Park Croft at Polegate and come to live at the Grange. One can imagine the two ladies being driven round the lanes in a carriage, hoping to catch a glimpse of the pack in full cry with the boys in pursuit. On a fine autumn day, sister Doris could be persuaded to join them. She was not a very serious beagler. In a photo album, Doris and a girl friend are pictured amusing themselves exploring farm buildings. The photo is captioned "Beagling"!

The big Victorian houses usually had big (and dull) Victorian gardens. It was an opportunity for men of the village to become gardeners instead of farm workers. Few of them had any training. They just used their common sense, and got enough tips on glasshouse management from acquaintances to get by. Employers were a trial. They intervened, according to their gardeners, far too often. A clever chap could see trouble coming and talk his way out of it. Keep the mistress happy, but get your own way in the end, was the slogan.

Lady Smythe of Twineham Court was undoubtedly in the class of an awkward employer. The local gentry were nervous of her penchant for going to law to protect her interests, and avoided becoming too involved. Typically, her employees were not worried by this; as an employer she was no worse than many others, and if you let her have her way most of the time, the job was all right.

This philosophical attitude did not always survive a serious disagreement, and one of these clashes occurred over a shrub. Shrubs seem to have attracted disputes in those days. The unbeatable ruction must be in the Estate Correspondence reproduced by Osbert Sitwell in his third volume of autobiography *Great Morning*. His father, Sir George, complained that he had been 'run in' for shrubs to be planted in the churchyard, when he had only intended to pay for forest trees. The shrubs had died. Ultimately Sir George agreed to replant at a cost of £10. "I will go to that expense, in another 'fatal gift'." So the expression 'fatal gift of shrubs' passed into the literary canon.

Lady Smythe only had one shrub. It was a bit special, as it was intended for a particular spot in her large garden. It arrived outside the real planting season and Sayers, her gardener, was told to plant it temporarily in the tree nursery. Sayers, brother of John Sayers the foreman at the Grange, had quite a different permanent home in mind. As the autumn advanced, Lady Smythe kept reminding him of the job of planting that had to be done, and Sayers was equally prompt in finding excuses for not doing it, but he realised that he could not go on indefinitely. He decided to put the shrub into his special place without telling his employer who might, just might, accept the *fait accompli*. His luck was really in one morning when the autumnal fog looked impenetrable. Collecting John as his assistant he had the shrub in a wheelbarrow by 6 o'clock and set to work on his chosen spot to prepare a good hole for planting. They became aware of a figure advancing on them through the mist. Inevitably it was Lady Smythe dressed in cycling bloomers and a cardigan. In spite of the provocative costume, the men kept their nerve and only straightened up when her ladyship greeted them with a "Good morning Sayers - an early start I see."

"Oh yes, m'lady, must get on, get the planting done." Lady Smythe gazed uncertainly into the hole as if to suggest they fill it in, but thought better of it and walked away. The brothers grinned and put the shrub in place. A convincing win for the Sayers brothers, and a successful defusing of a potentially 'fatal gift of a shrub'.

The enlarging and beautifying of the Grange did nothing to make the well water more drinkable. Big rain water tanks were built under the back yard which only provided water for washing-up in the Scullery. Bob was therefore a keen supporter of the plan to get the Burgess Hill Water Co. to bring mains water to the village. Negotiations over the cost dragged on for some time, and Dick Reece was brought in, as a Public Health expert, to add weight to the parish council's assertion that it was quite wrong for the village to be relying on possibly insanitary and unreliable supplies, while the company dragged their feet. For whatever reason the pipes were laid, and the summer of 1911 proved to be the first occasion when the villagers no longer had to worry if their wells were going to hold out. For the cottagers, being connected to the mains meant a cold water tap over the sink and nothing more. For years afterwards, wash day was heralded by the rattle of buckets around the well pump at some unearthly hour in the morning. Partly this was tradition, partly convenience, in that the buckets filled more quickly, but partly also a guilty feeling that they ought not to use too much of this piped commodity that was not their own. Even the gentry in big houses used very little. One bathroom was usual for guests and family to share as best they might, and wash basins in bedrooms were a rarity. For all the caution so obviously displayed the mains supply was a huge advance in living standards - the first of many that the century would bring.

The comprehensive scheme of church repairs and re-ordering in 1893/94 had not included the bells. By 1912 the 17th-century tenor bell had cracked and the frame was crumbling, leaving only the older bells in use. Bob saw this as a good opportunity to get a decent peal in the tower that would sound so much better than the ding-dong of the two bells being chimed. They could start a Twineham Band of Ringers. They alerted bell founders, Mears & Stainbank, who advised that a total of six bells could be fitted in. For reasons, possibly of cost, the wardens decided to order two new bells, quarter turn the old ones and reinstate the frame, at a cost of £264. The first donor before the appeal opened was Mr Huth, the Patron, with a promise of £25. They seem to have worked fast in those days, as the decision to go ahead was taken in June, and the bishop was booked shortly afterwards to take the Service of Dedication in October. Moreover the deadline was met. Even more astonishing is the revelation that the bells were brought back to the church on Friday October 11, and were all ready for ringing on Tuesday October 15.

The Homecoming was made into a great popular celebration. From the account in the Twineham parish magazine:

> On Friday October 11th, Mr Helme's "Bell" team (in charge of D Newman, sen) and Mr Fogwill's trolley were sent to Burgess Hill Station for the Twineham bells. When they arrived at Hickstead, a halt was made to enable Mrs McKergow, Mrs Helme and Mrs Gee to decorate the trolley with

bunting and flowers. Many thanks to Fred Sayers for his present of chrysanthemums from his own garden on this occasion. The only other halts on the way were for the purpose of throwing water on the axles to prevent their catching fire owing to the great weight of the bells" (Note. The pond they called at would have been Knowle Hill Dell).

On arrival at Slipe, the precious load was met by the Rector, Wardens, Choir and School, who were headed by the Twineham Fife and Drum Band. We were very pleased to see Mr Simmons, of Hickstead, the oldest living native of Twineham, following in a motor most generously lent by Mrs McKergow. The completed procession then wended its way to the church gates, singing hymns and the appropriate song 'Joy bells ringing'. Many of the children carried little models of the bells made of cardboard covered with silver paper and decorated with ribbons and flowers. At the church gate a halt was made when the Rector gave an address, in which he pointed out that Twineham people of today were simply doing their bounden duty to their church by improving and restoring the work of past generations, and the more they loved their glorious little Church the greater would be the desire to voluntarily embrace self-sacrifice to keep it worthy of the great traditions of the past ages of God's people in the Parish. Prayers and the Benediction brought the historic proceedings to a close.

The Dedication Service the following Tuesday did not start on time because the Bishop of Chichester lost his way. "The Bishop of Chichester will not forget his first visit to Twineham," reported the local paper. "To use his lordship's words he seemed to get all round it, and yet could not get at it, and while the Bishop was being puzzled by the Twineham and Wineham geography, a large congregation wondered for a quarter of an hour the cause of his delayed arrival.

"The Bishop gave a most interesting address on Church bells and deftly used the story of the bells being used to guide a lost shepherd on the Downs to illustrate his own adventure. On his next visit he would be guided by the bells of Twineham Church."

The Rector's next job was to form a band of ringers (his wife would be one of them) and get them trained. He called a meeting of likely members and proposed a set of rules for the tower which, as it happened, he had already drafted. One of the clauses provided for fines of 6d to be paid by anyone who missed a practice. The potential ringers were put out by that, but the rules were voted through at the meeting. It was not the end of the matter. When word got round there was enormous support for getting rid of fines altogether and the Rector was told, politely, that the plan to found a band of ringers would fail if fines were insisted upon. An Extraordinary General Meeting followed and fines deleted. This must be one of very few instances where the villagers were able to deflect the Big Wigs, but credit is due to Ernest Cresswell Gee, the very peace-loving Rector, for realising he had touched a very raw nerve and conceding defeat gracefully.

The year 1913 was important for Bob; he was elevated (that must be the right word) to the position of Joint Master of the Crawley and Horsham Hunt which was classed, at least by the members, as superior to all the other hunts in the vicinity. Since 1807 it had been run by the big landowners, who had chosen from their number Sir Robert Loder as Master, followed by Colonel Calvert, who after 20 years handed over to Colonel Charles Godman. Twenty-four years later Godman was still there, but criticism was mounting. The hunt was running an annual deficit, which showed no sign of getting less; the hunt servants' horses were not up to the job; and Charles Godman, always modest and retiring, was now thought, by some at least, not to be in control. The committee were in a difficult position. Charles Godman had been a very notable Master and his hound breeding policies were beyond praise. He was an institution in himself and showed no sign of being aware of any criticism of his conduct. How could the committee intervene without upsetting the Master and many of his supporters?

The committee did eventually agree on what is now called a 'package' with the master that included the acceptance of McKergow as Joint-Master. Bob was asked, in confidence, if he would say Yes. No doubt a good deal of discussion went on concerning his responsibilities, but he undoubtedly agreed in principle very quickly. He wrote at once to Dudley at Uppingham and got a congratulatory reply from his son, who looked forward to seeing better horses at the Kennels. A second letter followed, pointing out that this was going to cost a lot of money, and the Beagles which Dudley ran at Twineham might have to go. Dudley replied, "I quite see that it will be a great expense for you to keep the beagles if you get the Joint-Mastership, but we are very keen and will save every penny we can to help pay. I hope you have a good and dry time in [the Yeomanry] Camp, and that D-Squadron will come out at the top this year. With much love, I am your ever loving son. Dudley."

As the day of the annual general meeting of the Crawley and Horsham Hunt approached, Bob clearly got wind of some disagreements among the Committee about the package, and hints that the Master, Charles Godman, was only taking a Joint-Master reluctantly. He put his concerns to Lord Leconfield, who in his letter of reply said he agreed with Bob that the hunt should keep Godman at the head of affairs.

"I shall be at the meeting tomorrow," wrote Leconfield. "What the C & H want is a Master who will take his own line and not refer everything to the committee. The only function of this body ought to be to sanction expenditure on the upkeep of stables and kennels and to supervise the accounts. To my mind it is nonsense to allow them to dictate questions of policy, as happens now, especially when they make the awful hash that your hunt committee did of the Rawson affair."

The following day a distinguished company assembled at Horsham Town Hall for the annual meeting, when members were told what action the Hunt Committee were proposing to take, and were invited to give it their approval. Having carefully considered the accounts, and after consultation with Colonel Godman, ran the Committee's report for adoption, "it was agreed that he should continue to hunt the country in association with Mr R W McKergow, as Joint-Masters, on the following conditions: the Hunt Committee should collect all subscriptions and shall guarantee to pay to the account of the Masters a sum of £3,000 annually; the Committee shall undertake to keep in repair the walls, roofs and main understructures of the floors of the kennel buildings including the stables, kennels, mens' cottages and outbuildings; the present stud and stable 'tac' should be sold or taken over by the Masters at a valuation, the proceeds of the sale to be used in paying off the deficit on the Hunt Fund, and any balance be paid into the account of the hunt committee.... The Masters shall undertake to provide sufficient and proper horses to mount the hunt servants at their own expense, the horses to remain the property of the Masters. Colonel Godman having agreed, subject to the consent of the general meeting, to continue the mastership on these terms on condition that Mr McKergow was appointed Joint-Master with him."

This was proposed as part of the report which covered many matters of detail, the adoption of which was seconded by Sir Merrik Burrell. The members present who were not part of the inner circle were surprised and suspicious.

Asked by a member whether he approved of the arrangement, Colonel Godman replied that he had consented to it. Mr Harold Child, speaking as a farmer, said he was exceedingly sorry to see any change in the mastership. Colonel Godman had only said he had consented to it and, before he voted, he (Harold Child) wanted to be quite sure the Master was in accord with it. The matter seemed to have been sprung upon them quite unexpectedly, he said, though he hoped it would work well. If the Master was willing, of course it would.

The chairman said he hoped Mr Child would not think this had been sprung on the Master in any way. The Master had been present at the meeting of the committee, had taken part in their discussions, and knew exactly what was in the mind of the committee. Possibly it might have been rather a surprise to some members of the hunt. To them Colonel Godman made it clear that he did not want to raise any difficulties. "The only thing I say is that it was done after the 1st May. I perfectly agreed. I do not wish to differ in any way."

The chairman explained that the first of May was the date when the accounts were ready for consideration. The annual general meeting adopted the hunt committee's recommendations, and the contentious point of the possible snubbing of the grand old MFH did not arise again. Although Bob's entry into the joint-mastership of the Crawley and Horsham Hunt in 1913 was not totally without criticism, he had the cooperation of everyone once the deed was done.

The year 1913 was also significant for the Southdown Hunt. Siegfried Sassoon won his point-to-point race on Cockbird and, in May, Norman Loder, the admired 'Denis Milden' of the *Memoirs,* retired as Master. He had taken on the mastership of the Atherstone in Warwickshire, and he and Sassoon moved up there for the following season.

It must have come as a considerable shock to the part-time soldiers of the Sussex Yeomanry when, on August 4, 1914, Britain declared war on Germany, and they were called to the colours almost over night.

They were aware of the increase in international tension, and they had been putting in more hours of field training, but they had hardly bargained for war, let alone instant mobilisation, the orders for which included the reminder that cold steel was still part of their armoury and that officers should make sure their swords were sharp.

Bob McKergow was now a major in command of the Yeomanry Cavalry Regiment's 'D' Squadron. He opened the envelope containing the squadron's sealed mobilisation orders, and read that he had to proceed at once to Eastbourne. But then, as so often, events failed to follow the book. In the first place his command was switched from 'D' to 'A' Squadron, and he was told to proceed with it, not to Eastbourne but Bridge near Canterbury. He thought it unlikely that preparation would have been made for their arrival, and so it turned out. His men had to doss down in farm buildings, and make shelters from branches. They had to tie their horses to hedges and gate posts. Luckily the weather was fine and hot, so nobody suffered too much in their temporary quarters while they searched for proper billets.

The supply of horses to the army was top priority. The disasters of the Boer War of 1899-1902 were well remembered. Hundreds of horses died while being shipped out to South Africa and, once there, disease took a further toll. So, determined not to repeat those mistakes, in 1914 the War Office at once set about commandeering horses from private owners, racing and hunting stables - wherever they were to be found - in sufficient numbers to bring all cavalry regiments up to strength immediately.

In the history of the Sussex Yeomanry which Edward Powell wrote in 1921, he said this policy soon broke down due to confusion between the lists of horses registered for the British Expeditionary Force, which landed in France on August 8, with those registered for the Territorial Army, which consequently came off worse. He related one case when a Yeomanry squadron seized some, as they thought, unallocated horses, but were intercepted by the BEF buyer, to whom they had to surrender them. "The party returned to Brighton with the halters with which they set out, but no horses in the halters."

Major R W McKergow, OC 'A' Squadron, Sussex Yeomanry, got fed up with the low standard of horses the War Office sent him - they included six mares with foals - and decided to cut across all regulations by personally purchasing hunters from the stables of the Southdown Hunt, and the Crawley and Horsham Hunt, before they were commandeered, as he knew they soon would be, by the War Office. He wrote to Colonel C B Godman with whom he was still Joint-Master, suggesting swift action which would present the War Office with a *fait accompli*. He reckoned the men of Whitehall would never raise formal objection.

Charles Godman's response was immediate. On August 12 he wrote back to Bob giving him a list of the hunt's horses - which in the custom of the day were his private property - he had sent to Bob's squadron, indicating what he had originally paid for each of them. How much the War Office would be prepared to pay him for them he did not know. "I enclose list of the horses I sent with amount I gave for them," ran Godman's letter. "Your letter of yesterday seems to throw out a hint I get next to nothing for them."

The purchasing officer in this immediate district tells me they should really have gone thro. his hands. Now there is nothing more to be done. Send us a line someday. I don't doubt you are v. busy and working hard. I don't feel I am right doing nothing here at home but trying to help look after a

Bridge or so, but don't see what I can do. I have looked in at the Kennels a few times but this is far from a pleasure now. Have had some of the older hounds put away and think myself we ought to make considerable reductions yet, there can be no hunting next season even supposing any had the inclination, and besides there is the matter of food. What do you think if they were reduced to 50 couples now? There is I presume but one way of disposing of them. Send a line. Remembrances to old friends. I often think of you all.

Yours ever
C B Godman
South Lodge, Lower Beeding

Charles Godman listed 12 horses with names such as Whiteash, Limehouse, Belhus and Sensation. The most valuable was Tripoli, a 16-hand bay gelding with a long tail which Charles had once bought for £150. At the bottom of the list were Lloyd George and The Omnibus, for each of which he had paid £45. He had not paid anything for Osaka - "Bay mare, aged. I bred her - old favourite." He had paid £55 for Fanto "Br Gel. a stouter horse and thicker set but rides v. light" and £120 for Shiela "Br mare 7".

Bob was able to substitute the hunters he knew for the inferior mounts supplied to him through official channels, without any protest from the army's District Purchasing Officer who seems to have turned a blind eye to the irregular transaction. Bob had reckoned correctly. Whereupon, as the major i/c 'A' Squadron, he set about drawing up, and putting into action, a daily training programme which began with Reveille at 5.30 am and ended with Stables at 4.30 pm. There was Physical Training followed by Stables before the men sat down to breakfast at 6.45. Riding School began an hour later, and before Dinner at 1 there was Dummy Horse and Musketry training, and then Stables for two hours after 11. In the afternoon, there was Foot Drill, more Musketry (with a lecture) and the final Stables session.

Bob reserved the riding school for himself as something he could really enjoy. Armed with a ringmaster's whip, he stood in the middle of the circling riders telling 'the school' what he thought of them, and applying the lash impartially to man and beast. The men of the squadron concocted a song in his honour:

Major McKergow loves us so,
To his riding school we go.
If his horses won't go round,
He blinds and swears that we're hide bound.

Our major loves us,
Oh how he loves us!
Yes, how he loves us!

His kind words tell us so.

When we get up on our gees,
It makes us tremble at the knees;
If riding makes us ill,
He gives us C.B. and Pack Drill,

Our major loves us,
Oh how he loves us!
Yes, how he loves us!
His kind words tell us so.

C.B stood for Confined to Barracks.

Back at Twineham the Rector, Reverend Cresswell Gee, had to face up to the departure of parishioners on war service. "Twineham Grange is closed," he reported; "the East Lodge is empty, the stables are empty. It seems so dull in that direction. The Major is on active service, Mrs McKergow and Miss Doris have gone to reside near the field of operations for a time, and the boys are back at school. In a small place like Twineham this is a great miss. We look forward with hope to the future."

For the preparations that Britain was making to beat the Kaiser, however, Bob's absence on military duties was a gain. "Major McKergow is, at the time of writing, in the environs of Canterbury, and is from all accounts on very active service," the editor of the parish magazine told such readers as remained in the village. "He is engaged in instructing officers in the art of riding and in drill; and the men in the art of entrenching and digging themselves in. In addition to this, he takes an active part in the strategical movements of the large forces under his command."

'A' Squadron would have been surprised to find themselves a major part of the strategic force. As would Madge McKergow who, with her daughter Doris, witnessed what was going on at Canterbury at close quarters. She had to rely however on letters from Donald Seth-Smith, the sisal grower, to learn what was happening in far away British East Africa. "My Dear Mrs McKergow," he wrote in December 1914,

> This will arrive rather late to bring you any Xmas wishes I expect - even if it does reach you, which is doubtful as all mails are awfully disorganised, and it has to go 50 miles by runner from here before it finds a railway station.
>
> I did not arrive in Nairobi till November 1st, and 2 days afterwards was given a subaltern's commission in the Supply Corps and sent down here. This is about 10 miles from the German border and about 14 behind our main column which is now on Langedo Hill in G [erman] E [ast] A [frica], which we attacked and failed to take. 22 days afterwards the German evacuated. I don't know whether you have a map of BEA and GEA, but we are trying to attack GEA from 2 points: 1) from the seaport Tanga so as to get up to Moschi by rail; 2) along the Voi-Terete road which is close to Moschi.

He added a third line of attack which he considered the worst. That was Nairobi to Magadi, some 26 miles down the railway and then 60 miles across the game reserve with very, very little water. All the transport took that route by way of ox waggons, and they formed depots every 20 miles - fortified camps with one or two companies of soldiers, a small hospital, a telegraph office and some fifteen to twenty tons of provisions. It was very wild country between the depots. Every convoy of waggons had to be strongly escorted. What made it worse was that giraffes kept on breaking down the telegraph line, which was of course only a rough affair. Stray German patrols were always coming over the border, and wandered about spying for days on end.

Donald was made OC the camp, which consisted of a company of Kapunthalls, Imperial Service Troops from India, which he did not consider enough, since he had to find 40 men for pickets at night and he generally had to send twelve or so away to escort convoys.

> It rather amuses me, though, making them do fatigues of trench digging etc, and having false alarms. About 8 miles away there is a hill strongly held and fortified by us with some Calcutta Battery, 27th Mountain Battery etc. Nothing has been done here for a month since the 'Tanga' incident. I wonder if that got into the English papers. We tried to land 4000 troops from India at Tanga in GEA. Our cruisers were not allowed to shell the town first, as it was imagined it was weakly held and the buildings were wanted for the General's staff. So we landed and found it heavily fortified - maxims on housetops etc - and we had 1200 casualties in one day, and had to re-embark and sail away! The general has since gone on the sick list! The Loyal North Lancs suffered most. I believe we are now waiting for more troops from India - but the whole affair is disgraceful.

Donald did not believe the British would ever take German East Africa [today's Tanzania].

The British settlers formed a mounted Rifle Corps, some 400 strong, when war broke out, and did good work keeping back small patrols of Germans who tried to get through and cut the railway line. Nearly all of them, however, had now returned to their farms, since they heard that the idea was to give GEA to India as an overflow for their population - so let them take it! "There are Punjabis, Calcutta Batteries, Mountain Batteries and Loyal North Lancs, and a lot of useless Imperial Service troops over here, and rumours of a lot more coming."

> Martin [Seth-Smith] sits in Nairobi in the Intelligence Dept and grows fatter every day… I must stop now as I am expecting the General through here with his staff, and it is my duty to go out and meet him & report etc!!!! Excuse this awful writing, but I am sitting on an upturned whisky case with a packing case as a table & my tent is infernally hot.
> My kindest regards to all
> Yours very sincerely
> Donald F Seth-Smith

By the middle of 1915 the Sussex Yeomanry had settled down to the structure that was to stay with them through the next two years.

An active service battalion of *volunteers* was formed, based on the original Yeomanry regiment. The volunteering had to be genuine, since the men made it very clear to the powers-that-be that they had joined up on the understanding that they would have a Home Defence role. In the event, a high proportion of the regiment volunteered to join the active service battalion, which was put under the command of the officer whom Siegfried Sassoon in his *Memoirs of a Foxhunting Man* called Nigel Croplady, whose real name however was George Whitfield. After a period of intensive training, the battalion was shipped off to Gallipoli.

Fortunately they did not suffer many casualties in that disastrous campaign, and most of them were safely evacuated to Egypt. They went on to help Allenby eject the Turks from Jerusalem, and then on to the Western Front where the battalion eventually took part in the final push that brought the German surrender and the armistice of November 1918.

A separate Home Defence battalion was formed, stationed in Kent, with a remit to dash to the coast and repel invaders; and a 3rd Line/Depot unit under the command of Major McKergow to supply drafts to the other battalions. Apart from the CO, this had four other officers. It had the usual NCOs plus a Farrier Sergeant, two Shoeing Smiths and a Saddler - a total establishment of 157.

The letter which Bob received, dated June 12, 1915, from one of his old hunting friends at Brighton Drill Hall, telling him what his new unit would consist of, suggested that it might be as well to ask formally if he would be allowed any more officers.

> Green does not wish to leave Brighton again: it is very important you get a good man as S.2.S, as your pay etc will soon be in a muddle. I have written to the clerk at Shrewsbury to say he should not wait, but may hear from you. With complete knowledge of Payments Dept, he might be valuable. Inoculation going on.

The writer added a mystery PTO:

> Have a wire [telegram]. Roberts [?] arrested in London; sent escort with instructions to hand him over to 2/1st Maresfield Park for them to deal with. They have the facility & must help with this. Shall transfer him to them.

Maresfield Park was the regimental headquarters of the 2/1st. What 'Roberts' was arrested for I do not know, but apparently Bob did, and was glad of the information.

Bob's 3rd Line/Depot unit rapidly grew larger and, by the time it was converted from cavalry to infantry and moved to Crowborough, it was 757 strong. Bob could not but be pleased, but resented that he had a command of this size and was still a major.

~ 7 ~
Dudley Fights in the Air

F or Bob's son Dudley, his war began in 1915. In May he swapped the public
school life he had been leading at Uppingham, with term-time boarding and
holidays at home, for a double life - military and civilian - of weekday sol-
diering as an officer cadet at the Royal Military College at Camberley
(Sandhurst), and weekends at home doing what he had always enjoyed doing in
what had become 'Before The War'. He was 17.

He dropped beagling fairly soon, and became a motor-bike enthusiast. He
spent many weekends that summer riding over from Sandhurst to Twineham, and
on to Haywards Heath, to see his brother John at his preparatory school, and afterwards to whatever house Bob and Madge were occupying in Kent or East Sussex.
"My bike is going simply rippingly now, and ought to be a great success," he
wrote to his mother from Sandhurst on May 30, 1915.

> I propose to come to Maresfield via lunch at Colwood [the Seth-Smiths],
> call in at Parkfield to see John and on to Maresfield. They've been fairly
> shoving work into us this last week, and that abominable fellow Capt.
> Nettlefold always keeps us in after time. He tries to show us how to ride,
> but I've never seen such a terrible sketch on a horse in my life. His elbows
> and feet stick out, and he grips with the calf of his leg. A perfectly
> appalling fellow altogether. The new Major in command of this Coy. is an
> awfully nice fellow and behaves like a gentleman. 15 more fellows are
> passing out on June 15, and we shall be seniors then.

Bob took Dudley's assessment of the abominable Nettlefold with a pinch of
salt it seems since, after Dudley had successfully passed out, and indeed on the
day he was gazetted to the 5th Dragoon Guards as a second lieutenant, Bob wrote
the captain a letter of thanks for tutoring his son so well. Nettlefold wrote back at
once thanking Bob for his kind letter.

> It has been a pleasure to do what I could for your son because he had
> always been a real trier. As you say, he is a bit young and that is the reason
> that he has been here longer than average. I'm perfectly certain that he will

114

turn out a real good officer, though he may take longer to come to it than some.

He tells me that you propose to allow him £10 per month during the War, and £500 a year afterwards. That will see him through well, as long as he doesn't waste money continually knocking around London, and will be amply sufficient for him to hunt and play polo. We [the Dragoon Guards?] are not a rich regiment, and we are all keen on sport. I hope you will forgive my discussing finance like this, but I thought you might like to have the views of someone in the Regt on the subject.

I hope he will get on well and that you will never regret having let him join the Regt. I hope your son will come to me if ever I can be of use to him. I will always take an interest in him, as he was under me here.

Dudley's life then changed once again - no longer training and exercises, but the Real Thing - *active* service. It began for him in January 1916 with his arrival in the French town of Bethune. Like all cavalrymen he was on his feet alongside the infantry regiments. In the diary in which, like so many others, for the first few weeks he jotted down the bare facts of his introduction to what those at home - 'blighty' - called The Front, he noted that it was the 26th, "the eve of the Kaiser's birthday". From Bethune he "marched at 7.30 pm to Noyelle; slept on Estaminet floor". From then on it was life in the trenches.

January 27 1916
At 6.30 am marched to Lancashire trench east of Vermeilles. Took a working party up to the Kaiserine trench in the afternoon. Saw West and Harry Misa. They exploded a small mine close to us.

January 28
Still in Lancashire trench. The enemy bombarded the infantry on our left heavily. Our artillery retaliated. Peel's platoon and mine occupied Anchor trench for the night (second line).

January 31
Marched off at 6 am from Clarke's Keep to Front line. Gordon's, Turner's and Peel's platoons occupied the West Face and Kaiserine, Joredan's and my platoon in support. Northampton trench and Vigo Street respectively. Relieved 18th Hussars. Slightly troubled by Rifle Grenades.

February 1
The enemy fired a fair number of Rifle Grenades and Trench Mortars but without causing much inconvenience. The total casualties being 4 wounded.

February 2
Were relieved by the 10th Hussars and Essex Yeomanry and went back to Le Bourse for 6 days rest. A good mess and good billets for officers - not too good for men.

February 3
Our aeroplanes were shelled without any effect.

The next day Dudley took a party of 80 in motor lorries to Clarkes Keep, and at 7 o'clock in the morning on February 7 they practised gas alarm.

February 8
Marched at 6 am from Le Bourse to the front line. Azlewood's, Jordan's, McKergow's, Turner's platoons in the front line, Gordon's and Peel's in reserve. Took over muddy and sticky trenches from Leicester Yeomanry. Troubled for 15 minutes by trench mortars. RHA opened on the enemy. Duels in the air, otherwise quiet. Small defensive mine blown up by us. Enemy opened with machine guns and rifle grenades. Turner goes on leave.

February 9
A digging party was spotted in German 2nd line in the afternoon opposite my front. RHA open on them and stop their work. Our 15 inch gun opened fire at 11.30 am on force 8 and the mine works on our left, causing much damage. It ceased fire at about 2 pm. At 6 30 pm a German working party were seen carrying boards and straw along the top of their line. Azlewood's 4 D Gs opened with indirect machine gun fire on them. The night passed extremely quietly.

The next day Dudley's company was relieved by the Bedfordshire Yeomanry, and retired to the Lancashire trench in reserve. Two days later they "marched by platoon to Noyelle where motor lorries met us and took us to Bethune. Saw Jack Colvin. Dined at the France; men billeted in Orphanage." At 2 o'clock on the afternoon of February 13 they 'entrained' into carriages pulled by a steam locomotive, which left half an hour later and arrived at Montreuil at 11.30 at night after passing through Calais and Boulogne. They then detrained into motor lorries which took them back to Le Turne. It was Dudley's eighteenth birthday.

For some reason he felt unable to keep up the diary, and for the next six months, which saw the Battle of Verdun and the second Battle of Ypres, he would probably have had the opportunity to write home but, if so, the letters have not survived.

Trench warfare was restless, boring and dirty, and many officers saw air warfare as a decidedly more attractive way of 'doing their bit' to bring the Germans to their knees. From his muddy trench, Dudley had watched the British and German flyers fighting it out overhead, as he noted in his diary, and will have wondered whether one day he might become one of them, with the chance of shooting up the enemy on the ground from high above them, having duels in the air and then returning to a reasonably comfortable 'aerodrome', as they called it, for rest and relaxation.

Britain had created a Royal Flying Corps as part of the Army. Any infantry or cavalry officer wishing to join it could do so, provided he obtained his regiment's permission to become 'attached', and the RFC agreed to take him. Most young officers joined as trainee observers. Aircraft had, for the first time, given the High Command the opportunity to see what was going on behind the enemy's lines. To be able to spy in this way was one of the main reasons for forming the Royal Flying Corps. Two-seater planes were built to carry an observer/machine gunner and a pilot.

Dudley applied to move to this flying branch of the army, and was accepted, in September 1916. The first of the long series of letters to his mother which were to survive, describing his new life as an air pilot, was dated September 29, 1916. In it, he told Madge he had heard from his friend Kenneth Seth-Smith, to say he had been wounded in three places by machine gun, but they were only slight wounds and none of his bones had been broken. "He is very lucky; he says he would not change places with me for £1,000. He's got a nice blighty [send-you-back-home] one, but I think I would rather do without it."

> I'm afraid I am not allowed to name the kind of machines we have here [somewhere in France], but I think I may tell you that it is the only squadron that has this kind of machine out here. We do not do any photography work. We are simply for fighting and long reconnaissance. By what I hear, I think I shall be home on leave fairly shortly. We had a pilot and observer [Dudley was an observer] taken prisoner the day before yesterday. They were shot down, but the machine went down under control so they are all right. Other fellows who were taken prisoner sometime ago are being treated very well. They are playing tennis and hockey. The airmen of all nations are a sporting crowd because it is such international work... The German airmen are still a sporting crowd. At least we have reason to believe so. We do not attend any classes. When you have done your three hours a day you are finished and can do what you like, but mark you three hours can be, and often are, absolute hell. But when you come back you are always comfortable... My pilot's name is J L Trollope. He is nineteen and has got his head on his shoulders, and gives me the impression of a fellow who thinks before he acts.

Dudley's letters to his mother now came regularly, and subject to censorship, gave her a very vivid picture of what he was going through, in spite of the conventional cheery understatement so characteristic of all such 'jobs' as they called them.

October 2 1916
I left instructions at the Regt that they were to demolish any cakes that came from you, and Parker wrote and told me that they had eaten one of my very excellent cakes.

I am very sorry to hear that Geoffrey Wyatt has been killed, but I'm afraid he is one of the very many who will have to go 'West' (or 'East' as we call it being the other side of the lines) before this comes to an end. There is great satisfaction in the work we do, and I would far sooner do this work than to be continually training miles behind the lines. I have far more interesting news for you here in one day than I should get during a month with the Regt.

October 16 (uncensored)

I am sending this letter by Capt Vancour who is going on leave, so it has been posted in England. This squadron is at a place called Fienvillers which is a small village S.W. of Doullens. We fly Sopwith machines, and up to two days ago it was the only squadron of that type out here, but now No 45 have come out to this Aerodrome. There are two other squadrons besides this on this Aerodrome named Nos 19 and 27. Hedderwick was in No 19, and No 27 fly Martinsydes which are single-seater bomb droppers. Therefore you see we do our work in the Somme District over the 'Push'.

It was very cold today. Those thick socks you knitted me at the end of last winter are A1. I wish you could knit me two or three more pairs. Yesterday two machines [one of them his] did battle practice over the aerodrome for an hour on end. During which time we were turning sharply and doing vertical banks without ceasing. I stuck half an hour of being whisked about very well, but then began to feel bad. I asked my pilot to go down through the speaking tube, but he could not hear properly, and thought I was saying something totally different and took not the slightest notice of me, and I solemnly had to get rid of a perfectly good breakfast over the side.

He, too, had turned and twisted the machine about so much, he positively could not go on any longer, so we came down very shortly after I was ill. The observer and pilot in the other machine had had quite enough of it.

By the way, we do long reconnaisances right out to Mons, Manbeuge and Valencienne etc. It is quite interesting to look at the places where all the fighting used to take place at the beginning of the war, although you see it from 10,000 feet.

October 22

The [Dragoon Guards] regt are billeted in the next village and two of them came up for a joy-ride and Tattershall is coming for lunch today... It has been very cold the last two or three days and one can pick icicles off one's upper lip when in the air.

October 23

'Dud' weather and there was nothing doing. Tattersall had a joy-ride yesterday. The major took him up and I think he enjoyed it very much. Mitchell and Parker came up this afternoon and had a look round. While they were up there, one of our machines left the ground, and just at that moment a tender (which is a small motor lorry) came across the aerodrome and he just hit the top of it with his propeller which broke and knocked the hood of the tender and the machine crashed, but nobody was hurt. There were some officers in the tender but they merely had their caps knocked off. We always have some excitement in the crashing line... My pilot and

I have shifted from a tent into a hut now... I find my ordinary thick pants are quite sufficient under my breeches to keep the cold out without wash leather pants. It is most advisable to keep as free as possible in case you have a scrap with the Huns... The observer has to work a machine gun in these machines and he sits with his back to the pilot.

October 27
'Dud' weather and no flying. You will be pleased to hear that I come home on leave a week next Monday. These days are often changing, so I will wire my arrival from town... I will be awfully glad to get home so that I can explain everything about this show more fully... I do not think anybody is over anxious to come into the RFC from the Regt, as we have told them terrible yarns of our casualties, which are true as a matter of fact. However anybody in the RFC will tell you this is the 'cracked squadron'.

Dudley was right about leave days changing, and his was postponed for some weeks. Telling his mother on November 4 he was sorry to disappoint her but it would not be long now, he brought her the 'glorious news' that he, and two other fellows who had joined the squadron the same day as he did, had got their Observer's Wing, a breast badge of an O with one wing attached to it - "so look out in the gazette". He was gloriously bucked about his wing. "The next step is to become 'Flying Officer' observer. I am now a qualified observer."
And few days passed without his pilot taking him into the bright but cold air to use his observer's skill to pursue and destroy the enemy.

November 10
Yesterday we had a fine day for once in a way and we did a show. We were up at 16,000 feet, but I managed to keep more or less warm in spite of the intense cold. Two of my fingers have got slightly frost bitten, and my ears bled slightly. I think a pair of silk gloves would be a good thing for an under-glove, so will you please get me a pair next time you are in Brighton. I want all my fingers.

November 12
I think I shall manage it [leave] before December 3rd. At least I sincerely hope so. I shall not get home to fly until after January I don't suppose. We got some flying for two days, and two observers of their flight were killed. The Huns dived on them. We had no particular excitement on the other show. I again very nearly went up with a pilot whose machine was shot to pieces. I look upon them as absolute strokes of providence. Talking about that Norton bike, it needs very careful oiling...

November 21
I should be on leave if the other fellow had not had an extension of leave, but I shall probably get away on 23rd with any luck... I think I would like to go to one or two theatres, but we can arrange that when I get home.

There is no girl that I can think of that would come along too... Kenneth [Seth-Smith] wants to come into this squadron, and I am going to get the Major to apply for him [he had changed his opinion of the RFC].

December 15, 1916
The mud is simply appalling, as all our trench boards have been taken away and we are living like pigs. However we keep fires going, and manage to keep warm at night. We have a good many of our meals down in the village at the Battalion HQ mess. The Col. is a topping fellow by the name of Selby-Jones and is in the 13th Hussars. I got to know him by Gen. Swann's son who came to the sqdn just before I came home on leave [which must have been at the beginning of December when David Lloyd George took over from H H Asquith as prime minister].

December 16
Many thanks for the pheasants which look top-hole, and we are having the Major to dine and having them for dinner. The champagne has not yet turned up, but these things take a long time. By what method did Dad have them sent out? The cake and Xmas pudding arrived perfectly intact, which says a lot for your packing as the bag went through a good deal of banging about. The Flight very much like the [gramophone] records, especially the ones which you say sound like the nigger man at a point-to-point [buskers]... We have now got George Heasman, the amateur jockey, in the Flight and he seems to be a very good fellow.

December 19
The champagne has arrived safely, so don't bother any more about it. But I tell you that the records I bought [while on leave?] made a great hit. The Major loved the ones from Ciro's Coon Orchestra, and made us play them over and over again when he came into dinner the other night... The Major and the Wing Commander are leaving here [Lozinghem, six miles west of Bethune] for England on the 1st, and so three of us are going to form up and ask him if we can go home tomorrow. I hope we have luck. I propose to give [brother] John a hunting stock pin with a hare on it for Christmas, so don't you give him that please. I thought Dad would like a copy of that picture, framed, called "Far, Far Echo", one of the best pictures painted in this war. Do you think he would like that? What would you like, and what do you think would be suitable for Auntie [Maria Mockett]? I will give [sister] Doris chocolates or the RFC pilot's wings... I hope you got my Xmas card all right.

December 27, 1916
The champagne arrived in plenty of time for Christmas and it was absolutely topping. We had a jolly good dinner and danced. George Heasman and I went into one of the other flight messes after dinner where they were speechifying, and we had to make a speech each. We had a grand

evening on the whole, and finished up with dancing. I hope to be home in a fortnight's time.

Bob and Madge McKergow will have known better than to have taken Dudley's description of life in the Royal Flying Corps in France in 1916 - or such aspects of it as he saw fit to convey in his letters - as representative of the active service of all engaged in the life-and-death struggle which came to be called the Great War. Between them the French and British had sustained 600,000 casualties in the dreadful Battle of the Somme of which Britain, with 410,000, had suffered the most, though not as many as the 500,000 German casualties. The German line was longer and weaker by the end of 1916 and would have to be defended by larger forces than they had so far managed to muster. But, as J A Spender recorded, "The French too were near their last reserves, and even stout hearts among them doubted whether they could survive another year."

For Dudley's squadron the new year brought a new commanding officer who, in his letter to his mother of January 2, 1917, he said seemed to be "a very good fellow". This was A W Tedder, whose name he spelt Teddar - "I am not quite sure if this is spelt right." It was a name that most people came to know in the Second World War of 20 years later. By the time that broke out in 1939, Dudley's CO had reached the rank of Air-Vice Marshal and was in command of the contribution which the Royal Air Force made to almost every significant campaign in the West. In 1944 Tedder was Deputy Supreme Comander of the British & United States Expeditionary Force which made the assault on Europe with the landings in Normandy. He was promoted Marshal of the Royal Air Force in 1945 and raised to the peerage. A statue of Lord Tedder, the most distinguished airman of his time, stands in Whitehall.

For the 18-year-old observer/machine gunner who had celebrated Christmas 1916 in so enjoyable a manner with fellow officers of his Royal Flying Corps squadron in France, the coming of the new CO meant, presumably amongst much else, tightened discipline on the ground. "Every pilot and observer," Dudley told his mother in his letter of January 8, 1917, "now is responsible for the cleanliness of their machine, and they have to work at least an hour and a half a day on their machine. I think we made a bad move when we shifted here [?]. There is far more hot air knocking about. However, with any luck I shall be out of it soon, and it won't hurt us to do a little work on 'dud' days. Moreover, when one thinks of the hot air [lecturing?] in the other branch of the service [infantry] I was in, it makes one feel that one is well out of it."

January 13 1917
Please thank John for his letter. They must have had a clinking hunt with the beagles when they killed at Wivlesfield Station. I'd have given a good deal to have been there. 'Where are all your troubles and your cares ye melancholy ones; one holloa has dispersed them all' as Jorrocks would say.

I had a letter from Kenneth two days ago, and there seems to have been a row between himself and Mrs Seth-Smith over taking Joy Stewart to Burford Bridge on Sunday, because Mrs Scth-Smith objected to him spending Sunday in a car with a single girl. However, for goodness sake don't repeat it, as it's none of our business... John seems to be very useful on the farm, but he must look after himself during this cold weather with regard to his clothes or he'll very soon be in bed.

Ainger's and my name were sent in today, so I ought to be home by 20th easily (DV). I shall be able to tell you more about leave when I have reported to the War Office.

January 18

I have good news for you, namely that I leave this country on the 20th. I hope to come down to Twineham on the 22nd, but one never knows whether one will be held up on the railway journey or crossing or not, so I will wire you the time of the train I propose to come by. I hope I shall not miss John altogether. Please send any message you want to the Grosvenor Hotel and I will call there... Isn't it absolutely topping to be coming home for some time. There has been snow here for the last few days... Everything in a slushy mess.

Dudley almost certainly came to Twineham on leave on the date his mother expected him, and stayed for at least a week. Madge had always been against flying, although his time as observer in the back seat of the plane being flown by John Trollope had shown that it was possible to survive if you flew with a good pilot. But being the one in control of the plane was another matter, and Dudley's mother was very worried about his determination to train as a pilot.

She asked Mrs Seth-Smith to use her influence to persuade him to give up the idea. After all, he was not very quick thinking, and it seemed to her that you needed to be razor sharp if you were to get the better of the enemy. Mrs Seth-Smith would have none of it however. "The boy must do his duty," she insisted. So Dudley did not return to the squadron in France from which he was on leave but, after relaxing at home in Twineham, set off for St Patrick's Hall in Reading to attend a short introductory course, to give him a little engineering knowledge before being given the flying lessons which would qualify him as an air pilot.

February 8, 1917, Reading

This is a college which has been taken over by the Government for the duration in which to billet the officers on this course. Wantage Hall is also full of officers and some of them are billeted elsewhere in the town. It is absolutely impossible to go by train from here, because you immediately get nabbed, court-martialled and cashiered. However I have made arrangements with Hole to have the Morgan [his three-wheeled car, the model first made in 1910] down here by Thursday (today) week, and hope to come and see you on the following Sunday with any luck.

Our course does not start until about 10 days time so we are getting a good start. But to learn 7 different engines, 2 machine guns and a thousand and one other things, is rather a tall order in 9 weeks. However, most fellows manage to pass. I have received my flying tunic from Johnstone, and told them to send the bill to you, but they omitted to put a pair of RFC collar badges on, so do not be charged for them.

Madge sent him a fiver with which he bought a pair of fur gloves, a Flying Corps cap, a waistcoat and a scarf. Bob sent him a telegram wishing him all the best for the flying course.

Aunt Mockett sent him a letter, and so did Betty Hunt, enclosing a copy of a magazine *Court Beauties* - with good wishes from Shermanbury Rectory. He went by train - without being nabbed and court-martialled - to Croydon, and thence by taxi to Banstead to have dinner with the parents of John Trollope, who for so long had been his pilot in France.

"They are awfully nice people," he wrote and told his mother, "and their house is about as big as Twineham if not slightly bigger... There are two married daughters, another very plain and delicate daughter of 22, another daughter of 15, and the youngest daughter of 12 who is a marvel for her age. There is another son older than John." He stayed the week-end with them and celebrated his nineteenth birthday there on February 12. The next day Mrs Trollope wrote to Madge telling her how greatly they had enjoyed his visit.

Dear Mrs McKergow

Your son has been with us for the week-end and I was so very glad to meet him, as John our boy had constantly written about him and said what a splendid observer he was, and how dreadfully sorry he was to lose him. They seem great friends, and I do not wonder when they have been through so many dangers together. Your boy told me far more of John's work than he ever let on himself, so it was most interesting to have him.

Your son asked me to send John's photograph straight home for him, so I do now. Have you by any chance one to spare of your own son for John to keep here? What wonderful work the RFC is doing, but oh how terribly dangerous it all is! One can never forget them all day long. We hope John may be home next month, but he says he will stick on out there if he sees a chance of promotion, so we can't blame him, though we long to get him back.

With kind regards
Yours sincerely
C. L. Trollope

Dudley returned to Reading to complete his introductory course. One of the jobs given him in his last days at St Patrick's Hall was to escort an officer who was under arrest for being drunk - the court martial acquitted him. Dudley now shared his room with a Captain Hotsley of the East Yorks who had won the Military Cross. He also had to act as escort to "another fellow who did not get away with it".

Dudley saw March out at Reading and managed to get another period of leave at Twineham, seeing Aunt Mockett and old Will Matthews. Of the latter he got the impression that "he will soon be going home". In fact it was not long before he recovered. On March 5 Dudley told his mother that there was a rumour that everyone in no. 22 course were going to be posted to squadrons by the following Saturday, but he could not think that could be right, since a good many of the 21st course had not gone yet.

A few day's later he was gazetted Temporary Lieutenant - still in the army, but serving in its flying branch the RFC. "There is nothing about a Flying Officer yet," he told Madge on March 7, "so keep a look out for it please. This does not bring me any more pay, still it is quite nice to wear two stars instead of one."

He moved to Hendon for flying instruction at the beginning of April. "This is an absolute scream of a place," he told his mother.

> Apparently they have only just started it as a military school, and all the instructors are civilians. They take you extraordinarily steady at it, and they have not had anybody killed yet, so that is more cheering. It strikes me I have struck oil, as you can prolong the agony to an extreme if you wish to. The first thing they make you do is to taxi about in a machine with clipped wings that will not leave the ground.
>
> There are three or four different schools namely the Beatty, the Graham-White and the London and Provincial. I am in the Graham-White school and learn to fly on Gra White box kites. Very safe old busses; in fact as far as I can see its quite a rag time show at present.

A real air fight was far from rag time. "Did you see poor Duncan HLI & RFC of 70 Sqdn died of wounds?" Dudley asked his mother. "His name was in the casualty list just above Robin Loader's. He was Mason's observer on that show when they all got done down. Mason landed by Peronne with his petrol tank shot through - he thought he was still in Hunland and burnt his machine. He was the only one to get back." He told her George Heasman had said things did not look too rosy for them, and he dreaded flying with half the new pilots. He never heard talk of a Morgan now, let alone a horse. Heasman said most of his pilots were Canadians - "terrible fellows".

Heasman was in Mason's flight. He told Dudley that 20 Hun stunt machines with equally stunt pilots flew about together, and whoever met them God help them, for they would certainly be done down for a certainty. They did it to two flights of no 70 Squadron two days running, hence the casualties. "These Huns are known as the 'Circes' in France. However I heard on extremely good authority from a ferry pilot that the D40 got in amongst them the other day and shot down eleven of them and lost 3 machines themselves," Dudley told Madge on April 16, when he announced he had done exactly one and half hours flying, dual control.

> The Germans have ceased to be gentlemanly. They realise that if they comprehensively outnumber their opponents with a well trained 'pack' of fighters, they can wipe out the opposition in a few minutes. Their commanders achieve 'star' status.

April 22, Hendon

My instructor is useless. I have just been up with him for fifteen minutes and he will not let you have control at all, so I am going to have an extremely good try to get changed to another instructor today. I learnt more in 12 minutes with another fellow than I have in three-quarters of an hour with my present instructor. It's absolute waste of time.

It appeared in orders the other day we had all passed the exam at Reading, which of course we never went in for. Isn't it an absolute farce? All my observer friends will have gone soon as most of them have finished machine gun and flying, but I am in no hurry in spite of the classy crowd of officers here. They are gradually turning this aerodrome into an Air Acceptance Park, and Major Innes-Carr, Scots Guards (I think), is in command.

April 26

I heard from Kenneth the other day, and he seems to have firmly established himself in no. 70, and apparently his friends are my old friends... They are back at Fienvillers where I joined them, and they left Vert-Galand about 3 weeks ago. I'm awfully sorry to hear about Bob Hermon [of Cowfold] being killed. That really is a catastrophe. He was such an awfully good fellow.

I went to Bernard Weatherills and ordered a check suit at 7 guineas. This sounds infernally extravagant, but he assured me it was a real good cloth and a great many people had had them; and the material was too good for people of the 'Horse Coper' type to buy. If you think it is too much I will pay part of it.

I am now senior officer of the Graham-White school, and there are only three observers left in the whole place now. My instructor is better now because I kicked up rather a row about him not letting me have control.... There is no chance of me going to Shoreham after here, as Shoreham is an elementary squadron and so is this one... I hope to be in Twineham by Sat afternoon and stay the night at the Aunt's [who had a cottage at Henfield while Twineham Grange was being looked after by servants, who were able to attend to John's needs when he came home for holidays from Charterhouse].

Dudley enjoyed his week-end with Aunt Maria at Henfield. He got there by train from Victoria station and hired a bicycle on which he "pedalled madly for Twineham". There he found Major and Mrs Smith trimming the hedge down Crust's Lane, and left them to find brother John trying to teach his dog to retrieve on the lawn. At tea with the Smiths he thought Mrs Smith was carrying food rationing to an extreme - no crumpets? On Sunday he went over to the Grange and saw the young horses. They were doing well in his estimation, and should grow into useful horses. Then he and his brother biked back to the Aunt's for meat tea, after which, for Dudley, it was back to Hendon by train in the surprise company of old Charles Godman who asked for all the latest news of the McKergow family - and how was his father liking his new job?

It was a day to remember - when 'the war' took back place, and life came as near to normal as it could possibly be in such abnormal times.

Back at the flying school where he had 'at last and definitely' changed his instructor, he looked forward to making his first solo flight. "I want some practice in landing yet," he told his mother on May 1, "but I can take her off and fly her all right now." A week later he reported he was getting on with his flying pretty well. "I did not feel at all frightened when I went up alone for the first time, because I was absolutely confident I could fly the machine."

> I went up on Saturday morning when there was a pretty good wind blowing, and I've never been bumped about in an aeroplane so much before. However, I made perfectly good landing and felt jolly thankful to get safely down on terra firma. I only did one circuit of the aerodrome. I am now waiting for a less windy day on which to take my ticket. 10 figures of eight, two landings and a vol-plane. I have passed the exam on the Lewis Machine Gun and am now doing the Vickers which I find rather difficult to get hold of.

> *May 13, 1917*
> I took my ticket and finished my flying on Friday and am now waiting for a machine gun exam on Wednesday next. Then I hope to get three days leave pending posting to an advanced squadron.
>
> I took my ticket in record time. The first five figures of eight in six minutes, the second lot in seven and the Vol-plan in four minutes. Making 17 minutes for the whole thing. I did one hour & 31 minutes flying on Friday and as near as make no difference had a bad crash. I turned too soon after I took off and consequence was that the wind caught the upper planes and put more bank on and the lower wing was just about two feet off the ground, but I just pulled her out of it in time.

Madge's pride in reading the first part of this letter will have changed to horror, and then relief, on reading the second part, so casually added to hide what nearly put paid to his flying career before it had started. Dudley quickly passed to the news that Kenneth Seth-Smith, observer and machine gunner, had brought down his first Hun - "he is of course an excellent shot" and how he, Dudley the pilot, had "had the honour of going up with the great Claude Graham-White himself last Thursday and he taught me quite a lot". Graham-White was the most popular of the Edwardian aviators, and had founded the Hendon Flying School which he owned and ran until it was taken over by the Royal Flying Corps. He won countless awards for his activities, but became too independent a character to win the approval of the 'Establishment'.

So Dudley left Hendon - a qualified pilot - but before he went operational he was due to go on leave. "I will wire you when I am coming," he told his mother at the end of that letter of May 13, "probably Wed evening, but do not know for certain; the last two fellows had no leave at all." It is far from clear whether or not he managed to spend a short time with his mother, now living in Tunbridge Wells, and perhaps look in on Twineham, before reporting to a new aerodrome, which he knew would be in England, in his new status and rank. But as soon as he arrived at No. 20 RS, Royal Flying Corps, Wye, Kent, he notified Madge.

Sat night [no date]
As expected I have landed up here and I do not like the look of things very much. We fly Avros, BEs and finally go out on RE 8s. The latter machines are those which people refuse to fly etc because they catch alight and spin. However I will let you know more about it later.
   With much love from Dudley.

Not the sort of letter to calm her nerves. He followed it up with another next day, which enabled her to visualise the new life he was living.

Sunday
To explain the place more fully. The Aerodrome is pretty small and close to the racecourse. We live in huts and I am sharing one with Shewell who was at Reading and Hendon with me. He is a very nice fellow and a regular in the Gloucesters. The mess is cheaper than that at Hendon, but not so good, I am told, as the G. White men at Hendon.
   One has to be very light-handed with Avros, but with care I should hope everything will be OK. Trollope flew Avros when he was training, and they taught him a good deal. You finish up on RE 8s which they use for artillery observation out in France instead of the old BE 2C, and 2 Es. Artillery observation is about the softest job there is, but it's by no means 'all beer and skittles'. RE 8s are the machines which some people have been kicking up such a fuss about because they catch alight in mid-air, and if you get into a spin you cannot get out again At the same time I do not think they are half as bad as they are painted, and with care should be quite respectable machines to fly. Please send me another pillow-slip along, as one has been lost. One has no kit left after continually shifting. There is absolutely no leave going on as far as I can see.

Madge will have read, in the little news of events that got into the newspapers, why that should be so. April had seen the Allies on the Hindenburg Line advancing four miles by the end of the terrible Battle of Arras of which Siegfried Sassoon wrote so bitterly:

Men jostle and climb to meet the bristling fire,
Lines of grey, muttering faces, masked with fear,
They leave their trenches, going over the top....

And back went the line in the second battle of the Aisne. The conflict was spreading far beyond the battlefields of France to make it truly the First World War. The good news was that at the beginning of the month Woodrow Wilson, the

American president, had announced the United States declaration of war against Germany. For Dudley at Wye, as he told his mother, it was a matter of making himself technically competent to play an effective part in the new aspect of warfare which was in the air.

May 24, 1917

I am getting on well now with Avros, as I am beginning to get used to them. The feel on the controls is quite different to the G.W. because the former are so light. I can land them all right but they are very hard to keep straight when getting off the ground, and at first I swung all over the shop. I expect I shall be going solo very shortly. The place is six minutes in the train from Ashford. We are just the Canterbury side of Ashford.

I am looking forward to getting on to B E 2Cs. There one can leave the Aerodrome a bit and fly over to Twineham etc. When do you leave Tunbridge Wells? I cannot very well fly over the latter low in case the engine 'peters out', and then there is nothing but houses to land on; but I might fly over pretty high one day. I have got to do five hours solo on Avros before going on to B E 2Cs.

May 27

I saw the [press] cutting re the collision at Hove in the paper. Most unfortunate, but it shows how nippy you have to be when flying in formation. Flying in formation with inexperienced pilots always put the wind up old Trollope and I more than any 'Archie' [anti-aircraft fire]. Then of course Trollope knew what to do if a collision looked likely to come about.

Three fellows from here have flown over to Shoreham this morning and they hope to lunch in Brighton.

A fellow suffering from that fatal disease in young pilots, namely over-confidence, had a crash yesterday - totally wrecked the machine and has not gained consciousness yet properly. He is in hospital at Ashford. Another fellow from Devon landed and ran into hangars, smashed up the machine pretty badly, but immediately leaped out of the machine and took a camera out of his pocket and proceeded to take a photograph of his handiwork.

He was making rather slow progress on his handling of the Avro for his liking. So far he had hardly flown two hours in one, but no doubt he would get along soon enough. He looked forward to the time when he could career round the country in a B E 2C like his observer friends from Hendon were doing. Two of these, Captain Collie and Captain Tyrell, went to have a look at the damage which German aircraft had done in a raid on Folkestone that morning. "I think the Huns made rather a mess of the place by all reports, but of course they have every right to do so, it being a fortified town." He ended the letter by hoping that the hunt meeting had been a success, and then, before posting it, scribbled in a postscript.

P.S.

Since I wrote this letter I have got some important news, namely that on

Tuesday next we are shifting to Wyton in Huntingdon not far from Cambridge. This is to allow a Home Defence Squadron to come here, I suppose in consequence of the Hun's making that raid. I will let you know our address later.

May 31, 1917, Wyton
We arrived here on Tuesday evening by the 4.20 from King's Cross, getting in here about 6.0 pm. We left Wye at 11.30 am and got to Town at 2 pm. Four of us lunched at the Savoy, and then went on to King's Cross.

Well, having got here we are all very disappointed in our billets, left in a disgusting mess by 65 Sqdn. The billet consists of Houghton Manor House where we are squashed four or even seven in a room. This house, which has been shut up for a considerable period, is situated four and a half miles from Huntingdon and two and a half from the Aerodrome. Sundry lorries and tenders take us to and fro. There are no decent washing arrangements and no where to put your clothes. However, I believe there is a lot of furniture to come from Wye yet and, when once we get the place clean and settled a bit, it will not be too bad.

It certainly could not be as bad as a trench on the Western Front, and relief of the overcrowding seemed to be merely a matter of exorcising a ghost occupying the spare room.

There is supposed to be a haunted room in the house and we spent quite an hour trying to pick the lock last night, but our efforts were in vain. However we must get it opened as that is a room wasted.

The aerodrome itself is far too uneven for pupils to land Avros on, so I think 'A' Flight will do all its flying from another landing ground the other side of Huntingdon or all the machines will be without undercarriages in a couple of days.

Yesterday morning seven of us had breakfast in St Ives as there was nothing ready for us, and and I spent the rest of the day in Huntingdon and went on the river with Tyrrel and Shewell in the evening. There is one very nice hotel called the Bridge House Hotel, and the George is not too bad. But it's a pretty small sort of town on the whole, and has got the Canterbury dirty smelly style about it. So far, I think we were better off at Wye as it was a clean and well cared for place, and above all had decent washing arrangements and was pretty comfortable which I think is 50% of the battle. I would sooner be in a place miles from anywhere if you can get a bath when you like and it is generally clean, than be close to a third class town and live in dirt. There are about two servants so far to look after 40 people, as we left our batmen, belonging to a labour battalion, behind.

If the airmen did not like Huntingdon, neither did Huntingdon have any particular affection for the airmen.

The shop proprietors in Huntingdon are not very fond of the RFC as the louts in no 65 [Squadron] left without returning bikes they had hired, and they cannot be found now. I can tell you there are some extraordinary gentlemen wearing Sec. Lieut's uniform nowadays. I cannot say I am particularly fond of any of the staff in this squadron. I should like to have poor old Lawrence or some of [Squadron No.] 70 as C.O. Major Ross-Home of the Cameronians is the C.O. I have not had much to do with him yet.

Please excuse pencil but I am in No. 31's Mess, and none of their pens are working. They fly old G.White machines which I did at Hendon. They are always having minor crashes and do the most extraordinary things. I should think they must be pretty good fools if they cannot manage those machines better than they do.

It appears that the wind driving against his face in the open air cockpit was roughing it up and making it smart. His mother suggested his flying over to Twineham, landing in a nearby field and looking round the rooms in the Grange for a pot of something to soothe it.

I will try Hazeline Cream for my face. I have no intention of landing at Twineham because there is not enough room to land. There is just room, but it is too much risk of breaking something if you have not got plenty of room, and an inexperienced fellow does not know where and quite how he is going to land. However, nothing can prevent me flying there unless it is too far away from this show. I have only done an hour and a half on Avros so far - dual - and I expect it will be sometime before I do solo at the rate things are going on. As far as I can see, we are no nearer the end of the war than we were in August 1914.

A few final weeks flying Avros under dual control, plus several more on his own, led to confident mastery of the required techniques, primitive in comparison with the sophistication of modern aircraft, but demanding just as much concentration and intelligence, subject to just as much human error which experience could reduce but was not likely ever to eliminate. He was passed fit for overseas duty - for battle, that is to say - and in July 1917 was sent to Scotland for topping-up instruction on the latest models of machine-gun at the School of Aerial Gunners, Turnberry, Ayrshire.

On July 24 he wrote to his mother to say he had now finished this course, and was set to return to Dover in a few days. He was not quite sure what plans the CO there had for him, but he would almost certainly go to France "and possibly fly Sopwith Pups, but would prefer Camels". Soon after, Madge received a letter from Dudley headed Royal Flying Corps, Swingate Downs, Dover, telling her how pleased he was to get away from Turnberry. So was everyone else, he said. He met some very good fellows there, "and some appalling specimens".

The appearance of numerous junior officers, who were not 'gentlemen' according to the classification of the day, worried young men who had progressed through public school and Sandhurst. Most of it was letting off steam. There is not much evidence that the 'jumped-up' officers suffered much from their contemporaries, although they got into trouble from stuffy Mess presidents who took a delight in faulting their dress and conduct in front of their brother officers. Robert Graves, and other writers of war memoirs, have plenty of examples. Bob, incidentally, ran separate messes under a kindly major in his training battalions, so that the newly promoted officers could be coached in etiquette before being sent on to their regiments.

Dudley told his mother how, his last morning at Turnberry, he had his perfectly good flying helmet and goggles pinched off the hat stand. He never got them back. "There were an awful lot of blackguards up there, because several fellows had things 'pinched' off them and one chap lost £8 - 10s."

> I think I am doomed to go out on 'pups', and I do not think there is much chance of getting on 'Camels', at any rate this side of the water. At the same time I do not think it would be quite right to write to Gen. Trenchard, or rather to ask Mrs Wilkinson to write to him, asking him to have me sent to No. 70 Squadron if I have not flown Sopwith Camels in England, but I mean to have a desperate shot at it on my own when I get to AD St Omer.

General Trenchard commanded the Royal Flying Corps, and later saw the creation of a Royal Air Force, independent of the Army, and became its first Air Marshal.

It was nearly three weeks before Dudley finally set off for the war zone, and on the eve of his departure wrote to his mother from the Hotel Metropole, Folkestone, telling her what was likely to happen next.

August 11, 1917
My dear Mother
We arrived down here at 9.30 am this morning, but the boat does not leave until 4 pm this afternoon… Leslie Holman, who was with me at Sandhurst and in the 19th and joined the flying corps soon after me, is not killed after all but is wounded and is a prisoner of war. Charles (Cayser) said the cavalry are doing nothing at present and they have dismounted all the Yeomanry. The 1st Division are continually rushing up to the line to try and do something, but it is hopeless at present. I expect we shall go to the 'Pool' at 1 A.D. at St Omer first, before going to a squadron or perhaps 2 A.D. at Fienvillers where I was before. The sea looks moderate - slightly on the choppy side of affairs.

August 17
Just a line to let you know that I am going to 29 Squadron sometime today. They fly Nieuportes which I have been flying here. Please address all letters in future to No.29 Sqdn, R.F.C, BEF France.

August 18
I arrived at this Squadron yesterday afternoon and have lost my reputation

already. I completely wrecked a machine yesterday evening. It was absolutely my own fault. After going up to a fair height to try and improve my flying of this type of machine, I turned and twisted about and lost sight of the aerodrome. I was making for another close by, and coming down in a spiral, and the gun came down. So, while I was putting it up again, I was coming down very slowly and my propeller stopped - and it is impossible to get it [going] again with these engines. Well, I could not make the aerodrome, and found myself going into some huts. So I simply had to turn at a low speed, stalled and spun into the earth from about 20 feet. The machine was totally wrecked. The tail plane was the only thing intact, and the rudder bar was smashed back against the joy stick. I miraculously escaped with sundry bruises and grazes on my legs and arms, but apart from feeling rather sore all over I am feeling OK.

We do three jobs a day here if it is fine, and as usual I hear that it is always the new fellows who get done down, so I hope my previous experience will help me.

It is easy to imagine the fright which this letter will have given Madge in Tunbridge Wells - only by a miracle failing to get himself killed on the evening of his very first day! Dudley went on to tell her that in command of his squadron was the charming Sandy who had had been CO of 'B' Flight in his old No. 70 Squadron. He, Dudley, was practically the most senior fellow in 29 Squadron, so he thought he had a good chance of being put in command of a flight pretty soon. In command of his flight was someone called Collier, who had been at Uppingham with Dudley and was in fact junior to him there "but after last night's exhibition I should think they class me as a wash-out. The machine was a 'write-off'."

He ended the letter with a light-hearted reminder to his mother that "this is in the part of the country where Luke Smith was, and told you to think of the Christian name of the man who owned Gravenhurst." Presumably a family joke, the meaning of which is lost in time. Two days later he met another old friend to remind him of home - or maybe just an old regimental colleague?

August 20
The other evening I was surprised to see Gardener walking round here. He was with a digging party of the Regt close to this place, and I went and had dinner with him, Capt Wiley and Mitchell. It was very nice to see them all again, and they are very fed up. Pankhurst has made himself objectionable to Gardener, so he has put in for the R.F.C and I expect he will be going along soon. Joe Nettlefold is an A.P.M. [Assistant Provost Marshal] in a village close here, and they say the Col. will not have anyone who has left the Regt back again, but I do not believe it.

I have been doing some practice flying up to date and have got on petty well. At any rate I have had no more crashes - touch wood.

August 26
I am quite happy in this Squadron and think I am far better off here, as a

matter of fact. I am glad Dad is having a well-earned and much needed change, and sincerely hope he will not have to come out here… I have been flying considerably every day since I have been with the Squadron, and got 'archied' [shot at by anti-aircraft guns] pretty badly yesterday… We did a job this morning in appalling weather. Clouds at 1,500 feet and rain. Archie woke up and let me have a few, but I managed to dodge him all right… Practically all the effects of my crash have worn off now. The C.O. was very nice about it and did not say a word

September 5, 1917
We had a scrap the other morning, and Cudemore brought a Hun down and we did not lose anybody. This morning I was on a job and attacked one of a formation of 8 Huns. I was by myself and four of them turned on me but I got away all right, although I expected to be done in any moment. I quite enjoy the work here, but one gets rather a lot of it. We are now getting two hour jobs instead of one and a half hours.

I hope Dad does not come out here, but no doubt it would interest him; but at the same time it is no joke, especially his branch of the service.

Douglas Haig began his offensive in the third Battle of Ypres - Passchendaele - at the end of July 1917, which he carried through until the first week in November. The French slowly gained positions at the start of the second Battle of Verdun which opened on August 10, and raged until the middle of December. For the Allies, these were the most critical months of the whole war. No joke indeed.

Although the 'scraps' which young men like Dudley had with their German counterparts, in the air above the battles being waged on the ground, were a new feature of warfare, they were soon recognised as no mere side-show, but fully contributing to the outcome. In September 1917 Dudley was in the thick of it. In the letter he wrote to his mother on September 7, he told her, "I have had a scrap the last four times I have been on jobs.

The last one was the very devil. I dived on a Hun two-seater and got a scout on my tail. We both went straight for each other firing like mad, and that sort of thing went on until I had finished my magazine. I eventually got away all right, and another fellow drove him off but not before a bullet had come past my left arm and out by my right foot. I very nearly got a 'blighty' one that time, but was not touched.

He added that he had dined with one Vancour, who had been his flight-commander at no 70 Squadron, and he had told him that his old observer had written the articles in the *Blackwood* magazine which had been 'really very realistic'.

By now Madge was obviously desperately worried about Dudley. How could he possibly survive? She could not conceal her concern, and spoke about it to all her friends. It soon came to the ears of Isaac Baker, her 90-year-old father now living in Eastbourne, to whom she sent a brace of partridges. His letter of thanks will have been very comforting to her.

My dear Madge,

Many thanks for the birds which I am sure we shall enjoy. I hear that you are anxious about Dudley in the Flying Corps, and I quite share your anxiety, as I consider it very brave of the young fellows to come forward and offer themselves for the service as they do. This war is a terrible affair, and I shall be very glad when it comes to an end, but I can see no sign of that at present.

I am glad to say that I am keeping fairly well, but have to curtail my walks as I suffer rather from shortness of breath. Nell [his second wife] sends her love. She is busy going to s.c.a. canteen about twice a week to assist in making tea for soldiers.

With much love,

Your affectionate Father

As a postscript to his letter of September 5, Dudley had enclosed a cheque for £20 'for the Morgan stunt'. In his next letter to his mother he referred to it.

September 13, 1917

I am glad you received the £20 all right. I hoped it would come in useful for John's motor bike, and I am glad to hear that you have decided to give him one. I am sending the negligee to Doris by registered post and hope it will arrive safely. It cost 100 frcs, and the boudoir cap 28 frcs. I expect you think I am extravagant, but I thought perhaps it would be a chance missed and things with real Brussels lace on would be about twice the price in England. Sorry to hear about the General's accident.

We have been doing quite a few jobs lately. Of course we have to attack the Huns - that is our job. Our orders are 'to be as offensive as possible', but at the same time you can take care of yourself in most cases. The great thing is choosing your opportunities.

I had a very despairing letter from Kenneth today. He cannot seem to land Avros yet, but it is very hard to start straight away on these machines.

September 16

We have been doing one job a day lately, which is rather better owing to the weather not being so good as it might be. Last night we had a very successful scrap with 5 Huns. Payne brought one down and I got some shooting into the same one. He must have been a pretty 'dud' pilot, because he made no attempt at getting away. We got down very low over their side and we all got back safely. Payne was the fellow who drove the Hun off me.

We went up to see Capt White in my regt the other night who is in command of a large prisoners' cage, and every time we come back from a job we dive on it and zoom up again, which causes him great amusement, as the poor fellow is all on his own there. A terrible existence I should imagine.

How very funny John being mistaken for me twice the other day. He is so tremendous for his age. He seems to be having quite a good time.

September 18
Many thanks for your letter dated 14th. I am still in the land of the living as you see.

We had a terrific scrap yesterday. Four of us against 8 Huns, and Chapman shot one down out of control. We fought for about ten minutes, then several of us put ourselves out of control and got away with the assistance of clouds. One persistent Hun followed me down the clouds and got on my tail firing from about 50 yards, but I managed to shake him off by diving into another lot of clouds and steering by compass. I had four holes in my top plane but was not shot about any more than that, which goes to prove that these particular Huns were rotten shots, as we were fighting to great disadvantage from start to finish.... There is no more news at present so I will say goodbye. Love to all.

    With much love from
    Dudley

It was Dudley's last letter. On September 25 Bolney Post & Telegraph Office received a telegram from the War Office, which was immediately taken to Twineham Grange by a boy on a bicycle. It read:

Deeply regret to inform you Lt R.W.D. McKergow 5 Dragoon Guards attached R.F.C. 29 Squadron was killed in action September twenty first. The Army Council express their sympathy.

    Secretary

    War Office

Dudley's CO wrote to his father the day after he had been killed, telling him the circumstances.

    29 Squadron, Royal Flying Corps,
    BEF,
    France

    Dear Col. McKergow,
    It is with the deepest regret that I have to write and tell you that your son was killed yesterday. He was engaged in a fight in which one of our machines was shot down and fell on to your son's machine. I saw the doctor who was on the spot and he told me that he was killed instantaneously.

    I went to his funeral yesterday and he was buried by the side of the other officer in the English Military Cemetery at Ypres. The map reference of which is 1;40,000 Sheet 2817B2.2.

    Your son was one of the most popular members of this Squadron and had done very gallant work during the short time he was with us.

Please accept the deepest sympathy from the whole Squadron in your great loss.
Yours sincerely,
Charles M A Chapman
Major

One cannot suggest that the sense of loss and despair was more for any particular mother or wife than for all the thousands of similarly bereaved women at that time. But Madge must have felt the separation keenly, as she had expected almost daily bulletins from Dudley and become personally involved. Evidently other young men either did not write so often, or kept their letters to generalities. The Trollope family got far more out of Dudley than they did from their own son. Sometimes Dudley found his mother a bit too fussy. The crash on the first day with the squadron was a case in point. No-one in the squadron found it an unusual occurrence. The young pilots were crumpling their planes up all the time - it was part of the learning process. But for Madge it was a most worrying incident, and she kept returning to it in her letters. Eventually Dudley had to protest that an accident like that had been forgotten weeks ago, and hinted politely that she should do likewise,

So she must have gone over again and again in her mind the circumstances that led to her son's death. In November she wrote to the Squadron CO enquiring the name of the other pilot. Dudley had mentioned one or two of them in his letters. But the name the CO sent her was not one that Madge was able to recognise. He was a Canadian pilot to whom Dudley had had no occasion to refer in any of his letters.

Then Cis Breton, one of Madge's Mockett relations, suggested she visited a spiritualist medium. These operators were in great demand, as they gave the impression of being able to communicate with those who were now 'on the other side'. Madge duly attended a seance, but she found the medium far from convincing. The message which the lady purported to receive from Dudley "Tell mother I'm all right" was not worth paying money for. However, it probably helped to convince her that Dudley had gone. She packed his uniform and belongings away, and turned to her role as 'Colonel's Lady' with the Royal West Kents.

Kenneth Seth-Smith *did* get the hang of landing an Avro, as Dudley had forecast he would. That autumn of 1917 he flew one with great confidence from Gosport to Bolney to join a pheasant shoot and returned the same evening to his base - presumably logged as part of his training programme. However that may be, the feat greatly enhanced his reputation locally. On active service in the less friendly environment of war stricken France, he suffered the usual fate of being shot down. But he succeeded in being able to keep the plane under control, and landed in a shell hole on the British side of the front line. He was injured but not critically. He was sent to hospital in England, and on discharge was advised against rejoining the Royal Flying Corps, which he had at first despised, and to go back to regimental duties and take up his regular commission again with the Fighting Fifth.

At the time of Dudley's death, Bob was still busily commanding the Yeomanry unit of indeterminate size which he was supposed to be training as cavalry. Much of this training was taken up with sports and mounted events. The High Command were often more hindrance than help. On the other hand they were themselves subjected to pressure from civilian ladies who were wont to be even more frightening than 'Disgusted of Tunbridge Wells'. They were usually 'disgusted' at what the troops were doing. Unfortunately the war had been elevated to a crusade between the virtuous and chivalrous 'boys' on our side, and the barely civilised Huns on the other. Those representing the crusaders had to be whiter than white according to the self-appointed guardians of public morals. The CO of one army unit issued an order on how soldiers should, and should not, behave when they were in the company of women. It prohibited *inter alia* 'sitting around in public seats or any public place with arms around a woman'. Several men in his unit were outraged, and wrote to the Secretary of State for War to tell him so.

Such an order, they said, would appear to insult their relatives and themselves. When he heard of the men's action and what had led them to it, the GOC Eastern Command cancelled the order, except for the part about not putting arms round women. He could not overlook the disobedience of the soldiers who had written to the Secretary of State contrary to army regulations, and they must be suitably dealt with.

Having got that off his chest, the GOC appended to his Order, cancelling the CO's Order, a note expressing his views, with which he wished all commanding officers to make themselves acquainted.

> I am strongly of the opinion that it is no breach of Military discipline for either an officer or soldier in uniform to allow his wife or other female relative to take his arm or to be seen sitting with him on a seat in a public place. On the other hand, I quite agree that it is a serious breach of Military discipline and public decency for soldiers to be seen sitting on seats with their arms round women's waists, a practice which I have noticed with regret appears to have a tendency to increase. I therefore direct that the [CO's] Order is to stand.

> L Rundle, General Commanding-in-Chief, Eastern Command

The transfer of Bob's Yeomanry unit to Crowborough Camp, and the simultaneous conversion from cavalry to infantry, was a busy time for him, not least because he had to find NCOs to guide them through infantry drill. Whereupon, at the beginning of January 1917, no sooner had they settled in at Crowborough than the War Office decided to merge the Sussex Yeomanry with the Royal Sussex Regiment. Bob's command was abolished, and he received a letter of commiseration from one of Sir John French's Military Secretaries.

19th January 1917
Dear Major McKergow.

I am desired by the Field Marshal, Commander-in-Chief, to write and thank you for all the work you have done whilst in Command of your unit.

He is sure you will understand that the absorbtion that has taken place has only been done in the best interests of the Army.

He wishes to thank all who were under your command for the way they have loyally carried out the duties required of them, and is confident that the same spirit they have shown will continue in whatever sphere they may find themselves. Thank you again on the Field Marshal's behalf,

Believe me,

Yours sincerely,

Stanley Berry

Bob was not impressed. Before he filed it, he wrote what he thought of it at the bottom: "This is from a grateful country, cheap is it not." In other words, no promotion and no decoration - outrageous! At least not instantaneous. Promotion came in due course - to Lieutenant Colonel and command of the 4th (Reserve) Battalion, Royal West Kent Regiment at Tunbridge Wells. It was the new job to which Dudley referred in his letter to Madge saying he hoped he was enjoying it. And enjoy it he did - thoroughly. And he virtually insisted that everyone else involved should do the same.

The young officers, seeing out their last months of military service, looked back on their time in the battalion with affection for their commanding officer. Far better to have been having a bit of a laugh at the Orders of the Day than slogging out the never-ending war. And then there were the summer tennis parties with Madge and Doris in charge, the invitations to dinner and the Garrison concerts with the Queen's Own band. They were probably, after such a lapse of time, prepared to forgive Lieut Evans his impersonations and the humorous songs of Lieut Hartman.

At the eleventh hour of the eleventh day of the eleventh month of 1918 the Armistice was declared, and by the summer of the following year the reserve battalion was stood down. In Bob's period of command it had handled 1,523 drafts to France, Egypt and India, 1,398 transfers to labour camps and other units, 303 transfers to Machine Gun Corps and Tank Corps, 191 discharged and 14 commissioned.

But what pleased Bob more than anything else was the award of an OBE and permission to retain the rank, if he wished to, of Lieutenant Colonel in civilian life. He did.

~ 8 ~

Hunt Ball, Point-to-Point, Portrait as MFH

The war years were exceptionally difficult for the Crawley and Horsham Hunt. The hounds had to be severely culled, breeding was discouraged and more than 20 horses went to the army. At one time it was jokingly suggested that hunting would have to continue with the hunt servants on foot or, even worse, on bicycles. In fact they were able to continue by meeting two days a week and using horses too small for the army. Nominally Colonel Godman and Bob continued as Joint-Masters, with Mr W A Calvert as Acting Master. In 1915 the Masters tendered their resignation, as the committee could not promise to maintain their financial guarantee. The committee took over and Calvert ran the hunt under their jurisdiction for the rest of the war years, cleverly maintaining the hound breeding lines of Charles Godman.

As soon as Bob was out of the army in 1919 he came back as sole Master. The 1919-1920 season was as successful as it could be with only nineteen and a half couples of hounds in kennel. At the end of the following season he noted in the Hunt Diary, "It has been a hard season for our young hounds, having no help from the old hounds that could not keep up owing to age.

> The young hounds, especially the Berkeley draft [which he started to buy in 1920], have worked very well, and have pace and drive. We are now reduced to 21 couples of working hounds in Kennel, and four and a half couple of hounds purchased from the Whaddon Chase and seven and a half couple of young hounds of our own breeding.

The season of 1921-22 was possibly unique in the way of weather. The year also saw the retirement of the Huntsman and First Whip.

A hot summer did not worry the sportsmen too much, and some days of cub hunting were always likely to be lost in August if the ground was too hard. In 1921, however, they did not dare start until September 17, and it was not really fit then. Bob noted, "The ground is very hard. No rain had practically fallen since we left off hunting last season." On October 4 he wrote: "Scent was very bad and very hot morning, so came home." On October 8 it was the same story: "We had to go home early as hounds felt the heat so much. We must stop cubbing until rain comes." On

October 22 they had another try but "went home very hot and dry again". A remarkable turnround occurred on November 10 when frost intervened, and on the twelfth the hunt did not go out owing to frosty ground.

The opening meet had to be postponed until November 26 when over 100 mounted followers turned up and, typically for that season, had to tolerate a poor scenting day. On December 6 they eventually had a good hunt. After a disappointing morning, Bob was asked to draw Coolham Big Gorse, where they moved a fox that gave them a very fast 45 minutes before darkness made it impossible to continue. Then on December 8 Dick Kingsland, the Huntsman, had a bad fall that ended his career.

In an era of long lived hunt servants Dick Kingsland ranks high. He became First Whip to the Crawley and Horsham in 1882 and Huntsman in 1893. So after 28 years in the post he had to stand down but only, of course, through injury. The hunt members gave him a really good send-off, with a cheque for £1,000 and a silver tea service for his wife. In his 1930 'history' of the Crawley and Horsham, Geoffrey Sparrow depicted Kingsland as a severe, hatchet-faced character. In retirement he was almost the opposite. For years he was driven to convenient meets by his daughter, where he would stand by the roadside in a grey suit and brown trilby hat politely exchanging the time of day with the followers who knew him in his prime, and looking the mildest of men.

The First Whip, George Dean, also retired that year after 28 years with the hunt. Photographs show a distinctly Victorian figure in a full skirted coat from which his legs stuck out before him to the extent that his feet touched the shoulders of his horse. He was probably not easy to dislodge from the saddle.

Will Hale was engaged as Huntsman for the season 1922-23 and got a reasonably good summing-up from the Master: "Considering it was Hale's first season I think he has killed a good lot of foxes, and hounds have worked well all through."

At the end of the 1922-23 season Bob wrote, "I am sorry to say that certain followers are over-zealous and do not give either Huntsman or hounds a chance on a cold scenting day." Most of the regular followers were careful not to upset the Master - "we were terrified of him" as one lady who hunted as a teenager with him remarked. But there was at least one occasion when Bob took hounds home a little too early, having informed the field that they appeared to be taking no interest in hound work.

In the 1923-24 season 204 foxes were found and 59 killed. However, the Master had a hard time, as Will Hale was out of action following a fall and Harry Tyrell suffered a head injury. At one point Bob was hunting hounds with the help of Alfred Pankhurst (2nd Whip). Similar problems made life extremely difficult in 1924-25. Falls and influenza kept Will Hale out of the saddle for part of the season. Harry Tyrell had another accident which, as the Master noted, "meant my hunting hounds with the aid of Will Windley only, rather an arduous task. I did 66 miles on the road with hounds in one week, as well as the hunting".

At that time, and for several years afterwards, the Huntsman rode to the meet with the hounds and, of course, rode back again at the end of the day. The exception seems to have been meets in the Arundel district (the extreme south-west boundary of the hunt country) when horses and hounds either went by train or were housed overnight in the locality.

Anyhow, acting as Huntsman was a tough assignment for a heavy 58 year old, and Bob would not have wanted to continue hunting the dog hounds permanently. He was probably in charge when they had the freak run, which he described in his diary, after a meet at Mannings Heath.

February 17, 1923, Saturday
This was a red letter day as regards distance covered by hounds (but not by the "field"). We found close to the Schools at Mannings Heath Wood and ran North to Goldings, Leonards Forest where he turned back to Mill Shaw. He turned again there and ran back through the Forest to Roffey Park, Holmbush, Buchan Hill where the whole field had lost hounds. We had 5 ¹/₂ couple, the rest were gone. We rode on to the Faygate Road, the London Road to Crawley; no tidings of them so had to go home. At 6.30 I had a telephone message to say 7 ¹/₂ couple were at Horley. They ran their fox, so we hear, through Buchan Hill, through Cheals Nurseries to Gatwick Race Course, to Horley Mill to ground. Some man got hold of them and locked them up at the "Six Bells" Horley where we got them home by van late at night. The hounds travelled 15 miles and in all my experience of 40 years I have never gone home with so few hounds, leaving the other part of the pack out. Rumour has it that they hunted beautifully and their fox only got to ground a short distance in front of the leading hounds.

On December 23, 1923 they had an exceptional run after finding at Knepp Pond. The fox took them to West Grinstead, crossed the Henfield–Cowfold road to Kent Street, turned north, was headed and came back to the Henfield–Cowfold road where they lost him. They hunted two hours, and the dog pack showed great pace. As the crow flies they covered 11 miles from point to point.

These long distances covered on a good hunting day made second horses essential for those wishing to be up with the pack all day. The file, likened by Colonel Bob to a squadron of cavalry, left the meet after the mounted followers, the grooms maintaining strict discipline - no talking or looking around - until they were well away on their own. When the pack broke covert and vanished into the countryside, it was up to the experienced grooms to decide which road to take by dint of listening to the 'music' of the pack and the Huntsman's horn. If they made the right judgements, they would be on hand at the right moment when a fresh horse was needed. Only very occasionally did the system break down.

At that stage in the season feelers were out for a successor to Will Hale. Bob noted in his diary, recording a day at Muntham: "Bert Peaker (1st Whip Whaddon Chase) was out. Thinks of taking place of Will Hale. A nice looking man, good horseman; quick." Finally, "Have engaged Peaker."

Do we say "Here began the Golden Age of Foxhunting"? Possibly, but the whole inter-war period was pretty good and evidently the Crawley and Horsham flourished. The appearance of Peaker, seriously considering being taken on by the hunt, is instructive. Why would this most talented man, already with a prominent South-Midland pack, wish to come out into the provinces South of London? The answer may well lie in the operation of the 'bush telegraph' among hunt staff. The message could have been, "The old Colonel at the C&H is making something of it. Lot of support. A young chap could get himself noticed there."

Peaker put what is called his 'stamp of authority' on the Kennels straight away, added to which he was first rate in the field and extremely popular with the followers. Bob really could only sit back and let him reign - a most unusual situation. There are no comments from Peaker on his time in Sussex, but he must have enjoyed working with a pack that was accepted everywhere and under a Master, who had assembled a really useful Kennel of hounds and provided a good stud of horses to ride. By the end of 1925, incidentally, the hound-breeding had succeeded to the extent of 11 couple out of a total of forty four and a half were related to the pre-war pack.

Bob gave an enthusiastic report at the end of the 1926-27 season. "The season has been an exceptionally good one. The ground has been good going and not so deep as we had the year before. Foxes have been plentiful and our record this season for number killed breaks all records. I hear our Hunt subscription is the largest ever taken in the history of the pack. Harry Tyrell is leaving us and his place is being taken by E Ortin from Lord Leconfield's."

Hunts continued to be long, and, as in the case of the meet at Round-a-bouts on February 14, 1928, were sometimes curtailed through the non-arrival of second horses. "Found at Perretts at once," wrote Bob in the Hunt Diary of this meet.

> A brace ran hard to Wantley to Sandgate Wood, north to Warminghurst, to Hooklands, to Basingwood, through to south of Capite where he turned north and we went past Pot Hill through the Grinders nearly to Dial Post, back again to Hobb Shorts and we stopped hounds going into Lock. A great hunt of 1 hour and 50 minutes. We never got our second horses, so we had to go home.

The Sussex hunting fraternity obviously like the sustained nature of the hunts which the terrain of the Crawley and Horsham afforded; but the hunt's exceptionally quick build-up was due to a large extent to the ease with which they could now reach the different parts of the county where the meets were held - by motor car. In 1914 the automobile was fast taking over from horse-drawn transport; by 1919 it had won hands down. It meant that followers did not have to contemplate having to make a long ride to a distant meet. They could get into their car and be driven to it in comfort. The grooms, of course, generally had to ride there, but outdoor and indoor staff were plentiful and accustomed to long hours. As the hunt met three times a week, those with time to spare made friends with similar spirits all over West Sussex and, since the chaperone convention had also collapsed, a very lively social scene developed.

The 1928-29 season turned out to be the last one with Peaker in charge. The Fernie Hunt in Leicestershire had a vacancy for a huntsman which was exactly the opportunity Peaker wanted. Lord Stalbridge came down to see his preferred candidate in the field, and engaged him.

Bob arranged for Peaker to be photographed outside the Kennels and hung the print in his dressing room - the only member of the hunting fraternity to be so honoured. There was a particularly nice return gesture when, in 1934, Bob retired from the mastership. Peaker sent him the Fernie Christmas Card inscribed:

"To Colonel McKergow
Wishing you a <u>very</u> happy Christmas
from B Peaker"

As it happened the card featured two Fernie dog hounds, Trojan and Trimbush, that Bob probably wished he had bred, as they were exactly the old fashioned type he always favoured.

Bob began to comment in his diary on the 'big fields' which reached 160 horse-men (and women) on occasions. The Boxing Day meet in Horsham, put on for the townspeople's entertainment, drew about 3,000 to the Carfax, and the following year the crowds were so thick that it was difficult to extricate the hounds.

Not only those on foot but those in cars became a problem. After a meet at Ashington on March 30, 1929, Bob was moved to write in his diary:

A terrible crowd of motors etc in the main road. Must remember not to put meets on main roads in holiday time.

There was always a way of avoiding road congestion, but not bad scenting days or a shortage of foxes. The meet of November 29, 1930 was 'a rotten day' through having the extraordinary experience of being over-run with foxes and quite unable to hunt. Early in the day the prospects were not too bad. After a meet at Bines Green, they found in Station Wood, ran to Square Copse and back again to Hoadley's where scent failed. They found at Moore's Cottage, but the hounds never owned it. Holloas were heard in all directions, but hounds never spoke. The dog hounds Gainer and Gameboy owned a line across a field, but nothing came of it. The pack kept turning a fox in a covert. Some hounds threw their tongues, but never spoke in the open. From Caffyns six foxes came away with hounds whim-pering in covert. From Monastery Wood the Master was certain nine foxes moved. For the Colonel it was 'a very unusual day'.

For the followers who turned up for the meets, there was of course no knowing whether the day ahead would be Good, Rotten or Unusual; and the Crawley and Horsham Hunt continued to attract bigger and bigger fields. The gawping townees did not worry the farmers; the number of riders did. As one farmer put it, "It's a bit worrying to have 100 followers across your wheat." He added that, in spite of that, the hunt were still welcome on his land. It was Bob's major preoccupation to ensure that the farmers kept on his side.

To some extent the economic depression in agriculture helped him. Farmers found their corn selling for less and less and responded by not cultivating their arable fields, which then reverted to weeds. Bankruptcies increased; the big estates could not find tenants except on the humiliating terms of the 'first year rent free, second year 2/6 (12p) an acre' variety. Hunting people at least wanted hay, straw and oats for their horses. The hunt also paid up for any damage suffered and the claims were on the high side. The Master usually got a laugh at his Point-to-Point speech when he commended the farmers on the prosperity of their poultry farming. "The fox only kills pedigree chickens." It was a bit of a fiddle in many ways but kept the hunt tied in, as it were, to the local farming populace who could regard the fox-hunters as sympathetic to their difficulties. There was also the real generosity of the Master who was liable to give a present to anyone at any time - regardless of whether it was needed. A small farmer, small in stature as well as acres, had had to sell up and subsist in a dilapidated cottage. Bob turned up one day with bags of clothes, including an enormous overcoat that would have totally overwhelmed the little man, who was immensely flattered to receive such unexpected largesse.

Bob's characteristic was his talkativeness. If there was time, he would talk to anyone he came across. He generally found out who they were and three months later, to their surprise, remembered all their life history. For example, Bob comes across a farm worker.

> "Where do you work?"
> *Sayers Common, sir.*
> "Yes, yes. But who for?"
> *Mr Hole, sir.*
> "Which one? There are more Holes than foxes in Sayers Common."

He also encouraged the young enthusiasts - like young Goatcher for instance, the son of Cowfold's master butcher who, clearing up one evening at the back of his shop, heard a fearful roar from the front. "Goatcher!" It was a sound he knew only too well, and brooked no delay in dropping everything and hurrying out to confront the source of it. "Look here, Goatcher," bellowed Bob, "that boy of yours - went well today - needs a better horse - you'd better see to it."

Forty years later the 'boy' could still laugh about that confrontation - "Dad found me a nice little horse the following week, and I had a lot of fun with him."

The youths who knew the Master well were sometimes bold enough to be a bit cheeky.

A local lad was suddenly accosted by Bob who had ridden up at speed after losing the hounds.

> "Which way did they go, boy?"
> *The dogs is gone that way, sir* (waving an arm to the north).
> " 'Dogs' damn you? Don't you know they are hounds? You're nothing but a hobble-de-hoy"
> *Yes, sir* (delighted to have got a rise).

Bob himself was known to take delight - indeed a kind of boyish glee - in the discomfort of others, as on the occasion one day in the nineteen twenties, described by many, when the hunted fox had crossed Twineham Brook and the pack were disappearing over the far brow. The field pulled up as they saw the brook ahead, and there was some confusion, since no-one seemed inclined to give a lead. "Tommy, jump the brook!" shouted Bob. This was to Tommy Grantham, proprietor of the livery stables near the hunt kennels, a great supporter of the Crawley and Horsham and an extremely good horseman. Tommy jumped the brook with great poise with plenty to spare. One or two of the young bloods decided to follow suit, failed to make it and were deposited in the water. The Master's laughter, so the account goes, could be heard in the next parish as he headed for the bridge.

Any youngster with hopes of one day becoming a member of the Crawley and Horsham took care to treat the Master with due respect, like the one who wrote to Bob from St John's College in Southsea.

> Dear Coln McKergow
> I wrote and asked Mr G Mills Jnr to whom I should send the subscrip-tion and in return I received your address. He also said the subscription for me, if I lived at Worthing, would be £17.17. But that I had better write to you first and send my age, in case you would not charge me. My age being 11 years old. Last year I hunted two or three times but did not have to pay anything until Lady Burrell cornered me for the "Farmers Benevolence Subscription" (sic).
> Hoping to hear from you this week.
> I remain
> Yrs Truly
> R Bell

The Point-to-Point races in March each year provided the big opportunity for favourable publicity. The event was now far more formal. The course had been carefully laid out and the fences made up to something approaching professional standards. The parade ring could not be described as exclusive but at least it had a rope round it. The riders gave up their top hats and heavy hunting kit in favour of hunting caps and lightweight clothing. A few registered racing colours.

The Farmers' Lunch, given by the hunt in a large marquee, attracted much sup-port. Soon after the war Bob recorded 546 sitting down to the meal. Many of them were foremen and other farm men who had been given a ticket by their employers. Some of them were rather too boisterous. No sooner had the waitresses put down the plates of cold beef and bowls of boiled potatoes than some ruffian would tip half the spuds on to his plate and call out, "Do you want to starve us, gal?" "There's nothin' to eat. Cut us some more beef, there's a gal."

After getting more than two or three times as much as might be expected, topped up with pudding, and knocking back several bottles of beer, the company was ready to applaud Earl Winterton as he proposed the health of the Crawley and Horsham Hunt, and to raise the roof when the Master replied. Somehow proceedings were brought to an end so that the races could start. Before long the marquee was filling up again with family and friends for the complimentary teas - 1,675 of them the Master noted. In spite of all this generosity the Point-to-Point usually made money.

On a staider note the Hunt Ball could be relied on to make a profit while demonstrating that the High Society of the Country were supporters of the hunt. It is surprising that the ball was advertised to the *public* in the 1920s. One would expect word to be passed round the hunting circles and some details to be posted to members when they were notified of forthcoming meets, but to find handbills being distributed does indicate a different social world.

It was probably accepted that this was essentially a ball for the 'nobs', and even if you could afford the tickets it would not do to try and join in. On the other hand, if you were a hostess already in the swim, it was an excellent opportunity to make up a party of 'young things' glad to get an invitation to a country house for a night or two. So, without really trying, the organisers would automatically reach the sort of people they were aiming at. We also tend to assume the current dominance of the week-end. As the working man never had anything more than Saturday afternoon off, and a great many, including farm workers, did not get that, events such as the Point-to-Point relied on employers in the countryside giving some at least of their men an unofficial holiday to attend. The day of the week was irrelevant. So the races took place on a Tuesday or a Thursday. Those self-employed, of independent means, or 'something in the City' could go to a ball any time, and the village flower show was on a Wednesday.

The 1922 Hunt Ball was advertised as taking place at the Connaught Hall, Worthing, on Tuesday January 3 under the patronage of the Duchess of Norfolk, Baroness Zouche, Lady Burrell and many other distinguished ladies. Tickets cost thirty-two shillings (£1.60) if purchased before December 30, £2 thereafter. Considering that outlay included the ball and a good dinner with wine it sounds a bargain, but the farm worker was earning around half the value of the ticket per week, which puts it in better context.

The small print at the foot of the handbill added "Arrangements have been made for the provision of suppers for Chauffeurs. Tickets may be obtained before date of Ball from Lt. Col R W McKergow price, 3/- each (15p)."

Came the night and the *Sussex Daily News* had much to report: "Brilliant Scenes in Connaught Hall"; "Distinguished Assembly and Striking Success".

Their Social Correspondent's report was gushing: "The picture was a sparkling one, replete with life, animation and joyousness, and it is difficult to give it any sort of adequate description. The decorations were entirely carried out in white and red, and the ballroom was draped in these colours in front of the platform, and over the windows and in front of the spacious gallery, where light refreshments were served during the evening. The gallery was also a coign of vantage whence the dancing could be comfortably watched. A screened-off portion was reserved for Bridge for those who preferred a quiet rubber. At the back of the ballroom was a lounge which was much in request as a retiring room, and the charmingly appointed supper rooms were downstairs."

It was obviously a glittering occasion patronised by all the county's glitterati, which nobody who was anybody could fail to attend.

"The whole of the floral decorations in the twin supper rooms was carried out with pink tulips and feathery yellow mimosa, the effect being delightful. A big round centre table was reserved for Lieutenant Colonel McKergow MFH, the Stewards and his party.... Added to this were the pink coats of the hunting men, and a wealth of exquisite frocks, and the sparkle of wonderful jewels. Rarely have so many beautiful toilettes been seen, and they showed to perfection, for at no time was the ballroom unpleasantly crowded."

Then came the description of the ladies and their gowns. "Mrs McKergow was handsomely attired in black, glittering with bugles, and wore a lovely necklace and a pendant of diamonds. Her gown was of satin beauté and finished with long sash ends of net forming a train. Lady Burrell, who had a large party with her, looked charming in soft black tulle which gleamed with sequins, and a coronet of diamonds on bands of black velvet was worn round the head in bandeau form.... Lady Carberry was very picturesque in a lovely swathed robe of cloth of gold shot with Persian blue, and possessing draperies of the same tint. Lovely pearls and a Russian coronal of blue velvet leaves gave a most chic appearance". Dozens more "toilettes" were reported in detail, followed by 148 names of those "Among the Assembly".

It was undoubtedly socially important to get named in some form. For the hunt the publicity (a word not used except in a pejorative sense, but that is what the press report was) helped to make the C&H 'fashionable' to a quite unusual degree for a provincial pack. Later in the season the farmers held their ball, which rated no more than half a column in the local papers.

The departure of Peaker led to the appointment of Charles Denton from the Warwickshire as successor. In his history of the C & H, Sparrow noted that Denton had a successful first two seasons; and he did indeed prove his worth for many subsequent seasons, finally retiring in 1953.

In the 1927-28 season Bob had poor health and only hunted four days in four months, and he was also finding the correspondence and administration very burdensome. So from 1928-29 the Hon C Guy Cubitt became Joint-Master and hunted the bitch pack himself. As he was a young man living even nearer the Kennels than Bob, the arrangement secured the future without upsetting the traditions of the hunt - or so it appeared. In 1930 Bob told the committee he wanted to retire. Quite possibly rumours started to get around that an outsider would be appointed to join Guy Cubitt, and the farmers started to get worried. Would they get the consideration from a new man - an outsider - that they had become accustomed to from the old Master? Perhaps Colonel McKergow would change his mind if enough of them signed the petition that was going the rounds? In the event, 800 signatures were collected and appended to an illuminated address. Not everyone who signed were working farmers, but the great majority fitted that description, and were genuinely keen to back the Master. The petition said *inter alia*: "In the interests of sport, and because in the past Col. McKergow's relationship with us has always been most friendly and helpful, we hereon testify that it is our earnest wish that he be asked to continue to act as Master. Further that the Crawley and Horsham Hunt Committee be requested to endorse this our Petition, leaving no stone unturned in their endeavours to retain the services of the Colonel."

In the light of such a massive vote of confidence, Bob felt obliged to withdraw his resignation - for the time being at any rate. One can argue that few of the run-of-the-mill farmers would have refused to sign when the petition was backed by the top men of the county. However, the numbers who were happy to add their names undoubtedly surprised the organisers and delighted Bob, for whom it was a real triumph.

His decision to carry on as Master will no doubt have accounted to some extent for the enormous crowd of pedestrians at the March 31, 1931, meet at Sussex Pad, Lancing, along with 58 motor cars and 14 horse-boxes. "Drew Withybed and small gorse on hill, then Passmore's sheep feed and Steep Down blank," ran Bob's Hunt Diary for the day:

> Drew Charles Phillips's and Lancing Clump, and to Phillips's end of Cissbury Side Hill. Sent Tim on to 'ride' that divides Wyatt's from Phillips's, and he viewed a fox over. Denton tried to get hounds on, but some hunted another fox back towards Steep Down. Denton put his lot on the fox Tim saw, and immediately all was confusion. Three foxes came away south over hill - two of them hunted by some hounds. The remainder of the pack continued alongside hill to west end, then they divided, one lot that we stayed with up over the Roman Encampment, the others turning back. We continued into the square covert south of hill, where Alf joined us with one and a half couple, making 8 couple in all. Turned west over the earth we dug last year, and started away well as if for Clapham Wood, across Cissbury Farm, ran into some roots and divided again, three couple going on down the main road, the remainder going for Cissbury. Pack with Denton. Alf tried to stop the others and brought on one and a half couple again.
>
> As we were crossing Cissbury Park, the hunted fox (1) was viewed away to Stump. Denton made a gallant effort to collect his remaining pack and get on to his fox. He got them and was carrying on, when they hit another line. All left him bar four and a half couple with which we hunted to Stump Bottom. This was hopeless: no hounds, no whips, everything confusion. Took our lot back to Cissbury Park and met Alf with six and a half couple. Another two couple came from side hill. Put them back into side hill from Cissbury end. Tim joined us with one and a half couple he had fetched from Lancing Clump. A brace of foxes came away over hill again and hounds ran nicely over the golf course and back to side hill where we could do no more. Drew Hay Rick and Piggery blank, and came home one and a half couple short. Went back in car to find one and collected a couple, and heard of another one on the way home. Dreadful day for the hunt servants.

Unusually for the Crawley and Horsham, they had a meet on May 2 in 1931. They normally finished in April. They were out on 132 days, killed 100 foxes, and only stopped for frost on eight days. The following year they had two Red Letter Days in quick succession. The first was after a meet at the Fox & Hounds at Horsham when they found at Dog Barking, and after an eventful hunt lost their fox at Hurston's Warren.

> This in an eight mile point from College Wood to end, and hounds, after leaving Lakenhurst Gorse, were ahead the whole way except when we cut them off at Broadford Bridge. They were not helped once from start to finish and did not appear too tired at the end after one hour 54 minutes continuous hunting… A great hunt.

War preparations in 1914. Horses about to be sent to Bob at Bridge where the Yeomanry was based.

Bob ready and prepared for the riding school, Sussex Yeomanry 1915.

The CO gets ready to start the tug-of-war.

The 4th (Reserve) Battalion, Royal West Kents, 1918.

Dudley wearing his Observer's wing in 1916.

A partridge shooting party ready to set off.

A break for a good lunch.

After lunch.

This took place with the Crawley & Horsham Hounds at Park Farm Henfield.

THE HUNT BALL SEASON.

First Nut. "IT'S MISS SMITH-BROWN. SHE'S ALL RIGHT—THEY'RE LOOKIN' AFTER HER."
Second Nut (pulling up). "GOOD GRACIOUS, MY DEAR CHAP, IT'S MY TANGO PARTNER!"

Overheard as the Field take their line from Park Farm,
Henfield. In 1914 the tango was all the rage.

A meet at Washington with Dick Kingsland as Huntsman, 1920.
Kingsland served for 30 years before retiring after a bad fall.

Will Hale and Harry Tyrell as whipper-in at Arundel station.

George Dean, 1st Whip, receiving a cheque for £500 from the late Master,
Colonel Godman. Lady Burrell with her daughter look on, 1921.

Mrs Colvin congratulates George Dean.

Going to draw. A huge field at the Twineham Grange meet.

Bert Peaker who moved to the Fernie after three years, with hounds at the "Tabby Cat". Peaker followed Will Hale as Huntsman.

Bob with Charles Denton near Arundel in the extreme west part of the country. Guy Cubitt, Joint Master, in mid-rear.

With Walter Batchelor, head groom.

Some of the Field follow the Master at Poling.

The C & H members outside West Grinstead Park in 1923.

Bob as High Sheriff.

Bob's withdrawal of his decision to give up the mastership of the Crawley and Horsham did not alter the fact he could not delay resigning much longer. In 1933 he made it known that he would stand down at the end of the season and would not be persuaded to continue under any circumstances.

The hunt committee proposed to give him a portrait, and made the rounds again collecting signatures and donations. Madge heard of the idea and became quite nervous that the fashionable portraitists would be incapable of rendering hunting pink correctly. A visit to the Summer Exhibition of the Royal Academy was not reassuring; "Pillar Box Red" and other critical comments she scribbled in the catalogue. Sir Merrik Burrell cut across these anxieties. "Don't worry, Mrs McKergow, we have already chosen the artist, Philip de Laszlo - can't beat him. He has fallen out with the Academy, so you won't see his pictures there. I will get you both over to dinner to meet him."

The dinner party duly took place with Bob in full splendour of pink evening tail coat, black breeches and stockings. The artist said very little until he raised his voice to announce, "Very well, I shall paint you - but not in that coat. If you bring it, I will bury it in the garden." That created quite a hub-bub, from which de Laszlo finally got the message that the portrait would represent the Master in actual hunting kit. All right, but "bring your oldest coat" was his final instruction.

The sitting took place in early 1934 in the artist's London studio. Perching on a stool and trying to look if he had a horse under him became thoroughly tiring, even though the flow of good stories about de Laszlo's famous sitters helped Bob to pass the time.

The presentation of the finished picture was dramatically handled by Sir Merrik Burrell. He brought it, carefully wrapped up, from his house to the Point-to-Point field, and had it placed in a small tent with a farm wagon alongside. The hunt servants took up position on each side as a sort of guard of honour. The principal actors ascended the wagon and complimentary speeches made, concluding with the unveiling of the portrait. All the while de Laszlo was filming these unusual proceedings.

When it was all over, they brought the portrait to Twineham Grange by van. William Worsfold (one time coachman, now chauffeur), helped. "What do you think of it, Worsfold?" someone asked. "When I sees 'im look like that, I 'ops it," was the reply. Actually the commission suited de Laszlo, who was particularly good at painting older people. The portrait of the 'Master' is quite subtle. The strength and determination is there but, rising 68, he is beginning to age and be less confident. That is surely right; the disastrous Graham Sutherland portrait of Winston Churchill gave us the ferocity of the war leader, while omitting the gracious and humorous side of the man that was so attractive to the public who followed his leadership in the war.

The retirement of the Master had been unthinkable in 1930, but nobody was worried now he had actually gone. Or had he? As it turned out, he exercised almost as much responsibility as before. Guy Cubitt told the hunt committee that he would be delighted to carry on as Master in the field, but could not undertake administration and, in particular, would not be responsible for the stud of 18 horses at the Kennels - a considerable financial burden. The committee settled matters by taking over these aspects of the mastership, and then electing Bob chairman.

That suited everyone, and the Crawley and Horsham Hunt continued to prosper.

~ 9 ~
Grange Nannies, Twineham Worthies, Bognor Holidays

The musical retelling of the children's story *Peter and the Wolf* has a moment near the end when the narrator stops the action, as it were, and carefully reminds us where the characters are. Grandfather is…, the little bird is…, Peter is…, the wolf is…. I intend doing the same thing in relation to the events from the end of the Great War in 1918, when Twineham Grange was properly opened up and it once more became the McKergow family home.

Bob was kept busy with the Crawley and Horsham Hunt. He was also able to buy the 160 acre Park Farm in Twineham which ensured no anti-hunting landowner would obstruct his passage. More to immediate advantage, he purchased a string of cottages in Wineham Lane that solved the problem of housing staff, and made it possible to have a butler for the first time. Doris dismissed all her wartime suitors and pursued a lively social life from home. John was finishing his time at Charterhouse and was looking forward to going to Sandhurst.

It was Doris who created the first stir in 1920 by marrying Kenneth Seth-Smith, whom the papers somehow failed to describe as 'a childhood sweetheart'. As seen, Kenneth returned to the Fighting Fifth after his recovery from the plane crash, and stayed on as a regular army officer in peace time. They were married in Twineham Church, and the papers were able to highlight the link between the two local sporting families of distinction.

In 1921 excitement returned as it became known that Doris had expectations of a first born; and also that her mother Madge, very unexpectedly, was also with child - at the age of 45. Doris came to the Grange for the happy event, and both ladies perspired in genteel fashion in an exceptional heat wave. Doris produced her daughter, Diana, first; and then, two days later, stimulated by the fuss, Madge had a son.

This is the point at which the writer has to admit that he was that son, and Bob and Madge have to become Father and Mother. The memoir must now assume an element of autobiography, but my purpose is primarily to describe my father's conduct of events, in which I sometimes played a part.

Nurse Coleman took charge for a few weeks after my birth, and was always on call to come and look after anyone in later years. A boisterous and cheerful character, she inspired great confidence and devotion.

It is difficult for anyone growing up in the last 50 years to understand the conventions of child-rearing in a household like Twineham Grange in the years following the Great War.

A Nanny would take charge of the nursery and the night nursery where the child or children would live. The mother would visit once or twice a day. Friends and relatives in the early days visited the house for afternoon tea on a Sunday, and would then expect the baby to be brought down and admired. As the child grew older, special toys and games were kept in the drawing room to make this weekly event something to look forward to.

A nurse would, of course, take her charge out for a walk in the pram each day. Meals were brought to the nursery by the between-maid - the Tweenie. As the child became more active, it was permissible to wander round the passages and rooms of the first floor, but not to go downstairs on your own. I can remember building a steeplechase course out of toys in the long passage with Nanny Howe watching. In the next stage nanny could be abandoned and the garden explored, only accompanied by a dog. When a governess succeeded the nanny on the child reaching the age of six or seven years old, the nursery became the school room where arithmetical tables were learnt as well as the rudiments of spelling, reading and writing. Meals were generally taken in the (main) dining room at this stage.

In wandering about the house, stables and garden, one met some very cheerful and helpful people - the servants. It is supposed to be very bad form to spend much time talking about servants, as it may appear to be a form of boasting, but in all sincerity the long-serving senior men and women were totally part of the establishment, and also liked having your company.

Moorey, the head housemaid, loved babies and children; Aldred, the butler, followed the horse racing scene; Dan Newman, second gardener, was never known to miss a marauding blackbird at fifteen feet with his catapult; George King, third gardener, attracted the company of dogs; Walter Batchelor, stud groom, knew all about cats and their nine lives. There was enough entertainment round the house to last a lifetime. In the holidays Moorey, Mrs Golledge the cook and of course the nurses, liked to send and receive postcards. One which Moorey sent to me from Bognor read:

> Dear Master Peter
> I thank you so very much for your nice P.C. to me. I was pleased to see that you were nearly able to swim.

From Lewes she wrote:

> Dear Little Master Peter
> I hope you are quite well. I am having such a nice holiday. I am going to Eastbourne tomorrow with Betty.

Nobody could be as flattering as Nanny Webb, however

Dear Peter

I am sorry I was not able to get your tools but it rained hard all the morning and the shops were closed in the afternoon. I went to Barden to see Battle but he was poorly and today I went to Ambleside to see little Kit Wilson but he is not half such a nice boy as you are now. With tons of love from Lallie. Give my love to Moorey.

The tools are a mystery. I was just rising four at the time. Moorey was possibly standing in as part-time Nanny. Nanny Howe, who succeeded Lallie, left a memory of efficiency without getting involved, although one or two postcards suggest this is unfair.

My dear Peter

I am having a real good time here (Scarborough) and have got you a nice fishing rod. I hope you are a good boy and not forget your Nanny.

It is possible that this was a rod I used in later years when fishing under the supervision of Worsfold. If so, Nanny Howe had been as thoughtful as anyone could expect.

The season of good cheer could be discerned as on the way when the slate slabs of the larder suddenly filled up with glorious mounds of geese, turkeys and cockerels. The chauffeurs and van driver spent several days taking them out to the people named on the labels, who were generally those who had been particularly helpful to the Crawley and Horsham Hunt. The drivers, according to one farmer's wife, were not always very cheery; one got the impression that they thought the gov'nor was being over-generous.

As Christmas Eve approached, the shelves filled again in preparation for the ceremony of presenting the male staff with the constituent parts of a good Christmas dinner. Each man received a joint of home-reared beef, a Christmas pudding made by Mrs Golledge, a packet of tea and a bottle of port. The men assembled in ones and twos, well before the appointed hour, under the stairs and in the passage from the back door. Now was the chance for the butler to show off. The farm men were astonished to see this cheeky fellow marching about as if he owned the place, taking off his jacket, putting it on again, letting the door bang and God knows what. Surely the Gov'nor would have something to say! Butlers, who in former days ladled out the squire's soup on these occasions with due sarcasm, as a breed were not popular. In any case, they were despised for having a soft job. In defence, it can be said that the manservant did duty for many hours longer than the farm man, and when the master and mistress went out to dinner, he had to stay on duty until they came back. Our man, Aldred, was not personally unpopular as he liked a drink in the pub with the villagers, but he could rather put on airs - or so they thought.

The family then appeared, led by Father, in solemn step. John Sayers, farm foreman, came in view to act as M.C. and called the first name: "Will, Sir." This was his brother, the senior carter. As an ex-service man of the Great War, Will stood stiffly in front of the table, opening his canvas bag to have the joint of beef rammed home by Father, the pudding in its white cloth and bowl handed over by Mother, followed by the tea and the port. Will took one step back, came to attention and declaimed, "Wish you all a Merry Christmas and a Happy New Year." "And to you, Will," we said, "and to your wife and family."

Next to be called was Sid Walder who had fed the bullock for the past three months. "Ah, Sid," said Father, "do you recognise him now?" "No sir, no." "Well, do you think he will eat well?" "Should do sir, should do." "I think you're right, open up your bag."

In terms of smartness, nobody could beat Walter Batchelor, head groom. The white cloths were ironed to knife edge creases, completely ignored by Father who thumped the joint down scattering bloody patches everywhere. After 15 men had passed through, John Sayers stood on his own by the stair. "Is that the lot, John?" Father would enquire. "Yes, sir." John could then come forward and collect his own provisions and, as he disappeared to the back door, Father could remark, "Well that's that then. Half a minute, there's some beef and a pudding still here."

"That's mine, sir," the butler would say, darting out of his pantry as though on a spring. "Ah yes, so it is," Father would respond. "Take it with you when you go." The butler never got wished a Merry Christmas.

Christmas Day followed the usual pattern. Presents at the bedside brought by Father Christmas, Church, Christmas lunch, more presents off the tree in the drawing room and a chance to play the games that had been discovered under their wrappings. At some fairly relaxed stage, Moorey would appear at the door. "Excuse me, the Servants Hall, M'm. They would like you to see their presents." So we all immediately followed her along to the room off the back hall where the servants had their meals and which they used as a sitting room. By tradition the Servants Hall belonged to the servants, and no one else could go in unless invited. If the rain came in or the wall paper flaked off, the mistress would be asked to inspect and suggest the repairs, but in her normal visits to the kitchen and pantry the Servants Hall was by-passed. The main instigators of the Christmas invitation were the young kitchen maid and parlour maids. They had given each other presents, Moorey and Mrs Golledge had given presents to them, they had... it was a complicated roundabout affair and the cause of much excitement as the packets were opened. To round it off, Moorey would have said, "You are lucky. I expect you would like the Colonel and Mrs McKergow to see your presents."

So we moved slowly round peering at the pile on the sewing machine, the pile on the side table, the pile on the book case and several more. Original comments were difficult to formulate as every pile seemed to consist of warm underwear, stockings and handkerchiefs. The butler had to make it clear he was not part of this nonsense. "Don't know what they have done to deserve all this, madam," he would remark from his fireside chair. Mother put him right in a few words, and we could depart expressing every good wish to all.

Every week all the clocks in the house and the tower clock in the stables were wound and regulated by Mr Atkins, Clockmaker of Burgess Hill. It sounds ridiculous, but at a time when wrist watches were uncommon, the clock on the mantelpiece of every room ruled the day and all had to tell the same time. The embarrassment would be acute if guests were not ready for dinner when the gong sounded, because the clock in their bedroom was slow. Very few people had the correct time in the days before wireless, but Atkins, with his shop near the station, could use the station clock as his regulator - a single time which was 'right' for the whole of Britain came into being because the railways could not operate without one.

Atkins's visits to Twineham Grange worried him because he hated the idea of interrupting people. He disliked winding the schoolroom clock while I was having a lesson. On the other hand, I enjoyed the distraction. He would knock nervously and then appear round the door clutching the housemaid's steps. "Excuse me - the clock - wind the clock," he would say in a low voice. "Please come in, Mr Atkins," the governess would respond. He then had to find a path round the chairs, leaving the rocking horse on his right, and finish up in front of the fire. Next, he had to extend the steps which creaked and cracked disturbingly. "Sorry - the steps," he would whisper. Next he had to climb the steps - more apologies - and extract his pocket watch from his waistcoat - more apologies - and adjust the hands. By this time I had lost all contact with the important addition and subtraction I was supposed to be doing, and got a reminder from the governess. But I could hardly concentrate while the actual winding went on, followed by the descent, the folding of the steps and Mr Atkins's attempt to depart in silence.

The explosion of aircraft noise immediately overhead on a quiet summer's afternoon meant only one thing - the Fleet Air Arm preparing for a private display. Pel Clark, a Laing relation, served as a pilot on the early carriers, *Glorious* and *Furious*, and whenever his ship was near Portsmouth he took the opportunity to fly over the Grange in the company of another pilot, with the purpose of stirring up Father. It was all straightforward aerobatics initially.

We watched dives, climbs, looping-the-loop and rolls standing in front of the house, but then had to follow the two biplanes down to the stables to get a view of their next trick. The machines turned, and came down within a few feet of the ground. Then, slowing to walking pace, or so it seemed, with wheels brushing the grass, the intrepid aviators squeezed between two oak trees with only a foot or two to spare. They recovered a bit of height and turned threateningly in our direction. We realised we were the perfect targets, framed in the gates of the stable yard.

Cramming on every ounce of speed the planes sped fast and low towards us. Father dodged and weaved, but was too late to escape, and he finally had to turn his back and duck as the attackers appeared likely to fly into the yard and bring the clock tower down in ruins. But instead of an explosion, we heard a scream of engines as the pilots climbed safely away. We watched, decidedly shaken as the planes motored slowly back overhead and, with a waggle of wings, left in the direction of Portsmouth.

Father stumped back to the house muttering. "Damned young idiots. They'll be the death of us one day. I'll have to write to their C O." He never did.

An Italian accordionist seems an unlikely protégé for Father and no explanation ever came my way. It would seem that Monty entertained the holidaymakers on Brighton front in summer, but had difficulty in raising enough cash on which to survive in winter. Father organised a round of houses for him, at which he could play and be certain of a decent tip.

So, on a dull Friday morning in mid-winter I would be at my sums again in the school room, when there would be a flourish of accordion chords from outside which resolved into a Sousa march. Monty stationed himself in the lea of a shrubbery with his bicycle propped against a tree. Operatic selections followed, and I could then scurry down to the Hall, pick up two half-crowns and actually hand them over to the maestro. He had a pleasant smile, but we did not speak.

Before the Great War, a Village Flower Show had become an annual event in Twineham. It had attracted comment in 1911 when the young Rector acted as gateman and was classed as 'a man of the people' in the local paper. After the war, Father persuaded Mr Harris of Harris's Amusements to support the show with his roundabout, swings and traditional side-shows. Why Mr Harris should contemplate coming to such a small event was never gone into - it just happened.

As Commandant of the Show, Father had to ensure Harris came the previous evening and set-up in the right places. We made our way down to the field at the bottom of the garden after tea and checked the position of the marquee that would hold the exhibits the next day. That done, we waited for the Amusements to arrive. The outrider was Harris himself. We would be aware of something similar to a wardrobe moving slowly along the other side of the hedge. Harris and his roundabout organ, mounted on a pony-drawn flat truck, was about to enter. He did not allow anyone else to be in charge of the precious instrument. Soon the sound of steam engines could be heard, which speeded up as they descended the dip in the farm road. Then it was silence as the drivers engaged low gear, followed by furious puffing up the hill and a more measured entrance into the field. Father was satisfied, and we could return to the house.

Next morning the marquee was crowded with exhibitors putting their vegetables on to the staging. The Grange head gardener usually looked pleased with himself, because he was the only professional who could include peaches, grapes and hothouse figs in his fruit collection, and therefore be sure of the first prize.

Mother improved the attendance by arranging a garden party and tennis tournament for the afternoon. The At Home cards she sent to friends carried the words 'Village Flower Show' in one corner and 'Tennis Tournament Arranged' in another. In other words, don't bring your racquet unless invited. Her tennis tournaments, organised through the summer, were popular because she was a charming hostess and also an efficient organiser. The doubles partners were arranged in advance, with the ineffectual girl paired off with a man who could win a few points and, of course, vice versa. A Round Robin Tournament chart gave the order of play, and Mother presided at a table pouring out lemonade, entering the score of completed sets and despatching players to the courts. The couple winning most sets got a prize. On Flower Show day, she had to depute someone to run the tennis to allow her to greet the guests as they arrived at the house. Harris had his Roundabout going, which encouraged the visitors to head in the right direction. Nobody would say 'spend, spend, spend', but it would be apparent to all that this is what they were supposed to do.

In the year of the General Strike (1926) the Show was hit by the threat of a last minute 'down tools' by the men who ran the sideshows for Harris. Father relished the idea of personally saving the day. He appeared dramatically at the front door dressed in his loudest check plus-four suit, with a cartridge bag slung over his shoulder. Mother was astonished. "What are you doing, Bob?" "Doing?" he said "Doing? Why I am going on the Coconut Shy." "You can't do that," she said in exasperation. "Of course I can," he replied, "I know what they say - ROLL, BOWL OR PITCH, A PENNY A SHY." This expression of stage cockney alarmed Mother even more, but a messenger panted up the path to report that the strike was off. Father had missed his chance of starring as a showman.

In my younger days I would be escorted down to the field to try and win a prize on the Hoop-la and Rolling Pennies. Nothing could compare with the Roundabouts and its Galloping Horses. At one moment you would be in front of the organ getting the full blast of *My Blue Heaven* and spotting the little figures drumming away, and the next you would be watching young Harris poking small pieces of coal into the firebox of the steam engine that powered the Roundabout and, very important, gave the whistle that signalled the start of the ride. After tea, the organ would be silenced to let the prize-giving start. Two or three men dominated the Cottagers Classes, and tramped up and down to receive their envelopes of prize money. Finally, the overall champion was announced, who proudly walked up to receive a garden tool from Mother.

It sounds harmless fun, but the serious competitors geared the whole of their year's vegetable gardening to produce exhibits of top quality on the day of the show. If last year's champion was defeated, he would complain that he would have won if the judge had given him first prize for carrots which, in his opinion, he was entitled to. More seriously, rumours sometimes circulated to the effect that the winner of the cucumber class, for example, had no cucumber plants in his garden. The villagers who were not Show enthusiasts enjoyed spreading suspicion.

After the prize giving the fun of the fair started again, but I would soon be on my way to supper and bed. Sleep never came quickly, as the Roundabout Organ played on and on. It was *My Blue Heaven* again, and in my imagination I saw the electric light sparkling above the Galloping Horses.

Geoffrey Sparrow, sportsman, artist and historian, was asked to provide a hunting picture for reproduction in the 1939 Hunt Ball menu folder. He drew a sketch of Jim Heffer advising Charles Denton where to find a fox and accompanied it by a doggerel.

At Billsborough near Henfield town
There lives a worthy of renown
Jim Heffer is the name he bears,
and he's a man that has no airs
or graces either, for that matter:
There's no one claims to be his hatter.
He lays where he can find a bed
In haystack barn or open shed:

or else, in any sort of weather
He may be found among the heather.
He knows the country all around
and where good foxes may be found,
He hears the gossip in the towns
and what is doing on the Downs.
He knows who put a fox away
and has a poultry claim to pay!
In fact he is a fund of knowledge
as if he'd been three years at college!
For over 30 years they say
His Holloa's been heard when a fox goes away.
He never seems to be out of place
Or in front of Charlie to "Pook" his face!

The verse covers most of what can be said about him; he did wander around and he was totally dedicated to foxhunting. He normally slept in barns by permission of the farmer. This is in itself extraordinary, as it seems incredible that anyone could allow a tramp (not entirely a fair description) to lodge on and off in the same building with half his corn crop and several tons of hay stored there. But Heffer, and a few others like him, were totally trusted and they never burnt a building down or did any damage.

To impart his information, Jim relied on the apparently casual meeting. Taking his hounds towards a covert one day for the first draw, Denton came across him leaning on a gate. The old boy came to the point quickly. That covert where he was heading for, he told Denton, had not carried a fox for weeks. But the little Shaw on the left, and the old hedges leading to it, were worth a try. A dog fox lay there - pretty certain.

His approach to Father was similar. Almost on the dot of 9 o'clock, when most of us were finishing breakfast, Father would exclaim, "There's Jim Heffer." Sure enough, the unmistakable figure of the informer would be striding up the Park, several layers of coat flapping, the unbelievably whiskery face thrust forward and the trademark bowler hat, green with algae, pulled down to his ears. Father would jump up from the table and set off across the lawn, arms waving to attract attention. On one occasion he found he had his dinner napkin still in one hand and had to stow it away in a pocket. Heffer, who had timed his appearance perfectly, seemed a little surprised to see the Master, but was pleased to stop on the other side of the ha-ha fence and have a chat.

What they discussed was never repeated, but Sparrow's verse is a good guide. Firstly, which keepers were putting foxes away - no Christmas presents for them; and secondly, where to draw to be fairly sure of a 'find'. Some silver sailed across the ha-ha, and Heffer was soon out of sight.

There is a true story of two little girls who used to dare each other to cut across the field and see if Mr Heffer was in his barn. As they peered through the crack in the door, the tension was almost unbearable. Mr Heffer was never at home, but they would dash for safety regardless, giggling uncontrollably. The point is that they knew perfectly well that Jim Heffer would never hurt them.

When the 'worthy' died, the local paper gave him the privilege of an obituary column and called him Mr Heffern, which suggests contact with the Sussex dialect. Confusion over his name seems appropriate for someone who could never be tied down to time or place - nor evidently by name.

The pitch that George King had laid down in the Park survived the war years and came back into use in the 1920s. A number of village sides began to play on their recreation fields; Twineham just had a square in a grass field kept for hay. So they could not have any Home matches until the hay was cut and carried in July. It was not plain sailing then, as grazing cattle could easily get through the floppy wire fence and, in a wet summer, the grass outside the square would be several inches long. The square was mown, but it was difficult to get the bullocks' feet marks levelled out. So batsmen needed a good eye to keep the erratic ball out, and a powerful lofted stroke to make the ball bounce out of the grass.

Father would pull a cane chair from the porch and seat himself near the ha-ha to give advice. All teams needed a fast bowler to upset the opposition, and Twineham always had a man who could bang the ball in short. He got results, aided by the pitch. The hoof marks made the ball fly in all directions, and soon one made a direct hit to the ribs or, even worse, to the elbow, of the visiting batsman. When hurt, the Sussex villager of that time collapsed, rolled and twisted on the ground as dramatically as any Italian footballer. Father enjoyed the spectacle. "THAT'S IT - ROLL ABOUT," he would roar. "RUB IT WITH A BRICK." It was real attacking play by the home team, but the visitors all too often had men with enough technique to apply bat to ball. A good hit over square leg, and two bounces into the bottom of the hedge, would bring several fielders to the spot and shouts of "Lost ball!", which the batsmen did not hear, or were conveniently late in picking up after running five or six. The team's score began to look uncomfortably high. Sixty-one for five, and one good hitter still at the crease. Twineham did not usually reach that total.

One year the King's Cup Air Race stopped the match. During the afternoon, the sky became almost crowded with two-seater bi-planes making from west to east at various heights, and a few showing signs of non-airworthiness. One, with much popping and banging, slowly descended in the area of the brook. Both teams left the pitch and disappeared over the hedge in search of the plane. After half an hour or so, the engine was heard to start and the competitor took off. We heard from the players that the 'aviators' had cleaned up the engine, and then asked them to push the plane to the far end of the field to allow room for take-off. The flimsy machine had not appealed to the players. "Wouldn't go up in a thing like that for all the money in the world."

Some more usual afternoon arrivals were young couples with prams. The Park, after suffering several visits from the hunt during the winter, was heavily rutted. It could only be negotiated by the husband pulling the pram from the front, and the wife pushing from the back. An ex-parlourmaid often turned up on these occasions and, when tea was brought out from the stables, the couple manhandled pram and baby to the drive and went round to the back door of the Grange. Moorey's delight then resounded through the house. "Oh my dear, what a darling, the dear little mite! Oh I am glad you came." "Mrs McKergow will want to see you."

The action was suspended while Moorey hurried to the morning room. "Excuse me, but (Alice/Ellen/Betty/or whoever) is here M'm, with her baby, and oh, it is a dear little thing." So mother congratulated the parents on the health of the child, the excellent layette and the smart pram. After the seal of approval was given, Moorey asked them in for tea. The husband tended to hang back while all the baby talk went on, and had to be reminded. "You come in for a cuppa' tea, Mr Er-rer" (Moorey could never remember the husband's name). The kitchen maid was told to put the kettle on and bring the Servants Hall plum cake. It is likely that the visitors saw very little of the cricket thereafter.

Back in his chair Father could only watch and groan as the Twineham batsmen trooped in and out. Twenty-five for five in reply to eighty something meant defeat. The Twineham umpire did his best. A ball thudding into the pads after a missed swipe brought a confident appeal. "How was it, umpire?" "Not out." The Umpire had no hesitation. "What? Umpire!" the fielders shouted in disgust. "Not out." 'Break ball' was the verdict. The fielders would have liked to have explained the rules of cricket to the umpire, but the voice from the lawn demanded more action. "PLAY UP, GO ON, PLAY UP." So the batsman obtained his reprieve, probably for only a short time. When a ball was smacked into the outfield, bouncing about like a demented rabbit, Father expected vigorous running from the batsmen. "RUN UP, RUN UP," he shouted and, when the fielder got a hand on the ball, "AND ONE FOR THE THROW." Somewhere in the mid-forties the innings folded, and Father returned to the house dragging the cane chair behind him. Disappointing obviously, but a win would come one day.

"Mr Sayers is here, sir." Moorey, looking as though Methuselah had called, hovered anxiously at the bedroom door. Father's attacks of gout were sufficiently severe to induce what would probably now be described as septicaemia. Eventually the fever subsided and, although still in pain from the inflammation, he would decide he ought to find out what was happening on the farm. John Sayers, foreman since the early years of the century, was sent for.

"Send him up." As John emerged into the corridor, he looked odd without his usual hazel stick, and seemed uncertain whether to step on the carpet pattern or avoid putting a foot on it. Father looked exhausted. "Come in, come in John," he murmured. "Sit ye down. I'm no sense, no sense at all. Can't sleep for the pain." "No, sir?" John took it calmly, and then said the wrong thing altogether. "Thought you might be out with the hunt soon, sir." "Hunt! No chance of that, can't get a shoe on, let alone a boot. No idea when I can get on a horse - you can forget that." Then, expecting to learn nothing good about the farm, he continued, "It's rained ever since I've been up here, so I expect the men haven't turned a wheel and the horses are eating their heads off."

"No sir, no. We drilled the 7 acre yesterday."

Father was horrified. "Drilled did you say? Smarmed is more like. We shall never see a damned thing out of that." John remained calm, "It didn't go in too bad, sir. A fair season for the time of year".

"Can't understand it. Have you been to market? Did you sell anything?"

"Yes sir, sold a bobby calf from Herrings."

"How much?"

"Ten shillings, sir."

"Good God. That's nothing."

"Bought a good red calf with a bit of age about him, sir."

"How much for that?"

"Two pound, ten, sir."

"I'll be ruined at this rate"

"Mr 'odgson reckoned it was a fair price, sir."

"Mr Hodgson is a wealthy man, I'm not."

John invariably sat on a chair that let him look out on the corridor. Anyone passing, while these exchanges were going on, received what looked suspiciously like a wink. One could never be sure; John was concentrating on the next salvo.

Mothers with a full domestic staff did not go on holiday with their small children. Families in the top drawer of wealth and position had their house by the sea where the nannies and the children would have to spend weeks at a time. The less well-off booked into 'rooms' that provided all meals. The Rock Gardens terrace filled this need at Bognor. Nearness to the sea always came top of the list and, at Rock Gardens, you only had to cross a private ash road, skirt some dejected tamarisk bushes and you were there on the promenade.

Bognor was a marvellous place for children. At high tide the waves bounced and scrabbled on the shingle but, very soon, the first sand appeared. In no time the sea was retreating fast, leaving endless scope for sand castles and for exploring the pools round the breakwaters. Mother broke convention and came with us, sleeping in a brass bedstead and tolerating the dull food and dreary surroundings. The bow window to the north had never been cleaned. It is surprising we could all fit in, as Doris's children Diana and Mervyn came with their nanny, and another friend had his nanny in attendance. Most of the parents of the other groups in residence in the terrace came for a lobster lunch at the Royal Norfolk Hotel, and left for home after a decent interval of children's games. When we were all old enough not to have nannies and governesses in tow, our Bognor holidays went up several grades. Father decided he would take charge.

His conversion to the idea of fun at the seaside followed one of his rare visits to Rock Gardens when we put a dish of shrimps on the table for tea. We caught them, we explained, by pushing our nets along the sand in shallow water. Father realised that, if he hired a full sized net, the catch would increase excitingly. So it was soon settled - he would lead the shrimping expeditions next year, but only from a decent house near the sea. When the time came, we found we were living in Cecil Sharp's house at Aldwick, and very comfortable and convenient it turned out to be. As the pioneer collector and arranger of English Folk songs, Sharp might have been expected him to leave evidence of his musical attainments about the house but, apart from a good wind-up gramophone, the only personal memento was a collage caricature of the Cecil Sharp Quartet in the W.C.

We travelled down in two cars, with a van following carrying Mrs Golledge and a maid plus bedding and food supplies. The first evening must have been one of the best ever, with the garden to explore, the hard tennis court to test and the way down to the sea to find. The first morning was given over to a visit to Little Hawkes. Hawkes had joined the Yeomanry well before the War and risen to the rank of Quartermaster Sergeant in Father's unit. After the war he received a loan from Findlater Mackie & Co to start up a grocer's shop in Bognor. He hardly counted as a protégé of Father's, but it was right to patronise his shop for old times' sake. Advance notice as to when this important visit would occur filtered through, and Hawkes came to the door immediately the car drew up. He did not actually salute. but ushered his old CO (and the CO's lady) into the shop with respectful courtesy. "What have you got, Hawkes?" Father would ask with military brusqueness. "This Wiltshire ham is excellent, sir." "I'll have it."

Father snapped up most of the offerings that followed, and then asked mother to continue. When everyone had run out of ideas, Hawkes would say, "I'll get the boy to bring it over straight away. A great pleasure to see you sir - madam."

We were hardly back at the house before the unfortunate boy pedalled erratically up to the entrance, his huge delivery basket overflowing with provisions and barely able to keep the bike upright.

The daily shrimping session, tennis, visits to the cinema and concert parties entertained Father as much as ourselves, and we seemed set to repeat the holiday at our comfortable base. It turned out to have a snag. One of the most distinguished families in the county had a house and garden bounded by the sea wall and, what was worse, an inadequate hedge bordering the path to the beach. In brief, when Father set out for shrimping in khaki shorts he could be observed. For someone in his position this counted as a social gaffe. There was nothing for it but to find a house with private access to the beach and that, we found, was a rarity unless you were the Royal Family in need of sea air after illness. Even then, George V did not enjoy his substandard convalescent residence, just up the road from us. We did get our bit of sea wall and gate to the shingle, but the cottage adapted from stables had a damp problem, and Mrs Golledge with helper had to sleep in something like a chicken house. But Father felt he had essential privacy, and the other reservations were put on one side for a few years.

Wet days meant finding entertainment off the beach. On one occasion we were taken to Butlin's Menagerie on the sea front. A bare building had some parrots and macaws on perches mixed in with cages of small animals. A black monkey with a long tail sat on a log labelled 'Gorilla'. In pre-Attenborough days we were not quite sure if this was right or wrong. Not much to keep us there, so we marched into the amusement hall next door. It was totally deserted, except for the youths in grubby white coats manning the stalls.

Father decided we should play Rolling Pennies and put half a crown on the board. "Give me change, please." The youth pulled his left hand from the overall pocket and with his right thumb flicked quickly over the left hand. A fountain of 30 pennies arched upwards and clattered down in front of us. None of us expected such sleight of hand, but Father immediately got us rolling the pennies down the chutes and on to the board marked off in squares of different values. Someone soon shouted, "A six! I've got a six!" The custodian of the pennies would have none of it. "Doesn't count," he said: "It's touching the line." Father could only protest, "That's a bit hard." Then there was a claim for tuppence which got approved and the two pennies delivered by the same route. Father kept up a loud commentary on our efforts. "Too far, too short, that's a good-un, go for the six, miles out."

Outside, the holidaymakers drifted past the entrance. Some then seemed to back pedal and take a cautious peep at what was going on. There was no time for us to stare. We had to keep the pennies rolling. However we did become aware of strangers rolling pennies on our stall. Father eventually announced he was broke, and we would have to go home. Looking round, we saw that the place was really busy. Every sideshow had customers. Quite unintentionally Father's shouted encouragements had acted as a fairground barker's spiel! The youth in the white coat waved a battered toffee tin at us. "With the compliments of the management, sir." At the cottage we opened the tin. It contained screwed up newspaper with a handful of toffees on the top. We were most disappointed, but Father just laughed.

Hitler put a stop to the Aldwick holidays. In 1938 we sat beside our portable wireless in the sitting room of Garage Cottage listening to the development of a European crisis that could have ended as war. Then the nice Mr Chamberlain pulled off a diplomatic masterstroke that settled the dispute. Herr Hitler also promised to be good in future.

There was huge relief, but few people regarded the outcome as anything else than a temporary reprieve. Father, prompted by Mother, decided to take a modern house for next year's summer holiday, and wisely included a clause in the agreement that allowed him to withdraw In the Event of War or Rumours of War. In August 1939 he wrote to the agent cancelling the booking. Even the agent agreed it was a justifiable decision.

The Twenties and Thirties were marked by an increase in community activity. Those that led the way had their hands full, but it would be a mistake to assume that all ladies of independent means filled their days with voluntary work. Many of them kept well away.

Mother founded Twineham Women's Institute in 1921 and remained president for the rest of its existence. At one time it was fashionable to laugh at the W.I. with its tendency to organise pointless competitions such as a flower arrangement in an egg cup, but in the 1920s it provided a splendid social club for village women who, up to then, had no place to meet except the pub, and very few of them wanted to get involved there.

Mother gave a lead, and spent many hours making the soft toys, jam etc that the demonstrators decreed. The Institute were invited to meet in local gardens in summer and occasionally had coach trips to, for example, the Empire Exhibition at Wembley. The annual meeting of the Federation at the Albert Hall had excellent press coverage, but at the village level the members were far more interested in a nice cup of tea and a chat.

The Jazz Age had even less to do with social concerns. It is a bit mysterious how jazz percolated into villages. Dudley's letters from the Front recorded the great popularity of 'coon' songs in 1916/17. Dance halls became popular among returning officers and their friends in the 1920s. It is possible that small towns put on public dances at very cheap rates. The boys from the villages drifted in and became hooked on the fascinating rhythm. Whatever the reason youngsters demanded village dances.

To their credit the ladies who were running the Women's Institute, the Church and everything else, got out their violins, opened their pianos and tried to get the hang of the new tunes for the Foxtrot and Quick Step. One of the keen dancers of that period remarked with a grin in later years, "We must have been mad! We cycled miles to get to dances." The fathers of the village girls who begged to be allowed to go in were warned, "Now then my gal, you can go to the dance but only till 10 o'clock mind." Regrettably, Twineham Jazz Band never got anywhere near the top of the league. They could only muster a pianist, a violinist and a drummer. The customers pointed out that without a saxophone it was not a proper Jazz Band, so the outfit did not last all that long.

Talking Pictures finally killed the dances. It was almost compulsory for every male teenager to join the gang at the Orion, Burgess Hill on Saturday night for the latest epic. On Monday morning they were anxious to tell their elders on the farm what had happened to the old Indian Chief and the cavalry. "Lot of nonsense, boy; don't pay no attention to it." The boys with designs on the pub kept faith with the films until their 18th birthday - and then deserted Hollywood for good.

The relief of need in the community was still locally based to a significant degree. The direct feeding of the village poor by private soup kitchens had gone, and people like Mr Jago of Burgess Hill, who had pestered Father to take part in his theatricals in the 1880s, were now doing it for fun and not, as Mr Jago advertised, for the support of the poor. People still got into physical and moral trouble, and local committees raised money to put some sort of service in place. Mother belonged to both the District Nursing Committee and the Hurst Ruri-Decanal Branch of the Chichester Diocesan Purity Association - a quite splendidly titled body of which she was chairman for many years.

The *Mid Sussex Times* in 1925 wrote of the work of the Branch in dramatic terms :

In College Lane, Hurstpierpoint, there is a small house known as Shenley Cottage, where two hard-working Church Army Sisters act as godmothers to girls (often little more than children) who have become tarnished by contact with evil. Quietly and unobtrusively the Sisters carry on their noble work, bravely facing sordid facts and untold difficulties, dispelling ugliness by the magic of never-failing cheeriness and kind deeds, restoring self-respect and instilling a high ideal by their personal example. …not only to look after their 'family' at the 'shelter' (which not infrequently includes infants and wayward girls who require even more attention), but they journey on bicycles to distant parts of their district, face interviews of the most unpleasant kind, appear in police courts, attend all sorts of meetings, and yet still find time for needlework and cooking and all the hundred and one duties which the running of even an ordinary household involves.

The article's real purpose was to encourage gifts of money to pay for the purchase of the Shelter and the adjoining cottage, to be followed by the conversion of both properties into a more convenient centre. "The debt incurred," the article continued, "is a public debt of honour, since it is incurred in the best interests of the public, and it means the rubbing away of stains on souls meant to be white, the helping of fellow human beings wounded in the battle of life."

The work they did was similar to that of many other organisations looking after girls with illegitimate babies, who were often outcasts and needed temporary accommodation while a job was found for them and the baby adopted. I wonder if the committee meetings of the Hurst Ruri-Decanal Branch of The Chichester Diocesan Purity Association were among those that created something of a trial for the Sisters!

Later the Branch changed its name to Moral Welfare, that had less Victorian overtones, and then to Family Social Work, which conveniently abandoned the labelling of their clients as impure and 'sinners'. In fact Barnardos, and others in the field, all went out of their way to look after single mothers, broken families and children in the community, to emphasise they were no different from anyone else in any respect. No labels should be stuck on them, they said.

The District Nursing Association put that legendary figure The District Nurse on the road, looking after those who might never have medical assistance. To start with, she did her visiting on her bicycle until she was provided with a car. The cost of the car and the bills for petrol and repairs were a constant worry for the committee, and often made relations with the Nurse somewhat strained.

Country areas in the 1920s were enlivened in summer by army manoeuvres. Instead of using Salisbury Plain, the generals tried to simulate a battle around the lanes, woods and pastures of some convenient county - Sussex for instance. Father, as a Retired Lieutenant-Colonel, took part as an umpire and rushed about with a white armband emblazoned with a crown.

It must have been impossible to decide who was winning. The car owning families who clogged the roads at meets of the Crawley and Horsham Hunt, loaded up their children and went in search of the military action. One day a very large piece of artillery was spotted in a field near Cowfold, but disappointed the spectators by not firing any blanks. The Royal Tank Corps parked in a field at Hickstead and were highly co-operative. Endless children were lowered through the hatch to see the inside and twirl the brass wheels of the guns. A complete Highland Regiment with Pipe Band playing marched west up Bob Lane, and the Horse Artillery rattled eastwards. Puffs of smoke and feeble bangs confirmed that they were in action near Hurstpierpoint. Anything less like war would be difficult to find.

When the Depression struck in the late nineteen twenties and early thirties, Findlater Mackie & Co, the family firm, were not equipped to survive. John, on his return from the army, bought a new bottling plant that reduced labour costs, but the loss making pubs would have wiped out the company if it had not been sold to Fremlins, the Maidstone brewers. The loss of income and capital turned out to be manageable and, on the other side of the coin, Father had more time to attend to public work, especially after he gave up being MFH of the Crawley and Horsham

Hunt. In 1933 he became High Sheriff of Sussex; a role he thoroughly enjoyed.

The ancient office of High Sheriff could be seen as largely ceremonial, but some genuine responsibility had to be exercised. The person chosen by the monarch in the 1930s had to:

(a) Deliver the prisoners to the Assize Court for trial. Assizes were held three times a year in Lewes.
(b) Ensure that the Judge's Lodgings were in good repair and staffed.
(c) Accompany the Judge to Court.
(d) Ensure an ample supply of Whisky in the Judge's retiring Room.
(e) Engage Pierrepoint the Hangman to carry out executions.
(f) Attend executions (delegated to Arthur Farndell, Under Sheriff)
(g) Appoint a Chaplain to preach at the Assize Service.

The judicial process saw that the Assize proceeded smoothly without the active intervention of the High Sheriff, but some flair could be shown in the way he carried out his duties. The Sussex Assize was held in the county town of Lewes.

Father booked a horse-drawn coach to convey the judge from his lodgings to the parish church, and thence to the court on the first day. It was frustrating to receive an instruction from on high thereafter, forbidding the use of coaches in view of the national economic circumstances. A suitable limousine could be regarded as an adequate substitute. The judge therefore found himself motoring slowly along with two mounted trumpeters from the cavalry riding in front. At the entrance to the court they drew on one side and sounded a salute. As the assize judge on this first occasion was Mr Justice Amory, noted for his severity, this bit of showmanship may not have gone down too well. Incidentally, Amory was already 81 and brushed aside any suggestion of retiring. He fully intended to be back next year!

The judge who held the December assize at Lewes contrasted favourably with his predecessor. Mr Justice Charles was a fearful interventionist and wit. He always intended to be the star of the show, and as a result the public gallery of every court over which he presided was always crammed. The High Sheriff had the right to invite his friends to sit with the judge on the Bench, so letters and phone calls flooded in to Father from acquaintances humbly requesting a place thereon. The High Sheriff, Chaplain and others occupied their seats in court throughout every case, so it must have got quite crowded, especially for murder trials. M'lord evidently wasted no time in dealing with them. Asked when the two murder cases would be listed he replied, "One on Monday, the other on Tuesday."

At each assize the High Sheriff had to invite the Bar to lunch. Shelley's Hotel in Lewes put on an enormous menu which would have incapacitated the barristers if they had done justice to it. In the summer, the High Sheriff's Garden Party drew the great and the good to Twineham Grange. Fortunately the High Sheriff only held office for one year. It was an expensive privilege.

Hove General Hospital thought they could do with someone well known as their president and invited Father to undertake the duties. 'President' suggests someone appearing at the Annual Meeting and presenting prizes. In Father's case it meant responsibilities more akin to Executive Chairman. Various local councillors were always on the phone to him, and he had to chair the monthly board meeting, which had an uncomfortably active membership of surgeons who played their hand cunningly.

First they had to acquaint the board with the situation at Worthing Hospital. The board members settled back in their chairs, prepared to give some sympathy to Worthing although it was hardly well managed (no wish to be unfair but...). The surgeons had a desperate tale to tell. The ceiling in the operating theatre was flaking off, and it was only by good luck that pieces had not fallen into the open wounds of their patients (Good heavens!). They might have to stop operating there. Their difficulties were compounded by the situation at Hove (What's this?). The catalogue of faults and impending disasters at this very hospital seemed to outdo Worthing. Board members protested, quoted all the money they had raised and spent. But in the end they had to agree to an additional spending programme. Mother, who chaired the Ladies Appeals Committee, was asked to produce extra funds.

Father made his own special contribution to fund raising by organising a horse show at the Hove Greyhound Stadium each summer. In the morning, the show began with the greatest interest centred on the class for Milk Roundsmen driving their delivery floats round the ring, all with a beautifully turned out cob in the shafts. A dozen or fifteen entries made a grand sight, and most of them came from the Co-op Dairy. The commentator was then set a series of tongue twisters:

> Ladies and Gentlemen the results of this class are as follows:
> First No 20 The Brighton Equitable Co-operative Society
> Second No 17 The Brighton Equitable Co-operative Society
> Third No 8 The Brighton Equitable Co-operative Society.

It was an announcement extraordinarily difficult to get out without provoking mirth from the spectators. In the afternoon, the Cavalry Trick Riders Team entertained, and local horsemen tackled the Show Jumping.

One year Father had what he thought would turn out to be a masterly scheme for raising money. Bertram Mills's Circus came to Brighton on tour and rented a site from the Council. Suppose he could find them a free site in Hove? Surely it would be worth asking the Circus for one day's takings to be donated to Hove Hospital? He wrote to Cyril Mills with the proposition, who very politely turned him down. He made amends, however, by sending the family complimentary tickets for the Royal Box at one of the circus's Brighton performances. At the interval Cyril Mills came round full of *bonhomie*. "You were quite right, Colonel. I should have had your site. This lot are not worth two penn'orth of cold gin."

In fact, his regular spot on the Level, a park in the middle of Brighton, could never be improved upon, and the Big Top was full at all performances. The cost of taking a circus of that size on the road became impossibly high years ago and, coupled with the popular sentiment against keeping animals to perform tricks for public amusement, the days of the big traditional circus cannot return. Undoubtedly there is a real loss in this situation, as Bertram Mills and his contemporaries gave us show business of true excitement.

~ 10 ~
Home Guard, Evacuees from London, Cousin from Canada

The sense of relief following the Munich Agreement of 1938 did not last long. A year later Hitler was quite obviously going to attack Poland, on which he had no valid claims, and did a deal with the Soviet Union to ensure no interference. Britain and France now had at least to appear decisive, and promptly guaranteed the frontiers of Poland. In itself this was a meaningless pledge but had the consequence of a declaration of war against Germany. Hitler went ahead and cleaned up Poland in a matter of days. He probably gambled on neither country keeping their promise and, if they did, the German Army being able to defeat them within a few weeks.

In the months before the Polish invasion, the British Government had to forecast how Germany would fight a war and devise policies to cope with the consequences. There were clues to be found in the Spanish Civil War. German dive-bombers, acting in support of the Fascist rebels, had been extremely effective in creating panic among townspeople. Instead of dropping small bombs from on high, the dive-bomber pilot hurled his plane, with siren screaming, directly at the target, released the bomb at low altitude, and climbed away. The weight of high explosive dropped hardly counted; the attack succeeded by confusing and disorientating civilians who tried to escape and blocked the roads as a result. So the British Government's policy number one was to evacuate school children, and some women with children, to safe areas in advance of hostilities, at the same time telling those that remained to keep off the roads. Policy number two was to accept that poison gas bombing was inevitable so civilians must carry gas masks.

The procedure for the evacuation of London was well planned in advance. Local Parish and Urban Councils were told how many of each category of 'evacuees' they could expect, and were advised to make arrangements accordingly. Twineham was told to expect women accompanied by children. Father worked out where most of them could be billeted, but the number of cottages that were good enough (or big enough) to house these visitors proved limited, and some would have to live in the village hall.

The Government started the evacuation of London before any shots were fired, so it was on the day Hitler invaded Poland that a small coach-load of women were deposited at Twineham Village Hall. Very wisely the authorities in London moved

167

a whole street or part of a street together, so Twineham received a bloc of the Mile End Road consisting of true Eastenders dressed in black - the standard uniform of what would then be called the working class. Bringing friends and neighbours together in adversity helped morale, but undermined Father's billeting arrangements. Only two would go to the cottage assigned them; the remainder insisted on staying in the village hall. In the middle of the negotiations, fearful sobs and groans came from the road. A boy was rolling about under a hedge in a pitiful state. "What's the matter?" we asked. " 'E always goes to the pictures on Fridays'" we were told, "and there isn't a picture 'ouse here." We might have said, "Don't you know there's a war on?" except that there was not - not at that moment. So some comforting remarks were made instead. Extra beds were found and supper provided, as no cooking could be done in the hall.

For the next few days I seemed to be continually in and out of the village hall bearing huge dishes of steak pie and other goodies prepared by Mrs Golledge. The women, reclining on their beds, enjoyed it all. "Ooh you are kind! Keep coming dear, what've you got this time?"

As no hostilities had broken out anywhere in Britain, lounging about in a village hall far from home soon seemed pointless, and they quickly cadged a lift to the railway station and headed back to the East End. After a week Twineham's village hall was deserted.

The weeks and months that followed were called the Phoney War. It was difficult to keep interest alive. The British troops in France dug into a snowy landscape, fired the occasional artillery round and sent out patrols. One of these actually contacted the enemy and had a brisk exchange of fire and some narrow escapes. This quite trivial action made the front pages of the popular press, and the CO of the company involved was awarded the Military Cross.

By April 1940 the Germans were ready to move, and mopped up Denmark, followed by Norway, where the British Navy did some good work but the land forces failed to gain their objectives. They were extricated with difficulty. On May 10 the news broke that Germany was invading Holland and Belgium with overpowering force. The 'balloon' had well and truly 'gone up'. The extraordinary military dominance achieved by Hitler was strikingly confirmed by realising that, by the end of the month, France and the other countries were defeated, and all the British could hope for was to rescue as many men as possible from Dunkirk.

Politically there was, fortunately, a revolution. Neville Chamberlain, ill with cancer, finally convinced himself that the other parties would not serve under him to form a National Government, which was essential to unite the country. Winston Churchill received the King's invitation to form a Government. One is bound to say "surprise, surprise", as he was essentially an outsider in the Conservative Party. However, his talk on the wireless to celebrate the destruction of the German battleship in the River Plate a few months earlier had been so much enjoyed by a big audience that he had become indispensable. Unquestionably, if he had not given this broadcast talk the Conservative Party would have chosen Lord Halifax as potential premier and would have been rebuffed by the Labour Party. There was no campaign in support of Winston; it was just assumed by the public that he would get the job. Chamberlain and Halifax dithered and then, very wisely, suggested the name of the man they did not really like or trust. To be fair, most Conservatives in the country had spent the last twenty years distrusting Churchill after his part in the Gallipoli blunder and his poor record as Chancellor of the Exchequer in the 1920s, but they now swung round to support him en masse. He was in charge, but in charge just at the moment when the country seemed to be on the brink of defeat.

During the build-up to this situation I was up at Emmanuel College, Cambridge. The *Cambridge Daily News*, on sale opposite the college gates, told a sorry story each evening of our troops "retiring to previously prepared positions", with pictures on the front page of the evacuation from Dunkirk, which took place between May 29 and June 3, 1940. Perhaps for the first and last time the university admitted that their traditions were redundant. They declared the term over before the set date, and advised all who could do so to return home.

At Emmanuel we lined up on the staircase to be officially sent on our way by Edward Welbourne, the Senior Tutor. In his study he paced around, clutching his gown in a characteristic gesture and came to the point without further ado. "You have taken all your papers I assume? Well then, the university authorities have said you must go back home. No doubt you will find something useful to do. Don't do anything silly like joining-up. You will get called up when the Army wants you. I want you back here next term. Goodbye".

When I arrived at Twineham Grange a day or two later I found it on a war footing.

Nobody knew what Hitler would now do - send an invasion force within weeks? Evidently there was a lively belief that he would attack because, it was said, his secret agents were already here. The fall of France was blamed on the cunningly disguised spies who spread false information and demoralised the population. Some of them even impersonated nuns! It is doubtful whether any eye witness came forward to confirm the story however. A nun descending by parachute in army boots hardly sounds the ideal start to a spying mission. Nevertheless, retired generals and colonels in the South-East were roused to action. If the ex-service men in their villages were fitted out with sporting rifles and shotguns, and told to keep a look out for parachutists, they could jolly well guarantee that none of these spies would escape. The local calls to arms made a good story in the papers, and from then on villages followed suit in huge numbers.

The War Office were worried. If the German Army did come and was fired on by these civilians, there would be a wholesale massacre. It was essential to make them part of the British Army and so be protected (in theory at least) by the Geneva Convention. The Civil Service came up with an accurate, but uninspired, title for these unconventional recruits - Local Defence Volunteers - and began to issue arm bands with LDV embossed on them.

The prime minister did not warm to these decisions, and on June 26, 1940 said so in a memorandum to the Secretary of State for War.

I don't think much of the name 'Local Defence Volunteers' for your very large new force. The word 'local' is uninspiring. Mr Herbert Morrison suggested to me today the title 'Civic Guard', but I think 'Home Guard' would be better. Don't hesitate to change on account of having made armlets etc, if it is thought the title of Home Guard would be more compulsive.

Nobody challenged Winston and a further memo followed a week later.

Prime Minister to Secretary of State for War 27.6.40
I hope you liked my suggestion of changing the name "Local Defence Volunteers", which is associated with Local Government and Local Option, to "Home Guard". I found everybody liked this in my tour yesterday.

It was no surprise to find Herbert Morrison backing 'Civic Guard'. As the top wheeler-dealer of the London County Council, he regarded local government as far more effective in getting things done than Parliament. Winston Churchill, the lover of the great stage, on the other hand hardly recognised the existence of Town Councils. A Town Hall to him was a place to make a speech from, but to Morrison, now Labour Home Secretary in a Coalition Government, a Town Hall represented the place where political guile could be executed and power accumulated. But romance won.

In spite of the operational disaster that had just overwhelmed them, the War Office acted promptly. Soon bundles of battle dresses, boxes of boots and forage caps were delivered to the village platoons. The great coats were a bit slower in coming through, but heartily welcomed when they did. No farm worker had ever possessed such a coat before, and they did good service on farms for years afterwards.

The War Office had no hope of handing out the Lee Enfield 0.303 rifles that the British Forces used; too many had been left in France. Instead they issued Browning 0.300 rifles which had become surplus to requirements in Canada. To have rifles of differing bores in the same army could have been a nightmare but, as the Home Guard were never called on to fire their rifles in anger, it was a perfectly sound solution.

Father responded immediately to the idea of local militias. He raised a Twineham Defence Force overnight. He summoned all the ex-service men from the Great War of 1914-18 to parade at Twineham Grange one evening, along with likely younger men and youths. He set up a table in the study to take the old drill manuals from his Royal West Kent days, together with the new Standing Orders, Orders of the Day and Duty Sheets.

The routine settled down to an evening parade at Twineham Grange stables for Drill and Other Instruction for the non-ex-service men.

Everyone had to undertake the night watch duty, however. Four men reported to the Stables at the Grange by 9pm. Two of them then stood by the iron fence looking south until 1am, while the other two gossiped in the harness room, drank mugs of tea and finally dropped off to sleep on straw palliasses. At one o'clock in the morning they were rattled up to do their watch until 5 am. Father did not want to be left out, so during June and July he would emerge from the front door at 4.30 am wearing a dressing gown, and approach the night watch. "Attention!" the ex-service man would snap, and be immediately told, "Stand at Ease, Easy, Seen anything?" "Nothing." "Never mind - this is a time the enemy might drop people, keep a good look out."

When September came and the mornings were darker, these visitations ceased. By July 21 the LDV armlets were being recalled and all men were warned of manoeuvres to come.

> A scheme is to take place shortly, as practical manoeuvres which will not take long, and it is hoped, if properly carried out, will end by 6.30 am. It is essential that all should be present as soon as possible after the alarm is given."
>
> R W McKergow OC No 8 Platoon, Twineham

The one-day Scheme, the erstwhile Field Day, carried out by no 8 Platoon of C Company, Twineham Local Defence Volunteers (yet to assume the title of Home Guard) that August day in 1940 was watched by an Umpire, and by the CO of D Battalion of LDVs, of which they were a part. When it was all over these gentlemen issued a report on what they had seen and heard, and my father made a precis of it which he circulated to all concerned.

He began this by telling his men that both the Umpire and the Commanding Officer of the Battalion were most pleased with the quick turn out on the alarm being given, and also to see the keenness which was shown by all ranks in carrying out a scheme which was marred by fog. "The Umpire said it was impossible to follow the doings of the different sections; in fact two sections of attackers never came in contact with the defending force, and much therefore which could have been instructive failed."

> One section of the attacking force attained their objective in cutting the wires at the Post Office and also claimed to have destroyed one pylon. One remark made by the Umpire and Brigade captain was that they were sure it was most necessary for the LDV to take part in field operations to obtain efficiency. No doubt in the absence of fog, the attack and defence would have developed and it would have been interesting to see how, or where, the attacking force could have been held up.
>
> I hope we shall have another scheme, when the Platoon will have more rifles to work with and better weather conditions.

It is surprising to find the LDV (in process of becoming the Home Guard) had so soon acquired a full complement of Field Rank Officers and Staff Captains. The Platoons only really thought of themselves as a village unit and, in fact, the Home Guard never had a co-ordinated plan to resist an enemy advance.

Meanwhile, in the air, one of the crucial battles of the war was developing. The Battle of Britain had the unusual distinction of being fought, in part, over home territory, with the public watching the loops and whorls of the vapour trails, and hearing the rattle of machine gun and cannon fire as the fighter aircraft of both sides tried to engage each other. After each German attack the Air Ministry put out the score of kills for the day. Almost always the German losses exceeded our own which gave the comforting impression that we were going to win. The public did not truly grasp how important it was not to lose. The air attacks were directed at the Fighter Command airfields in Kent and Sussex, with the object of knocking them out operationally and destroying as many aircraft as possible in the air and on the ground. If the British air force could be pushed back north of London, the way would be open for the German Navy to escort an invasion convoy across the Channel. It would have been an exceptionally risky operation, but Hitler was confident it could succeed. It was never tested, of course. The RAF held their territory - just - and the Germans found their losses too high to continue.

Twineham was on the western edge of the battle, and only saw the vapour trails two or three times. A single Hurricane fighter crashed vertically into the ground on one occasion, fortunately without its pilot. Other areas were obviously more actively involved, and needed to be well primed with regard to what to do, and what not to do, in a wide range of circumstances. Even so, Twineham LDV platoon were on the circulation list of the War Office memo on how to distinguish enemy from friendly aircraft, and the reminder that the man coming down out of the sky on the end of a parachute might be one of ours. This read:

INFORMATION AIRCRAFT
Parachutists
   There is still a tendency in some quarters to regard all parachutists as hostile. While it is a good thing to take no chances, it must be remembered that friendly pilots sometimes have to 'Bale out' or more frequently Germans come down wishing only to surrender.
   It has been suggested that anyone speaking with a foreign accent must be immediately dealt with as a German. While the greatest care should be exercised in dealing with parachutists who cannot speak English properly, it is pointed out that there are now a large number of foreign airmen, particularly Poles and Czechs, serving with the RAF and some of these can hardly speak any English at all. It is therefore impossible to adopt a policy of shooting all non-English speaking parachutists on sight.
   As a general guide, it can be taken that any party of parachutists over six in number will be hostile and should be treated as such and fired upon.
   Parties of six or less will not be shot at unless it is definitely confirmed that they are hostile, and showing fights or attempting to escape.
   Remember not to fire at an areoplane unless either:
   (1) It behaves in an unfriendly way.
   (2) The International Markings can be seen.
   Be careful to distinguish between an enemy attacking and one of our aeroplanes coming down to drop a message.
   Finally, you have a very effective weapon in your rifle and your LMG Enemy pilots hate small arms fire as they cannot bale out. USE THIS WEAPON RUTHLESSLY ONCE YOU HAVE RECOGNISED THE AIRCRAFT TO BE AN ENEMY.
   In future, German Airmen coming to earth in this area and captured by either the Military or LDV will be disposed of in the following manner:

Police Station, Horsham (Horsham 122); Police Station, Haywards Heath (Haywards Heath 18); Police Station, Brighton (Brighton 4141).

The memo went on to describe how crashed aircraft should be guarded. The idea of aircraft dropping messages was clearly a hang-over from the First World War.

The possibility that the Germans would invade was still in the forefront of military thinking as no-one on this side of the Channel knew that, after mid-September, the High Command in Germany were going to postpone the invasion. One was thought to be less and less likely, and for that reason Father's suggestion that they should flood Twineham Brook to act as a barrier was not adopted.

The Twineham Platoon had, like all others, a fair share of 'characters'. Private Dollimore, Dolli to his friends, found the uniform and accoutrements a stimulus to Great War memories. As he stared out from the Guard Hut with his rifle in the corner, he could relive his triumphs as a destroyer of snipers. The Germans used sharp shooters from their trenches to harass our men dug in opposite them. You had to be able to pinpoint where they were firing from, and then knock them out with a single shot. He had it all worked out, and other platoons further up the front line would send for Private Dollimore if they were worried by snipers. Even other regiments would call on his services. The Royal Sussex were proud of him; the officers said so.

The 'Shop Steward' was unquestionably Arthur Small, who openly supported the Labour Party and ensured that the interests of his fellow volunteers were looked after. The topic of the Allowance ruffled a few feathers, as it obviously derived from the presence in Government of good Trades Unionists skilled in the art of manufacturing bonuses and special payments on grounds that were flimsy but difficult to refute entirely. It was consequently accepted by the Government that members of the Home Guard doing night guard duty incurred additional expenses in providing food and drink to be consumed in off-duty moments. They agreed to pay a sum of one shilling and sixpence, or something similar, for each night on duty. The military men who had raised their village platoons were not happy. By all means give the Army a bit extra, but the men in the Home Guard were defending hearth and home and had come forward voluntarily. Payments were against the spirit of the whole thing. In any case, it was said, the men did not bring food with them on duty.

The announcement of the proposed allowance appeared in the press. Arthur Small was determined his CO should not overlook it. At the next parade, Father drilled the platoon and then told them to Stand Easy.

"Permission to speak, sir?" said Arthur.
"Yes. What is it Small?"
"The Allowance, sir. It was in the paper that it would be paid for guard duty."
"Nothing official has come through. We cannot act on newspaper reports. Anything else?"

173

The next week the same thing happened and the following week, with Father's "What is it Small?" getting steadily more dejected. Then, three weeks later, a table appeared with brown envelopes on it. The Allowances had come through.

The first detachments of the impressive Canadian Army began filtering in to London in 1940. A Social Club was set up and the King and Queen very soon visited it. Among those who exchanged words with the Queen was a Sergeant McKergow, whose name appeared in the press reports. He immediately had an invitation to spend a night or two at Twineham Grange.

The Canadian McKergows of Montreal had surfaced in the 1930s. Their local newspaper had published, rather in the vein of Strange but True, an extract of a speech given in England by the Hunt Master at a Point-to-Point lunch. The editor had evidently found it a very curious, but entertaining, example of English eccentricity. The speech had been given by a certain Colonel McKergow.

The Canadian McKergows, much more numerous than ourselves, had already drawn up their family tree. It took them back to the part of Scotland that Robert McKergow, my father's father, came from. At that point the trail petered out, and they were never able to find the link between the Canadian and Scottish families. It was assumed, however, from then on that the relationship existed, even if undiscovered.

Sergeant McKergow turned out to be a quiet man but with definite views. Our suggestion that perhaps he would shortly be taking a commission were brushed aside. The Sergeants' Mess suited him very well. We felt obliged to commend those splendid men the 'Mounties', but that was even worse received. "A pain in the neck" took care of them.

At about seven o'clock on the first evening, we mentioned that dinner would be at 7.30 when the gong would be sounded. In the meantime, we said, we would get into something a bit smarter (evening dress for dinner had been dropped when the war broke out). "Sure," said the sergeant, and reached for the paper.

When later we came downstairs slightly tidier, we passed him on the way up. A check on the clock showed he had five or ten minutes to wash and brush up. Brockbank, our butler, sounded the gong sharp at half past seven and took up his place in the dining room. Five minutes passed, ten minutes, fifteen minutes, and no sign of our guest. Brockbank was sent up to enquire. He came back with one of the best lines any butler could have wished for. "He says he's changing his pants, Madam."

Hitler realised that the air attacks had not succeeded, so he tried to break the will of the English by night-bombing ports, manufacturing cities and, in particular, London. He was confident that he could erase, as he put it, any city he chose. He came close to it with Coventry. The defence system of searchlights, anti-aircraft guns and night fighters were at first ineffective, but the latter soon acquired the ability to intercept some of their bombers.

A searchlight operated within 500 yards of Twineham Grange, and the guns were distributed in the High Weald as the first line of defence. The Home Guard were glad of their hut when fragments of anti-aircraft shells whistled down. The dock areas and the City took most of the bombs in London. Surprisingly few of the people moved out. Among those who sought a safer billet were some sharp Eastenders who took rooms at Twineham's Castle Inn.

They looked very out of place among the locals, but money talked, and they were soon to be seen propped up at the bar, dispensing hospitality from the fist full of notes that never seemed to diminish.

They would quickly summon a diffident youth they saw hovering in the doorway. "Now then young man, what's your poison? A pint of Mild if I remember right."

"Thank ee, sir."

"Don't call me sir, lad. I'm Frank."

"Thank ee s... Frank."

"And your friends over there?..."

Such loud-mouthed showing-off went down badly with the older regulars, who liked their visitors even less when boasts about female conquests and french letters (condoms) circulated. It was generally concluded that the outsiders were a lot of windbags trying to make fools of the locals. But then the day came when the pub's septic tank was emptied and, as plain as you like, the infernal contraceptives were floating on the surface. The news of the discovery went round the village without attracting too much comment. Those Londoners could carry on like that, it was said, but nobody round here would copy them.

The Crawley and Horsham Hunt had an easier passage than they had experienced in the First World War. It is true they had most of their horses taken by Army Remounts in 1939, which suggests that at least one section of the Armed Forces were living in a totally different world. All the young men on the hunt staff went with the forces, leaving an adequate team to continue hunting in a quiet way with a total of 20 couple of hounds in Kennel. The saddest moment came in 1943 when it was reported that the Master, Guy Cubitt, had been badly wounded in the face while serving in Italy, and would probably be nearly blind. This proved correct, and it had to be accepted that he could never resume the mastership. Mrs Molly Gregson, who had been invited to take over in 1939, was the obvious successor. A great admirer of the Colonel's long experience at the head of affairs, the two of them were soon in virtual partnership. Hardly a day passed without a long phone call to analyse what had happened and the way ahead.

In 1942 Lord Leconfield decided to give up his hounds. It could not have been very surprising, since he was in indifferent health and the cost of keeping a pack going must have looked difficult to justify. Father was most upset ("Great mistake, Colonel") and did not cease to try and get him to continue. The Hunt Puppy Shows went on each summer, and Lord Leconfield always came over. He got a tremendous talking-to by Father one year, which went on so long that the spectators had taken their seats at the ringside and the first of the puppies were in front of the Judges, before Father suddenly wound up by saying, "Well, you don't want to listen to me" - and marched off to supervise the Show. His Lordship smiled at the retreating figure, murmured, "Always so silent" - and wandered down to the benches to find somewhere to sit. It was hardly the way to treat an honoured guest but Leconfield was used to Bob's behaviour. Their friendship dated back to 1901, and the Third Baron still did not really know what Bob would do next.

The Government soon brought in regulations to ensure that everyone in their early working lives had jobs in Essential Work, as they called it, which contributed to the War Effort. They could transfer themselves to jobs of their own choosing or be drafted into suitable employment by the Ministry of Labour. Domestic servants were absolutely Not Essential. Father accepted that the girls had to go, but "I'm not having them sent all over the country". The outcome was that as many as possible were taken on by an electrical contracting firm in Brighton where tracer bullets were made. The second Gardener also went into munitions.

The Second War differed from the First in the social revolution it encouraged. When the servants packed their bags to go into War Work, that was the end of domestic service as previous generations had understood it. They did not offer to come back, nor did any girls come forward from school. Alternative opportunities opened up for them, and to some extent for the boys as well, who no longer chose to be gardeners for Big Houses. At Twineham Grange, Moorey was the only resident maid. In future, housework would be done by part-timers, and the size of the gardens under cultivation went down rapidly.

Father's war years, and the aftermath, were exceptionally busy for a man approaching 80. When the Home Guard dropped night guard duty following the switch to the east of the German invasion force, the rather half-hearted attempt to turn the HG into Territorials made it pointless to stay on, and he resigned.

Other jobs came up as the middle-aged men who might have filled them were at the War. He was elected Chairman of the British Field Sports Society, President of the Brighton and Hove Conservative Association and Chairman of the Brighton and Hove Property Owners Association. None of them proved to be sinecures.

The Labour Government elected in 1945 made it known they were minded to ban fox hunting. The BFSS were immediately in the front line of protesters against such sacrilege, and speeches had to be made and tactics discussed. (Fifty years later hunting remains unbanned.) The Brighton Conservatives seemed to be proceeding towards the 1945 election smoothly, lined up their sitting members as candidates and were then suddenly confronted by one of them wanting to retire. A delegation persuaded him to continue and he won the seat. Property Owners meetings were difficult to manage as there were always groups determined to raise long running disputes that were not the business of the association.

At the end of the war, Lord Leconfield asked Father to join his committee set up to raise a large sum of money to ensure the future of the Army Cadet Corps in the country. In Brighton an Exhibition Match between the top darts players was expected to make a good profit, but Father's planning came to nothing when the champion and the runner-up refused to compete, and the event collapsed. Luckily other areas came up with successful promotions and the cadets got their finance.

In the midst of this activity Father suddenly died.

One day in October 1947 he did his usual ride round the farm with the groom in the morning, and then decided to have the horses out again after lunch. A good circuit of the village followed. After dinner he admitted to being 'pretty whacked' and departed to bed a bit earlier then usual. Mother looked into the bedroom an hour later and saw his book on the floor. He was in bed but unconcious. The doctor drove over at high speed but could only report that the Colonel had passed away.

On the day of the funeral the coffin was brought from the Grange in a farm wagon with Will Sayers at the reins, and followed by the older hunter saddled up, led by the groom.

When sufficient time had elapsed for them to reach Twineham Church, we drove down by car. The coffin had been transferred to a wheeled bier and was suddenly almost swamped by the farm men who crowded round looking very bewildered. Perhaps they felt they ought to be with the Guvnor at this moment. "Get back," hissed the undertaker. "Let the family in." So, more or less sorted out, we processed down the path and found a Guard of Honour at the porch. On the right side a line of nurses from Hove General Hospital, and on the left the hunt servants in their hunting livery. Glancing towards them, one was conscious only of their absolute disbelief that the old Master had gone and was in the coffin. They leaned forward to keep it in view as the undertakers lifted it through the door.

A friend gave an interview afterwards to the local paper. One remark rang very true: "He will be missed by thousands." It sounds absurdly exaggerated, but in reality was an accurate assessment of a career that was unique in the first half of the century and totally impossible to repeat subsequently.

I have lifted a window on a past lifestyle, past manners, past attitudes and assumptions from which time has distanced us, and had a peep at the private lives of my father and mother's circle straddling the end of one century and the beginning of another; the intimate correspondence between my father and the young girl who became my mother, the uninhibited accounts which my airman brother Dudley sent home in the Great War of his last months in the land of the living, the exciting big game hunting interlude, the daily round on the farm, in the hunting field, on the polo ground, officiating at point-to-points, playing cricket, driving dogcarts and four-in-hands, singing at concerts, giving dinner parties, sharing in the running of village and church. My reporting is less focused than when they speak for themselves. I hope however I have gone some way towards re-creating a lost world to which many of us, though every year fewer and fewer, once belonged.

~ Index ~